ROUTLEDGE LIBRARY EDITIONS:
HOUSING POLICY AND HOME OWNERSHIP

Volume 12

BUILDING BY LOCAL
AUTHORITIES

ROUTLEDGE LIBRARY EDITIONS:
BUILDING AND CONSTRUCTION

Volume 17

BUILDING
CONSTRUCTION

BUILDING BY LOCAL AUTHORITIES
The Report of an Inquiry by the Royal Institute of Public Administration

ELIZABETH LAYTON

Routledge
Taylor & Francis Group

LONDON AND NEW YORK

First published in 1961 by George Allen & Unwin Ltd

This edition first published in 2021
by Routledge
2 Park Square, Milton Park, Abingdon, Oxon OX14 4RN

and by Routledge
52 Vanderbilt Avenue, New York, NY 10017

Routledge is an imprint of the Taylor & Francis Group, an informa business

British Library Cataloguing in Publication Data
A catalogue record for this book is available from the British Library

ISBN: 978-0-367-64519-9 (Set)
ISBN: 978-1-00-313856-3 (Set) (ebk)
ISBN: 978-0-367-68419-8 (Volume 12) (hbk)
ISBN: 978-0-367-68424-2 (pbk)
ISBN: 978-1-00-313744-3 (Volume 12) (ebk)

Publisher's Note
The publisher has gone to great lengths to ensure the quality of this reprint but points out that some imperfections in the original copies may be apparent.

Disclaimer
The publisher has made every effort to trace copyright holders and would welcome correspondence from those they have been unable to trace.

BUILDING BY
LOCAL AUTHORITIES

BY

ELIZABETH LAYTON

*The Report of an inquiry by the
Royal Institute of Public Administration
into the organization of building
construction and maintenance by
Local Authorities in England and Wales*

Ruskin House

GEORGE ALLEN & UNWIN LTD
MUSEUM STREET   LONDON

PRINTED IN GREAT BRITAIN
in 11 point Baskerville type
BY SIMSON SHAND LTD
LONDON, HERTFORD AND HARLOW

Royal Institute of Public Administration
Members of the Steering Committee

PREFACE

In 1952 the Royal Institute of Public Administration decided to undertake a series of major research projects on subjects of current importance to the public services. *Building by Local Authorities* is the fourth in that series.

This subject was chosen because of the major responsibility placed upon local authorities since the war for the provision of housing, and the large number of schools they have been called upon to construct in recent years. Indeed, during the last fifteen years local authorities have spent many millions of pounds a year on new buildings and, as the country's largest property-owners, they are now faced with maintenance problems of unusual magnitude. The salient questions which the Institute thought worthy of study were how various local authorities organized themselves to discharge these responsibilities, and whether there were opportunities to improve existing methods of organization and management.

The cost of this study was met by a grant from the Nuffield Foundation, and the Royal Institute of Public Administration wishes to record its warmest thanks to the Foundation for their generous support.

This study was undertaken by a full-time Research Officer, Mrs Elizabeth Layton, assisted by a study group. The members of the group are listed on a preceding page, and the Institute would like to emphasize the value of their contribution to this enterprise and to thank them for their expert assistance and unflagging interest over a period of two and a half years.

Mr Eric Adams, Managing Director, Dolphin Development & Management Co. Ltd., was Chairman of this group at the inception of the study, but midway through it he left this country to take up an appointment in Canada. He influenced to a considerable extent, however, the lines on which the study was developed, and its final shape and content owe much to him. He was succeeded by Mr G. F. Darlow, Town Clerk of Reading, who had been a member of the group, and who was kind enough to assume the additional burdens of Chairmanship despite the heavy obligations to which he was already committed.

Mrs Elizabeth Layton was responsible for the detailed

9

investigations and for drafting the final report. The quality of the book which has resulted reflects in large measure the skill and energy which she devoted to her tasks, and the Institute considers itself most fortunate to have had her service and talents at its disposal.

The terms of reference for the study were as follows:

1. To investigate the basic forms of organization employed in local authorities of various types, populations and areas for:

(a) designing new buildings and securing their erection, and (b) maintaining existing buildings,

by contract or by direct labour.

2. To pay regard in this investigation to the extent to which councils delegate authority to their committees and to their officers in these matters.

3. To examine the forms of organization used for building construction and maintenance by other public authorities and by privately-owned undertakings.

4. To consider how well the local authorities' forms of organization meet present needs, and in what respects they might be improved.

The investigations were confined to England and Wales and the term 'building' was not taken to include civil engineering activities such as sewerage and water supply. Some preliminary enquiries were made into the methods used by various large private enterprises and by other kinds of public authority, but it appeared that the kind of buildings concerned and the type of operations did not generally provide conditions similar enough to those existing in local authorities to make comparisons fruitful.

Many of the enquiries were carried out by personal interview, and these were supplemented by correspondence and three different sets of questionnaires which were completed by some 65 authorities. The pages of the report show the large number of public officials and others who were consulted in the course of this enquiry. The Institute knows all too well how burdensome to busy people these demands for information and opinions can be. Much of the success of the enquiry is due to their willing response, for which the Institute is sincerely grateful.

CONTENTS

LIST OF TABLES

LIST OF DIAGRAMS

CHAPTER I

LOCAL AUTHORITY BUILDING
AND THE NATION

*Change from private to public patronage accelerated by war
—scale of local authority building—comparison with total
building—emphasis on housing and schools—adjustment
to slum clearance—importance of educational building—
future developments—functions of local authorities.*

BUILDINGS have a special fascination for the human mind. In
a shifting world they are reassuringly solid. They outlive by so
long a span the generation which conceived them. They are a
tangible memorial to wealth, power, social success, spiritual
dedication, philanthropy or public service. In their day the
Pyramids, Babylon, the Acropolis, castles, cathedrals, colleges,
country mansions, alms houses, town halls and housing estates
were built to satisfy these human aspirations or to record their
achievement. Few ceremonies embody so much expectation as
the laying of a foundation stone or so proud a sense of fulfilment
as the formal opening of a building. By these acts man struggles
to make real the insubstantial fabric of his vision.

In the modern world the individual benefactor or patron is
disappearing under the pressure of taxation. In his place public
authorities have taken over many of the functions of patronage
and many of the services hitherto run by private benefaction.
The responsibilities and powers of central and local government have grown gradually for many decades, but the rate of
change was greatly accelerated by the Second World War and
by the emergence of the welfare state. It is now accepted that
the state will provide from rates or taxes, or both, many services which were hitherto provided, if at all, from private
sources.

During the changeover at the end of the war the local authorities lost a number of responsibilities, which were taken over by
central government. Local authority hospitals and a number of

trading services, for example, were transferred to public boards controlled by central government. At the same time bigger responsibilities for housing and education devolved on local authorities. Both these responsibilities involved very large building programmes. For more than ten years after the war local authorities were heavily engaged in meeting the demands for new housing and new schools and in all the administrative and social problems, which the running of these two major services demanded. It is only within the last few years that the momentum of house building by local authorities has slackened. School building is expected to pass its peak after 1960.

THE SCALE OF LOCAL AUTHORITY BUILDING

Between 1945 and 1959 local authorities had erected 2 million out of the total of some 3 million new dwellings which were built, and had provided about 3 million new school places. The effort involved in building these houses and schools during this period is of a different order of magnitude from anything which was done by local authorities before 1939. Local authorities have been clients of the building industry on a large scale and have had an important influence on the demand for labour, materials and for the professional services of architects, engineers, surveyors and others with technical experience.

Capital expenditure on new housing and schools has dominated the building activities of local authorities. Over the past ten years there has been a crescendo and a diminuendo of total expenditure by local authorities on these two services together, but in 1958 this expenditure was still fifteen times larger than local authority spending on all other types of building. (Table 1.)

TABLE 1

CAPITAL EXPENDITURE BY LOCAL AUTHORITIES
£ million

	1949	1953	1958
Housing	263	399	251
Education and Child Care	38	72	122
Total	301	471	374
All other building	12	21	25

For further details see Table 4 Chapter 2

16

Since 1958 there has been a further decrease in local authority housing programmes, and an increase in sanctions for such buildings as clinics, fire stations, municipal offices and swimming baths. Houses and schools are still, however, by far the biggest responsibilities in the field of local authority building. They are likely to remain so, and to continue to make large demands on the resources of the building industry. Most of the large urban authorities have only begun to tackle the problems of slum clearance; there remain years, if not decades, of work to be done here, quite apart from the problem of obsolete property which must be renewed by one means or another in the near future. The replacement of old schools has barely started, while the school population will be rising again before long.

If other types of building absorb only a small part of the local authorities' building effort, they are of much greater importance than the scale of expenditure suggests. Many socially desirable schemes have been frozen during the past years. In 1958 and 1959 there was a slight thaw, but past experience has shown how precarious such improvements can be. The field of social and recreational services has been starved of buildings for twenty years, while resources were concentrated on housing and schools. Plans for sports centres, community centres, and concert halls have grown dusty in pigeon-holes. Maternity and child welfare services have struggled in cramped premises. The fire and police services have, in many places, operated under conditions of great physical difficulty. Town halls are bursting at the corners. If the thaw should continue, even at only a few degrees above its earlier freezing point, local authorities will be able to produce a number of interesting and worthwhile new developments and to show municipal building in a greater variety of forms than has been visible for many years.

In the 1950s local authority building found its most interesting and vigorous expression in school building. For reasons which are discussed later in this book the development of school building in this country has been outstandingly successful. In the field of architecture it is Britain's most known and acclaimed achievement. School building has benefited from an intensity and originality of effort not yet matched elsewhere. This effort has given the school building programmes a special vitality and produced exceptionally good value for the money spent on them.

17

There are signs that this effort is now being harnessed to other types of local authority building, and that similar research, experiment and development work will be applied to these. Much of the initiative for this must come from central government. But local authorities have their own part to play and a few are starting to pioneer along these lines. The very fact that the development of slum clearance schemes will mean more flats, with their social handicaps, and less traditional two-storey housing, and that a wider range of other types of building is now being planned, will provide a fresh stimulus.

Local authorities are responsible for so large an annual expenditure on building work that the efficiency of their organization must be a matter of public concern. The cost affects the pockets of all. The designs affect the comfort, happiness, safety and health of a very large number of people. It is a sobering thought that in recent years, local authorities have been spending from £400 million to £500 million annually on new building, and that 2 million families and 3 million school children are daily influenced, for good or ill, by the way local authorities have designed and built their new houses and schools since the war.

THE CHANGING SCENE

The years between 1945 and 1960 have provided a succession of strains and stresses in local authority building. The end of the war found the building industry reduced in strength. Local authorities were faced with the reconstruction or repair of heavy war damage, shortages of labour and materials, a huge housing demand and a rising birthrate. Housing had the first call on national resources; schools had a strong claim. During those early years very little else received any help beyond essential repairs.

The problems of meeting the physical demands upon them would have been difficult enough during the immediate post-war years without the complications of financial crises as well. From 1947 onwards the country was faced with a succession of economic crises which further complicated the local authorities' task and constantly threw their preparations out of balance. The effects of these crises on local authorities and their building programmes are discussed more fully in the next chapter. In retrospect they assume a diminished significance. At the time they seemed to obscure the whole horizon. Coupled with the problems of recreating their own building organizations and of assimilating the standards and procedures demanded by central government, local authorities had an exacting task.

Gradually physical shortages diminished, systems of priorities and allocations were suspended and technical staffs were built up. Gradually the output of schools and houses gathered momentum. Had they not been shaken brusquely and at roughly two year intervals by the succession of national financial crises, authorities would have been more aware that by the early 1950s their building organizations were running fast, in top gear. By then the pressure on the housing lists was beginning to ease, and the output of schools was rising steadily on the basis of firm programmes, fixed well in advance. Local authority building had reached its peak by 1953 and then declined.

The crisis of 1957 with the 'credit-squeeze', which was its outward expression, made more manifest the new change in emphasis in local authority building. School building, it is true, continued to rise but the scale and balance of housing changed. Slum clearance has now become the dominant preoccupation of local housing authorities. If this change has meant a diminution in the total volume of local authority building, authorities are now concentrating their efforts on a large and difficult problem, which will demand all their skill. It is the centres of cities which will now be developed rather than the new housing estates on the fringes. Redevelopment poses much tougher problems than building on virgin land.

It is dangerous to predict the future trends of local authority building. Prediction has so often been falsified by political and economic changes. But assuming a continuation of present policies there remain large tasks for local authorities in slum clearance, school building and in making good the neglect of all other types of building since 1939. Quantitatively these do not add up to the peak years of building before 1954, but they make a significant total.

Local authorities will have to meet demands not only as they are visualized now, but as they will develop and change in the future. These demands will be affected by three major social

19

changes:

> the rising standard of living and with it the demand for space and a higher standard of services, of housing, education and public health;

> the birthrate which, contrary to the earlier forecasts of population trends, is again rising. This will affect the scale of services and increase the problems of congestion in the cities;

> the continuing movement of population from the industrial North towards the Midlands and South-East England.

These changes will set local authorities all kinds of problems. In their solution new housing standards will be needed and new kinds of buildings will be required. Perhaps new types of public enterprise will be developed to check the drift of population from the older towns.

Quite apart from these larger social problems there are important changes going on on the supply side of building:

> building methods and techniques are at last showing signs of breaking through into the modern world of technical advance. Until recently the technological progress of building has been slow; research has been minimal and the building industry has lagged behind many other industries. In future local authorities will have to adjust their ideas to the new techniques at a quickening pace;

> this technical advance requires a new kind of co-operation between clients, architects, engineers, surveyors and those responsible for actual building. To reap the benefits of this advance may mean some difficult change of attitude and procedure within local authorities and the adjustment of some standing orders and departmental boundaries.

These are some of the problems which face local authorities in the organization of their building services. They show how much thought is needed, how many new fields are to be explored, how great an opportunity lies ahead.

DIVERSITY OF LOCAL AUTHORITIES

There are no simple answers to questions about how to get greater efficiency, lower costs, or better designs for building. These are the product of able men working within the framework of an efficient organization. No single formula, not even a dozen different ones, would provide solutions for so wide a variety of local authorities, of such different sizes, and with such different powers and responsibilities. Not only do authorities vary from the London County Council with a population of 3·2 million to district councils with populations of less than 3,200 and from authorities with no housing responsibilities to ones building many thousands of houses a year. Even when authorities with similar responsibilities and powers are compared, their problems and the organization designed to meet them can be strikingly different.

This diversity in size, function and organization is a characteristic feature of English local government. It greatly complicates any description of the building organizations and makes generalization difficult. The county of Middlesex with a population of 2·2 million is almost wholly urban; it contains no county boroughs and no rural districts. It could hardly be more different from Shropshire, where half the population of 300,000 lives in rural districts or from Lancashire where 3 million people live in seventeen towns, all of which are county boroughs and independent of the county council.

Diversity among the county boroughs is perhaps even greater. They vary in size from 1·1 million people to 30,000. They may be industrial, commercial or administrative centres for their region, or they may be dominated by industry alone. They may be working ports or seaside holiday resorts, market towns or cathedral cities. All these authorities have broadly the same range of responsibilities, but the circumstances in which they operate are so different that they have evoked very different solutions. Slum clearance and re-development may be the most intractable problem in towns which had their main development in the nineteenth century. Seaside resorts undertake large annual programmes of painting and repair to keep the sea front gay and inviting for visitors, and may own and run swimming baths, piers and pavilions for entertainment. Services connected

21

with the old are of special importance in areas of declining population, just as the maternity and child welfare services and education will require an exceptional number of new buildings where there is a young and expanding population, for example, in the new towns.

Some non-county boroughs are no more than villages of 3,000 or 4,000 people, often with a long history but a declining population. Others are hovering on the verge of county borough status with populations of 100,000 or 200,000. Clearly the building organization of a large urban authority on the fringes of London will be quite different from that of a small town in a rural district. Similar disparities are to be found among the urban and rural district councils. Size is, therefore, of as great importance as the functions of any particular type of authority.

NUMBERS AND TYPES OF LOCAL AUTHORITY

There are five main types of local authority, with the metropolitan boroughs as a variant on the non-county boroughs. These are shown below. (Table 2.)

TABLE 2

NUMBER OF LOCAL AUTHORITIES OF DIFFERENT TYPES

Types of Authority	Number
County Councils (including the London County Council)	62
County Boroughs	83
Non-County Boroughs (excluding Metropolitan Boroughs)	318
Metropolitan Boroughs	28
Urban District Councils	564
Rural District Councils	474
Total	1,529

The *County Councils* are mostly large authorities, large in terms of area, population and power, although there are five in England and six in Wales with populations of less than 100,000. The counties are the upper part of a two or three tier system, with the non-county boroughs and urban and rural district councils in the lower tier. The county councils are responsible for the following main services: education, town and country

22

planning, police, fire protection, local health and welfare services, highways, weights and measures, and certain agricultural services. Of these, education makes much the biggest demand for buildings. The county councils are not housing authorities, though they do provide houses for policemen, midwives and others who must live within the locality they serve.

It is important to distinguish between a geographical county, known by its county name such as Yorkshire, Lancashire, Essex, Warwickshire or Shropshire, and the administrative counties. The county councils are responsible only for the areas which are included within the boundaries of non-county boroughs or district councils, and not for the county boroughs. This is an important difference. In a rural county there may not be a single town of county borough status, so that the whole area of the geographical county comes under the jurisdiction of the county council. In some counties half the population may live in county boroughs, so that the area and population covered administratively by the county council is relatively small compared with the area and population of the geographical county. In Yorkshire the area is so large that it is divided between three county councils. It is thus important to distinguish between administrative counties which are controlled by the county councils and geographical counties which are not local government entities at all. This book is concerned only with the former.

The *London County Council*, in spite of its name, does not fit into the county council pattern. Like the county councils it is part of a two-tier system, in which the metropolitan boroughs correspond more or less with the non-county boroughs elsewhere. But the London County Council is wholly an urban authority and has responsibilities and powers for housing as well as education. Housing is in fact its largest single responsibility and absorbs the largest share of its capital expenditure. As far as its building organization is concerned, London is closer to the large cities such as Birmingham or Manchester than to the other county councils, who are chiefly concerned with school building.

The *County Boroughs* are mostly the larger cities. They are single-tier, all-purpose authorities and combine responsibility for the services run by the county councils with most of those run by the non-county boroughs or district councils. They can be thought of as independent islands within the boundaries of the geographical county.

The county boroughs are thus responsible for both housing and education, each of which makes heavy demands on their building organizations. These twin responsibilities coupled with the size of many of these cities have meant that the county boroughs usually have large and elaborate arrangements for the design and control of building and large maintenance organizations. Because diversity is great and different county boroughs may meet the same problems in completely different ways, generalizations about building organizations are particularly difficult. Often it is only possible to illustrate the diversity by examples.

The powers and functions of the *Non-County Boroughs* include: housing, sanitary services such as baths, wash-houses, cemeteries, refuse collection, street cleansing and sewerage, libraries, markets, museums, street lighting and parks. Of these only housing entails any significant building programmes, though individual buildings for the other services may be important for the particular authority.

The powers and duties of the *Urban District Councils* are similar to those of the non-county boroughs.

The powers and duties of the *Rural District Councils* are also similar to those of the non-county boroughs with the exception of highways, libraries, markets and museums, though in some minor instances these may be shared with parish councils. Again, housing is the main building activity.

It will be apparent from this brief summary that in the field of building organization authorities divide sharply into three main groups:

the county councils, who are mainly concerned with school building;

the county boroughs, who have two major building responsibilities—housing and education. Of these housing usually makes the larger demands;

the non-county boroughs and district authorities, who are concerned almost entirely with housing.

24

Any discussion with a particular authority is overshadowed by the dominant building responsibility of that authority. In a county council four out of five of the architectural staff are likely to be designing schools. In a non-county borough almost all of them will be designing houses. In a county borough the balance between the two will be rather closer. A similar difference of emphasis will be found for maintenance. In the district councils the maintenance organization is geared to the maintenance of houses. In the county councils it is geared to the maintenance of schools.

The design and maintenance of schools present different problems from the design and maintenance of housing, and each has to be discussed in its particular context. Nevertheless there are many lessons to be learned from the one which are applicable to the other. This applies throughout the field of local authority building. While there is no talisman to efficiency which can be applied by all authorities even of the same type, there are many common problems. It is hoped that the descriptions and discussion of the various methods, which is the subject matter of this book, will stimulate and help authorities to improve their own building organizations.

If the next decade is to see the consolidation of building in the hands of public authorities it is more than ever important that these buildings should successfully fulfil their purposes. To satisfy the social, technical, financial and aesthetic requirements of these buildings is a task of great difficulty but also one of lively interest and of lasting value.

SUMMARY AND RECOMMENDATIONS

1. Over many decades there has been a shift in the balance of resources devoted by public and private bodies to building. The rate of change was accelerated by the war, the emergence of the welfare state and the establishment of new public boards controlled by central government. In the process public authorities took over many of the functions of private clients.

2. In the realignment of responsibilities local authorities lost certain functions to central government. But they assumed bigger responsibilities for housing and schools, and building programmes for these have occupied much of their energies. These

two services overshadow building for all other local authority services.

3. Local authority building reached its peak in 1953. Since then the volume of house building has declined. School building, however, continued to rise. The demands of slum clearance and school building are likely to keep local authorities very active for many years ahead and to make big demands on the building industry. Other and more varied types of building increased after 1958 though its total volume remained small.

4. The main housing effort of local authorities is being orientated to slum clearance and redevelopment. This presents local authorities with difficult but challenging, social, administrative and technical problems. Other changes can be expected in the future due to the rising standard of living, the higher birthrate and shifts in population. These changes will demand new responses from local authorities. There can be nothing static about their building organizations in the future.

5. The building industry is itself changing. Local authorities, like other users of building resources, will have to adapt themselves to the new techniques and methods of management.

6. Local authorities are so diverse in size, function and organization that it is difficult to make valid generalizations. The book draws upon a wide field. It is hoped that local authorities will be able to select from the material ideas and methods, which they can adapt to their own particular circumstances.

CHAPTER 2

CONTROL OF BUILDING BY CENTRAL GOVERNMENT

Aims of control by central government—economic and political factors—type of buildings controlled by each department—methods of control over capital programmes, standards and costs—use of these methods for schools, housing and other buildings—lessons of present methods.

THE close interrelation of central and local government is nowhere more apparent than in the control of capital expenditure. This control has a character which is all its own. It is more dramatic and more definite, and it can stimulate much stronger feelings than are usually aroused by the more routine controls over day-to-day services. Most local authority members are barely aware of the regular examination of their services by inspectors from government departments. They are even less aware of the routine checking of accounts by the district auditors of the Ministry of Housing and Local Government. Maintenance expenditure on buildings is paid for from revenue either directly or by way of a repairs fund: such expenditure is rarely the concern of government departments. Council members are, however, very much alive to the approvals or refusals they receive from government departments for new schools, new housing schemes, new libraries, clinics or town halls.

Public investment in Great Britain constitutes nearly half the country's total fixed capital formation. In 1958 the aggregate gross fixed investment by the nation was just over £3,500 million. Of this some £1,500 million consisted of public investment by central government, by local authorities and by the public boards. Less than one-fifth of this public investment was expenditure by central government. Local authorities were responsible for rather under two-fifths and public corporations for rather over two-fifths. (Table 3).

27

TABLE 3

GROSS FIXED CAPITAL FORMATION (at home)[1]

£ million

	Personal sector	Companies	Public corporations	Central government	Local authorities	Total
1948	233	554	180	113	372	1,452
1953	383	689	487	217	608	2,384
1954	478	803	534	186	577	2,578
1955	554	982	568	194	543	2,841
1956	584	1,168	591	220	574	3,137
1957	610	1,310	655	244	581	3,400
1958	677	1,359	696	241	543	3,516

The level of capital investment is an important factor in the country's economic situation. Too much and it may accelerate inflation; too little and it may encourage unemployment. Since the Government has little direct control over the volume of private capital investment, much of its effort to maintain economic stability is concentrated on the public sector.

In the exercise of this control local authorities are subject to a more detailed supervision of their capital expenditure than the public boards. Generally speaking the control by central government over the capital expenditure of the boards is concentrated at two points only; on their long-term capital programmes and on their annual capital budgets.[2] The long-term programmes determine the main lines of development, and the framework within which each board will bring forward new capital schemes. The annual review of capital expenditure settles the share of national resources which the Government can allow a particular board in a particular year, and is influenced by the current economic situation. Having agreed the annual estimate of capital expenditure a board is normally free to spend this money within the agreed limits without further consultation with its Ministry.

It is part of the special relationship between local authorities and central government that central control covers not only the total volume of capital expenditure and the general pattern of its distribution between services and authorities, but the design

[1] Source: *National Income and Expenditure 1959*. This expenditure includes civil engineering as well as building, plant and machinery.
[2] *Budgeting in Public Authorities.* A Study Group of the Royal Institute of Public Administration. George Allen & Unwin Ltd (1959).

and costs of each particular scheme. Local authorities are not only told how many houses, schools or fire stations they may build each year, but the plans and costs of every scheme must be submitted for approval. In the case of schools and two-storey housing, of which local authorities have a great deal of experience, the scrutiny has in recent years become less rigorous provided the standards and costs are acceptable. In the case of less familiar types of building, however, the scrutiny may be very detailed.

The controls exercised by central government over capital expenditure by local government have four main aims:

to control the total share of national resources going into this sector of the economy;

to decide how much shall be allocated to each of the main services out of this total;

to secure a reasonable degree of equity in its distribution between one authority and another; and

to ensure that the money on individual schemes is well spent and gives good value.

It is the Government of the day which makes the first two decisions. The total figure and its distribution between the services is determined partly by the current economic situation of the country and partly by the Government's political aims. Throughout almost the whole post-war period the country has been faced with the problems of inflation and with difficulties in the balance of payments. These have erupted at roughly two-year intervals into a situation of financial crisis. Each crisis has had immediate repercussions on the local authorities, since this is the sector of the economy, apart from its own operations, on which the Government has the most direct influence. Calls for savings in costs, re-assessments of programmes or for the post-ponement of less essential schemes have succeeded one another so frequently that authorities have felt much uncertainty and frustration.

The commotion created by each crisis has had a very unsettling effect upon authorities and has adversely affected the efficiency of their building services. In terms of total building output the effects of these crises have been small and concentrated on the smaller programmes. Looking back over the past fifteen years it is now possible to see that the main programmes for housing and schools have remained but lightly affected by financial crises. Their rise or fall has been for political rather than for financial reasons. It is the other services which have had the severe casualties. At each earthquake their schemes have been buried and have had to be painfully dug out again, when the tremors had ceased.

The main trends of local authority capital expenditure in recent years are shown in Table 4. At its peak in 1953 housing absorbed four-fifths of the effort of local authorities on new building and education about a sixth. Even after six years of declining expenditure housing still absorbed five-eighths of local authority capital expenditure in 1958. Educational expenditure in the same year had risen to one-quarter. The total of all other expenditure on building is trifling compared with the two largest services.

Housing and education would in any event have been heavy users of building resources. They have, however, enjoyed and, in the case of housing, also suffered from their political importance. Throughout the post-war years housing has been a highly controversial issue, with a sharp cleavage between the two main political parties on the role to be played by private enterprise. This divergence is reflected in the downward trend of local authority house building which became evident some time after the change from a Labour to a Conservative Government in 1951. This fall, which is seen still more clearly in Table 5, is not attributable to political factors alone, but it was accelerated by them. Yet in spite of the influence of the views of successive Governments on the balance between public and private enterprise, housing by local authorities remains too important a need and too inflammatory an issue to be neglected.

Education has also been a live political issue, but both parties have been agreed on its importance. Since 1945 Ministers of Education of both parties have succeeded in increasing education's allocation of the total capital investment programme of local authorities. First the demands of the years of high birthrates and subsequently of technical education and the training of teachers have given the building programme for education a high priority. The battle of the 'bulge' has kept Ministers, the Ministry of Education and local education authorities at full stretch and infused them with a notable unanimity of purpose.

No such political horse power has been harnessed to the building of other types of local authority buildings. There is much less political kudos to be gained from building police and fire stations, maternity and child welfare clinics or municipal offices. As a result the services which required them have made do with a pathetically small total allocation of resources for new building. Their demands would in any case be modest compared with those for schools or houses. Table 4 shows in what reduced circumstances they have lived.

While it is politics rather than economics which have determined the long-term rise or fall of local authority capital investment, the effects of the financial crises must not be underes-

TABLE 4

CAPITAL EXPENDITURE BY LOCAL AUTHORITIES ON BUILDINGS[1]

(*United Kingdom*)
£ million

Type of Service	1948	1949	1950	1951	1952	1953	1954	1955	1956	1957	1958
1. Housing	267	263	264	288	352	399	365	318	304	294	251
2. Education and Child Care	25	38	50	62	71	72	74	82	103	121	122
Total of 1 and 2	292	301	314	350	423	471	439	400	407	415	373
3. Health	2	3	3	3	3	3	3	3	3	3	3
4. Care of aged, handicapped and homeless	1	2	3	3	3	2	3	3	3	3	3
5. Police[2]	1	2	4	5	7	8	7	8	8	7	7
6. Fire Service	—	1	1	2	3	3	3	3	3	3	3
7. Other[3]	4	4	5	7	5	5	6	7	10	9	9
Total of 3–7	8	12	16	20	21	21	22	24	27	25	25
Total of 1–7	300	313	330	370	444	492	461	424	434	440	399

[1] *National Income and Expenditure 1959.* Table 39. Capital Account. Gross fixed capital formation.
[2] Includes police houses.
[3] This includes a number of miscellaneous buildings, such as town halls, swimming baths, crematoria and some minor capital works.

31

timated. The succession of crises has had three important effects on the organization of local authority building.

First, it has engendered uncertainty and decreased the efficiency of local authority building operations. Such operations can be efficiently organized only on the basis of continuity. Every crisis, whatever its final outcome, has broken continuity to a greater or lesser degree and undermined the willingness of authorities to plan ahead. Many of the practices criticized in this book owe their origin or continuance to the repetition of these uncertainties.

Secondly, the problems of each successive emergency have made it necessary for central government to retain or re-impose a close control over local government. In more propitious circumstances it is probable that controls would have been relaxed progressively and local authorities would have gained greater independence. In practice each crisis tightened once again the grip of central government because of the need to restrain capital expenditure.

Thirdly, almost every crisis has intensified the drive to obtain more building for the same or less cost. Even when total programmes remained unaffected the squeeze on costs increased. Much of this effort was salutary, and could be applied without impairing the efficiency of the buildings. Some will produce a crop of problems in the future.

RESPONSIBILITIES OF DEPARTMENTS

Once the Cabinet has fixed the broad outlines of government spending, it is for departments to secure a fair distribution between authorities and to see, as far as possible, that the money is spent to the best advantage. This is done according to the local authority services which each government department controls. Each department has its own methods and these differ from one another in important ways.

Four central departments between them control virtually all the schemes for new building by local authorities. They are the Ministry of Education, the Ministry of Housing and Local Government, the Home Office and the Ministry of Health. The responsibilities of these four departments work in different ways and affect the relations with authorities correspondingly. Their responsibilities for the different kinds of buildings are as follows:

Ministry of Education—All school buildings, colleges of further education and training colleges for teachers.

Ministry of Housing and Local Government—Housing, and all buildings which do not come under the jurisdiction of another department. These include municipal offices, public libraries, markets, buildings for public entertainment, crematoria, swimming baths, depots and miscellaneous small buildings.

Home Office—Police buildings, fire stations, local court buildings, approved schools and buildings for the care of children.

Ministry of Health—Clinics, health centres, ambulance stations, occupational and training centres for the mentally disordered, homes for the elderly, the handicapped and the homeless.

Ministry of Education

The allocation of functions between the four departments has meant that the Ministry of Education alone has undivided responsibility for a single major service. The advantages have proved to be great. It is a compact and homogeneous department bent with singleness of purpose on clear objectives.

It also has the advantage of dealing with relatively few local authorities. Since the 1944 Education Act responsibility for local education services has been concentrated in the hands of the county councils and county borough councils. This means that the Ministry is dealing with less than 150 authorities, most of whom have experienced staff and sizeable administrative and architectural organizations. The balance between central and local government is more even when a ministry has to deal with a few large authorities than it is when it has to work with a large number of small authorities. The administrative machinery for transmitting and receiving information is also greatly simplified.

The Ministry of Education has had three main preoccupations in the field of building; schools, technical colleges and training colleges for teachers. Of these schools is by far the most demanding.

Local authorities have a statutory obligation to provide

schooling. The Ministry of Education thus has a clear responsibility to ensure that they can and do meet the demands upon them. The steep rise in the birthrate immediately after the war set the local education authorities and the Ministry a large, definite and urgent problem to provide extra school places. The Government's decision to raise the school leaving age in 1947, from fourteen to fifteen, increased it. The combined effects of the higher birthrate and the extra year at school necessitated a very large school building programme. There were $5 \cdot 1$ million children in grant-aided schools in 1946; in 1961 when the numbers will reach their peak there will be more than 7 million. The Ministry has addressed itself energetically to helping local authorities to provide the extra school places, and for over ten years no one has disputed the urgency and importance of this task.

The responsibility of the Minister and the local education authorities is only marginally affected by the provision of education in private schools. It is true that the half-million children in private schools relieve the public authorities of a large burden. But the existence of these private schools does not alter the local authorities' duty to provide education for all who demand it, and it does not make possible any deliberate shift in emphasis from public to private facilities. The Minister of Education cannot, like the Minister of Housing, decide that the weight of school building shall be transferred to private enterprise. The vast majority of school building remains inalienably in the hands of local authorities.

The second major task of the Ministry is in the field of technical education. This task is now in the ascendant since the present bulge in the school population is half-way through the secondary schools and most of the buildings to meet it are now built, under construction or in design. Quantitatively, the work of increasing technical education involves much less building than schools, but it poses complicated physical and administrative problems. The country is in the process of a big change in the scale of technical education and the colleges of further education are an essential element in that change.

Thirdly, there is now an urgent need for more facilities to train teachers. The training period is being increased from two to three years while the Government has declared its aim to reduce the size of classes. Within a period of four years, between 1958 and 1961, the number of places must be increased by 50 per cent and 100 colleges must have major extensions added to them. Again, the capital investment is nothing like that needed for schools, but the operation has had to be carried out with exceptional speed, and is the direct result of policy decisions by the Government.

The singleness of purpose, the clear definition of responsibility, the closeness of the contact between the Ministry and local education authorities and the consistent political support which education has enjoyed have had important results. They have enabled the Ministry of Education to develop methods of controlling capital expenditure and of working with local education authorities which are the envy of other Ministries and authorities. The Ministry has been a pioneer in building development and control. Much of the rest of this chapter and many other parts of the book show how much more successful the Ministry has been than other government departments in this field and how its example is being followed elsewhere. The repetition of praise for the Ministry of Education has sometimes seemed embarrassingly frequent. However deserved, it must be emphasized that the Ministry has enjoyed exceptionally favourable circumstances in which to evolve its new methods of controlling local authority building. Its success now makes it easier for other departments to follow suit.

Ministry of Housing and Local Government

To move from the Ministry of Education to the Ministry of Housing and Local Government is to move into a different climate. The Ministry of Housing's responsibilities are far more diverse. Though they are limited almost entirely to local authority activities, the Ministry is concerned with a much less homogeneous range of functions, and covers all local authorities including nearly 1,400 non-county boroughs and urban and rural districts. The Ministry deals, therefore, with far more authorities about far more things and its energies are dispersed more widely both in the centre and on the periphery.

The range of the Ministry's functions derives from its general responsibility for all local authority activities. Its Minister speaks for the Government in all major negotiations with local authorities collectively. The Ministry, for example, handled the negotiations and the Bill which revised the grant arrangements between central and local government in 1958. It also covers the revision of local authority boundaries, and changes in the status of individual authorities. With the exception of certain borough accounts most local authority accounts are audited by the district auditors, who are a part of the Ministry's staff. All loan sanctions for capital expenditure pass through its hands. The granting of loan sanctions is largely a matter of routine for building schemes approved by other government departments. But the fact that all such sanctions pass through the Ministry of Housing gives it a general view of the total volume of local authority expenditure and of the total commitments of each individual local authority. Other duties for which the Ministry is specifically responsible include the control of bye-laws, the oversight of all water and sewage schemes and the control of new towns. The Ministry also deals with town and country planning.

As far as local authority building is concerned, there are two quite distinct divisions in the system of control. There is the major responsibility for housing, and the minor responsibility, in terms of total cost, for a miscellaneous number of buildings such as town halls, swimming baths, crematoria, public libraries, depots and markets. Housing is important because of the size of the programmes, its political overtones and its social significance. The other more miscellaneous types of building come into the Ministry's embrace because they do not belong to services under other government departments. In the absence of other guardians and by virtue of its overall responsibility for loan sanctions the Ministry has assumed responsibility for overseeing these buildings also.

Local authorities have less specific statutory obligations to provide housing than they have to provide education; the Housing Acts[1] lay down some statutory duties on local authorities to review housing conditions and to submit proposals, and authorities have been required to carry out a survey of unfit houses in their areas. But the obligation to meet housing needs is much less clear cut than for schools and action is dependent largely on the initiative of the local authorities themselves and

[1] For example: Housing Act 1957, Sections 171–6.

on local pressures. Only the local authority can effectively judge the local needs for housing: the Ministry cannot be closely in touch with housing requirements in the areas of nearly 1,500 authorities. At the same time the existence of private enterprise as a second and important agency for house building makes it still more difficult to define the responsibilities of the local authorities from Whitehall. The Minister has almost no power of control over the numbers, standards or costs of houses built save such as he can exercise by virtue of his power to withhold loan sanction. For the rest he must depend on exhortation, inducement and advice.

For the other types of building, which come under the control of the Ministry of Housing and Local Government, the initiative rests even more with the local authorities. Many of them are connected with services which are not grant-aided. The Ministry's control over these buildings stems from its power over loan sanctions and not from any positive responsibility for the services they provide. If local authorities are not under any statutory obligation to provide buildings for, say, swimming or cremation, and meet the full costs of these buildings from rates, control by the Ministry of Housing and Local Government is particularly delicate.

In practice these distinctions become blurred in the every day contacts between authorities and ministries. Nevertheless, the source of each ministry's authority and the closeness of its knowledge of local needs conditions the initiatives it takes and the responses it receives.

The methods used by the Ministry of Housing to control local authority house building have been strongly influenced by the political and financial policies of successive Governments. There are three main phases, which cover the post-war period.

Between 1945 and 1951 it was the policy of the Labour Government to concentrate most of the housing effort in the hands of local authorities and the Ministry had the responsibility for stimulating and controlling this effort. The task was enormous, and it was carried out in the political limelight, with ceaseless criticism inside and outside Parliament. During most of this period shortages of men and materials were severe. At the same time interest rates for local authority borrowing were low and housing waiting lists high, so that most local authorities

37

were eager to build. The Ministry had, therefore, to attempt to keep a balance between demand and supply by a fairly elaborate system for agreeing building programmes with individual authorities.

The change of emphasis did not immediately follow the change of Government in 1951. The Conservative Government aimed at a larger total volume of building and gave a freer hand to private enterprise. But during this second phase local authority building continued at a high level, and the resurgence of private enterprise was slow. To achieve more output without a proportionate increase in capital outlay local authority housing designs were rigorously examined and pruned, and an all-out effort was made by the Ministry to keep housing costs from rising as fast as building costs and to economize on the use of scarce materials. In this it achieved considerable success, though at the price of a detailed scrutiny of housing schemes, the sacrifice of many amenities and the risk of higher maintenance costs during the life of the houses.

The third period coincided with the further rise in interest rates in the mid-1950s and the withdrawal of the housing subsidies for general needs in 1956. The Government considered that the time had come for local authorities to concentrate on more specialized tasks rather than to continue to build for general needs. The changes in the subsidy arrangements were designed to steer the local authorities towards slum clearance. By making borrowing more expensive and doing away with the housing subsidies except for slum clearance and the rehousing of old people, financial deterrents became more important than physical controls.

House building by local authorities is highly susceptible to changes in interest rates, more so than most other types of local authority building. This is due in part to the larger volume of such building, but also to the methods by which housing is financed. The impact of higher interest rates on rent is immediate and severe unless it is cushioned by higher subsidies. Every half-per-cent rise in interest rates increases rents significantly. For other types of local authority services interest charges on buildings are only a small part of total running costs and may be partly met by grant. For housing, interest payments are the main charge on rents. If, as in 1956, the rise in interest

38

rates is followed by a withdrawal of some of the housing sub-sidies, the curtailing of housing operations is certain.

TABLE 5

PERMANENT HOUSE BUILDING[1]

United Kingdom

1. Construction Begun

	All houses	For local housing authorities[2]	For private owners	For other authorities[3]
1953	354,860	246,716	84,890	23,254
1954	336,961	211,885	108,911	16,165
1955	320,000	180,441	130,113	9,446
1956	285,014	153,987	122,676	8,351
1957	281,223	148,138	127,792	5,293
1958	263,249	119,675	139,076	4,498
1959	324,976	147,721	172,336	4,919

2. Completions

1953	326,804	244,916	64,867	17,021
1954	354,129	239,318	92,423	22,388
1955	324,423	196,024	116,093	12,306
1956	307,674	170,710	126,431	10,533
1957	307,590	169,629	128,784	9,177
1958	278,633	143,283	130,220	5,130
1959	281,568	124,545	153,166	3,857

The effects of these changes in government policy are re-flected in the output of local authority housing and the balance between public and private enterprise. Up to the end of 1951 local authorities had completed nearly 800,000 dwellings and private enterprise less than 200,000 (Table 6). Local authority building continued to rise until 1953. After 1953 it declined steadily. In 1958 the number of local authority houses started was half the figure for 1953. During this period the number of private enterprise houses increased by 75 per cent. Taken together, public and private enterprise produced 1·0 million dwellings by 1951, 2·0 million by 1955, and 3·0 million by 1958.

[1] Source: *Monthly Digest of Statistics.*

[2] Including New Towns Development Corporations; in Scotland, the Scottish Special Housing Association; and, in Northern Ireland, the Northern Ireland Housing Trust.

[3] Including housing associations, other than the Scottish Special Housing Association and the Northern Ireland Housing Trust, and houses provided or authorized by government departments for the families of police, prison staff, the armed forces and for certain other services.

39

The change in interest rates and subsidies would have been less effective if they had not also served to narrow the gap between the costs to the occupier of public and private housing. In the early years the rents of subsidized housing were extremely attractive compared with what private enterprise could offer, if indeed it could build at all. Gradually the impact of the higher interest rates, the reductions in the statutory subsidies and the withdrawal of many of the additional rate subsidies altered the balance between council rents and the price of private housing. Families, who had been willing to wait years for a low rented council house, were no longer so anxious to do so when the rents ceased to compare so favourably with private housing.

A further important restraint on local authorities was the success of their own efforts. It is impossible to build steadily at the rate of more than 200,000 houses a year without making an impact on the shortage of dwellings. Gradually the pressure began to diminish in many areas outside the main towns. Gradually families moved off the waiting lists. The housing shortage changed from being an overall national problem to a series of local problems.

TABLE 6

HOUSES COMPLETED BY PUBLIC AND PRIVATE ENTERPRISE
(Cumulative Totals) *United Kingdom*

Year	Total[1]	By local[2] authorities	By private enterprise
1945	3,095	1,936	1,099
1946	59,074	27,181	31,665
1947	199,959	125,209	73,152
1948	432,422	318,757	107,542
1949	637,679	489,563	135,999
1950	843,106	657,480	166,239
1951	1,044,962	823,963	191,724
1952	1,293,281	1,023,140	228,394
1953	1,620,085	1,268,056	293,261
1954	1,974,214	1,507,374	385,684
1955	2,298,637	1,703,398	501,777
1956	2,606,311	1,874,108	628,208
1957	2,913,901	2,043,737	756,992
1958	3,192,534	2,187,020	887,212
1959	3,474,102	2,311,565	1,040,378

[1] This includes certain other agencies not included in Columns 3 and 4.
[2] Excludes temporary housing.

40

After 1956 the main emphasis was on slum clearance. By 1959 about half the houses were being built to meet the needs arising from such schemes. One quarter were one-bedroomed houses mainly for old people, and one quarter were for general needs, and without subsidy. This change was partly forced on the local authorities by the financial pressures. It was also a reflection of the change in the pattern of needs.

During the greater part of the post-war period capital expenditure on the other types of building for which the Ministry is responsible has been very restricted. Only the most urgent schemes could pass the net, and many of the larger projects awaited approval for years. Taking all local authorities together only perhaps a third have at any one time any schemes of this kind under consideration, and of these a still smaller proportion are of any size.

Recently there has been an increase in the number of buildings which have received loan sanction. In 1958 expenditure on buildings such as public libraries, town halls and swimming baths rose sharply and approvals continued during 1959 at a higher level.

Administrative control of this miscellaneous range of buildings is a very different problem from the more homogeneous programmes for housing and schools. It is more difficult to determine priorities between dissimilar buildings. Authorities themselves are more changeable in their plans, and the importance of such schemes can wax and wane for political and other local reasons. Authorities are also particularly liable to misjudge the period necessary to prepare them, owing to their unfamiliarity. The Ministry finds that such schemes regularly mature later than authorities estimate.

It is against this complicated background that the control of building operations by the Ministry must be judged. As will become clear the Ministry has not succeeded in providing a simple framework for the exercise of this control such as the Ministry of Education has done. If there are shortcomings they must be judged in the context of their day, the political and financial vicissitudes of housing policy and the low priority of other kinds of building. And it must not be forgotten that in exercising this control the Ministry has had to deal with a very large number of local authorities, and has been controlling a much larger volume of capital expenditure by them than any other government department.

Home Office

The Home Office is the department which controls law and order. Its functions are not confined to local authorities as are those of the Ministries of Education and Housing. Some of the Home Secretary's most important responsibilities have nothing to do with local government and relate to such things as prisons, naturalization, control of aliens and immigration regulations. As far as local authorities are concerned, the police, the fire service, the children's service and civil defence are the main points of contact.

Like the Ministry of Education the Home Office's work is mainly with the larger authorities, the counties and county boroughs, who control these services. Indeed it has to take an exceptionally wide view, geographically, of most of its functions. Crime has no respect for county borders. Fire services may be called upon from far and wide to deal with major fires. Civil defence is nation-wide. The Home Office, therefore, has responsibilities for securing co-ordination between authorities which are not required by other departments.

As far as new building is concerned, only £7 million to £8 million was spent annually on police buildings between 1950 and 1958, of which quite a large proportion was on houses for police families (Table 4). The annual capital expenditure on buildings for the fire service has been only some £3 million a year. The children's service uses mainly domestic housing and other new building is negligible. This volume of building necessitates only a very small architectural staff. Building programmes for local authorities are for the Home Office a modest responsibility compared with their importance to the two departments already discussed. After 1958 there was some increase in the capital expenditure allowed, but it remained very small compared with that for housing or schools.

The Ministry of Health

The Ministry of Health is occupied even more than the Home Office with responsibilities which fall outside the scope of local authorities. Its largest responsibility is for the national health services, including hospitals, the family practitioner services, the dental service and the pharmaceutical services. These absorb a great part of its energies.

The local authority services it controls cover maternity and child welfare, home nursing and domestic help, health visiting, the ambulance service, control of food and drugs and welfare foods, port health services, mental health services and welfare services for the old and the handicapped. Many of these are carried out by the personal visits of nurses, health visitors and others to people in their homes and require no special buildings; others are administrative services carried out from the offices of the Medical Officer of Health in the town hall. Until 1958 expenditure on buildings for local authority health services had been running at about £3 million a year and on buildings for other services at another £3 million. It was expected that the lifting of some of the restrictions on capital expenditure would permit new approvals for the year 1959/60 to increase to £9 million.

Methods of Control

Once the Government has decided the total share of capital resources which local authorities may have and the distribution between the different services, individual departments are concerned with three main questions:

will the aggregate of all the schemes submitted by local authorities for a particular service come within the limit of total expenditure laid down by the Government?

does the design of each scheme meet the accepted minimum standards for the type of building or the standards laid down by the department?

is the cost of each individual scheme reasonable and does it fall within limits of cost laid down by the department?

The first question is designed to secure that the volume and direction of local authority spending will accord with the Government's views on priorities, on its estimates of what the nation can afford, and its attitude towards the activities of local

43

authorities in any particular field. The second question aims at maintaining or raising the minimum standards so that public money is not wasted on buildings below the current standards of design and construction. The third serves to avoid extravagance in public spending and to permit the largest possible output of houses, schools or other types of building within whatever total level of expenditure has been laid down.

These three questions resolve themselves into the three basic aspects of control—the control of programmes, the control of standards, and the control of costs. The rest of this chapter is devoted to discussing how these three controls are exercised by the different departments and the effect of the various methods on local authorities and their buildings.

CONTROL OF CAPITAL PROGRAMMES

The financial system of the country is run on the basis of annual budgets. Government departments prepare annual estimates which include current and capital expenditure. These are approved annually by Parliament. A high proportion of the Government's capital expenditure is met from current revenue, and these items appear in the same section of the budget as its current expenditure. Indeed, until recently the annual estimates of many government departments showed no clear distinction between expenditure on capital works and on current services, since they were financed in the same way.

This blurring of the distinction between capital and current expenditure is made easier for central government because its capital expenditure is a relatively small part of total expenditure and much of it is concentrated in the hands of three government departments. The Post Office, the Ministry of Transport and the Ministry of Works are responsible for the greater part of the building and civil engineering works undertaken by the central government. Included in the Ministry of Works' operations are agency services paid for by other government departments, such as the provision of offices. Apart from their own office buildings many government departments have little capital expenditure.

Because Parliament sanctions central government expenditure only on an annual basis, and because so small a proportion is for capital projects, there has in the past been little machinery for long-term capital budgets. Such long-term programmes as existed were usually of an informal kind. They might be discussed with the Treasury but carried no guarantee of Treasury or Ministerial approval. They were a working guide for the department. The Post Office and the Ministry of Works, for example, have such programmes, and these provide a valuable method of settling priorities between schemes. Nevertheless, certainty is obtainable only for the year immediately ahead, since the Treasury only fixes the allocations to departments in the autumn for the following financial year. Such figures as may be tentatively agreed for the year after have often been seriously curtailed later.

The relation of revenue to capital expenditure by local authorities is very different from that in central government. In 1958 local authorities spent on current account £1,534 million while their expenditure on fixed capital formation was £543 million. Thus over a quarter of their expenditure in that year was on building and civil engineering projects, building being the larger part. Almost all of this was financed by borrowing, this being the normal method of meeting capital expenditure by local authorities.

This means that fluctuations in the volume of capital expenditure authorized by the Government have a much more disrupting effect on local authorities than on most government departments. A far greater proportion of the energies of local authorities is devoted to new building. A much higher proportion of their staffs is occupied in designing and controlling building operations. Uncertainties and sudden changes in Government policy on their building programmes are thus much more disturbing than for central government.

Education Buildings

Government departments differ very much in the methods they use to control building programmes of local authorities and the degree of certainty they offer. In spite of the Treasury's normal insistence that capital expenditure shall be fixed on an annual basis, the Ministry of Education has been able to establish a system which gives local education authorities a high degree of certainty over a period of two-and-a-half to three years ahead. The credit for this is partly due to the unanimity of the political parties about the importance of school building, which has caused few major changes of programme. It is also due to the lively appreciation by the Ministry of Education of the relationship between building efficiency and building programmes, and its success in persuading the Treasury that the benefits merited a change in the normal procedure.

The procedure used by the Ministry of Education works as follows:

authorities are asked to submit in about February of each year details of schemes they wish to start in the next financial year. For example in February 1958 they submitted schemes to be started in the year 1959–60;

at the same time they are asked to submit a further half-year's programme as a reserve list. In the example this would be for 1960–61;

these requests are generally approved in May or June of the same year; in the present example in 1958. Authorities were then free to design a programme which carried them forward from June 1958 to October 1960, a period of twenty-eight months;

the same procedure then follows the next year; in the present example this would have been early in 1959. By that time the authority should already have been well advanced with the design of the schools in the current reserve programme. This covered schools to be started between April and October 1960;

in 1959 for the first time the Ministry called for schemes to be submitted for the whole of 1961-62 as well as 1960-61, instead of asking for a half-year's reserve programme for 1961–62. This was an important new departure which it is hoped to maintain in the future.

Not all education authorities take full advantage of the advance programmes the Ministry of Education can give. And

46

sometimes a change of view or a difference of opinion between the Ministry and an individual authority may delay agreement on the programme. But in general these arrangements work to the time-table which has been described, and are far superior to those offered by any other government department. They enable the Ministry to divide the total capital allocation for education well in advance and with a full knowledge of all the competing claims. And they give authorities confidence in their programmes and permit them to plan the architectural work involved more efficiently. It would be difficult to over-emphasize the value of this programme procedure for Ministry and authorities alike.

Housing

It has already been explained that the change of Government in 1951 meant a gradual shift from physical to financial controls of the volume of local authority house building. Those controls which were necessitated by shortages of labour and materials would have diminished in any event. Whether the kind of programming, which gives advance notice of government intentions, would have been discontinued without a change of Government cannot now be determined. What is clear is that there was a complete change of method.

The control of local authority housing programmes can be divided into three main phases.

The first phase coincides more or less with the period of building licensing between 1945 and 1954. During this period there was a detailed system of housing allocations, operated through the Ministry's regional offices. It was closely related to the availability of men and materials. By 1950 the programming system had settled down to an annual return by local authorities of their housing requirements and a decision by the Ministry transmitted to each authority of the number of dwellings they might build in any one year. This was coupled with a general statement of future prospects. This policy was summarized by the Ministry in the following terms:

Local authorities may assume, when the Ministry informs them of the number of houses they may build in any one year that, subject to any over-riding changes in Government policy, their approved cur-

47

rent annual rate of house building may be repeated for at least three years . . .[1]

This system was less definite than that provided by the Ministry of Education, but it gave both the Ministry and authorities a reasonable basis on which to plan future building.

The second phase began when building licensing came to an end in 1954. This marked the end of an era. House building by private enterprise was then given its head. The release of the building industry from the licensing system made it unnecessary to continue such allocations to local authorities as were based on physical shortages. In the process of abandoning physical controls, programming was dropped too. There were political advantages in leaving local authorities to make their own adjustments to rising interest rates without too overt a limitation of local authority building. These advantages, coupled with the administrative problems of agreeing programmes annually with over 1,400 housing authorities, made the case for stopping the machinery for programming.

The change meant that authorities were free to build as many houses as they wished or felt able to, taking into account the higher interest rates, the structure of the subsidies, the efforts of private enterprise and the emphasis laid by the Government on slum clearance. The cumulative effect of these restraints and pressures was very great, and it is doubtful if authorities recognized the new situation as one of greater freedom.

The third phase started with the financial crisis of 1957, known at the time as the 'credit squeeze'. Local housing authorities were asked by the Ministry to make a cut of 20 per cent in their expenditure, to review their programmes and to consult the department. Local authority housing programmes were already decreasing so rapidly that the actual adjustments were much less than the nominal 20 per cent. The crisis, however, marked a return to an annual allocation system which was still in operation at the end of 1959.

In 1958 there was some relaxation of the pressure; housing programmes were discussed with authorities and some cuts were imposed, but less than in 1957. For 1959 local authority demands were so far reduced that the Ministry had to exercise

[1] *First Report of the Local Government Manpower Committee.* Cmnd. 7870, 1950.

few restraints. Overall demand from authorities equated more or less with the volume of local authority housing which the Ministry was empowered to approve. In December 1959 authorities were again asked to submit their requirements, this time for the 1960 housing programmes which, as previously, ran for the full calendar year. It was expected that demand would again balance fairly easily within the planned capital programme.

The reduction in the volume of local authority expenditure on housing has thus been achieved with little direct limitation of programmes. There is a great deal to be said for a system which encourages self-restraint, rather than a restraint imposed from Whitehall. But the programming system exists, and exists on such a short-term basis that it is difficult for authorities to operate efficiently within its framework. Whatever latitude they may have had from time to time, and particularly between 1954 and 1957, they are far more conscious of restriction than of freedom. Certainty is limited to a period of less than twelve months ahead.

While it is true that most housing operations are a continuing process and most authorities are drawing on their own programmes when they send their requests annually to the Ministry, there remains a significant element of uncertainty about what will be approved. This discourages the more cautious authorities from carrying out as much of the preparatory work as the continuity of building operations demand. Conversely, the more impetuous authorities are liable to incur additional loan charges for land acquisition and site development if their expectations are disappointed by the Ministry. In these circumstances it is small wonder that building schemes get bunched together towards the end of the programme year, and that design work is rushed. Such results lead to higher tenders, less efficient work on the site and costly settlements of accounts.

Housing is so large a part of public investment that it cannot be insulated from the economic situation of the country and exempted from cuts when these are necessary. But looking back over the last few years it is clear that the economic crises have been minor fluctuations in a much more fundamental change of trend. By fixing housing programmes two years instead of one year in advance some later adjustments would have been necessary, but the main effort would have been unaffected. The psychological effects on authorities of fixing their programmes at least a year further in advance would have been profound. Many of the extra costs and inefficiences dealt with later in this book must be attributed to the failure to help authorities to bring their schemes fully prepared to the starting line and to start on time. This cannot be done by asking authorities in December what they want to build in the twelve months immediately ahead.

Other Buildings

It was stated earlier that only housing and schools had had a strong political momentum behind them. Apart from their low place in the queue politically, the buildings controlled by the Home Office and the Ministry of Health and the miscellaneous buildings controlled by the Ministry of Housing and Local Government suffer two other disadvantages. At times of crisis cuts are imposed where this can be done most easily. The apparatus for preparing large schemes is normally too complex to be quickly halted. Thus, minor works and small schemes nearly always contribute more than their fair share to such economies. Secondly, these schemes are not protected by formal procedure for advance programming such as the Ministry of Education has for schools.

In spite of the comparatively modest annual expenditure there are certain types of buildings which are numerous enough to call for some programme procedure. These include many of the buildings controlled by the Home Office and the Ministry of Health such as police and fire stations and maternity and child welfare clinics.

In such cases authorities are usually invited to submit their requests to the Ministry concerned in the autumn for the coming financial year. This is only some six months before the programme year starts in April and eighteen months before it ends. Large schemes may have been the subject of preliminary discussions, but not of any firm decision.

These requests are then reviewed by the department with its knowledge of authorities' needs and the relative importance of the different schemes. They are discussed with the Treasury in broad outline in the light of the current economic situation and

50

the allocation of capital expenditure to the various services. Authorities are then informed by the department which of their schemes may go forward. This decision at best will reach them three or four months before the new programme year starts. It is an essential part of the whole programming system that schemes approved in this way shall start within the programme year for which they are approved. Those that fail to start within this period will lose their place in the queue.

A typical example of the procedure for settling programmes is given at the end of this chapter. It is drawn from the Home Office and covers police buildings. It accords with the usual arrangements of government departments themselves for drawing up annual estimates and is primarily adapted to revenue expenditure. It is a system which produces great difficulties for all authorities who are dealing with building time-tables.

Some of the inefficiencies which arise from a system of programming building operations only from year to year have already been touched on. When, to this annual system of approvals, is added violent fluctuations in the volume of these approvals so that authorities have frequently to put schemes, which are ready to start, back in the plan files, discomfiture and inefficiency are greater still.

The figures of capital expenditure on the buildings controlled by the Home Office and the Ministry of Health (Table 4) give a misleading impression of continuity. While school and house building have risen and fallen on fairly steady curves, police stations, fire, ambulance stations, clinics and so on have been subject to sharp changes. Table 4 shows expenditure which covers payments on schemes under construction. Since the building of a particular scheme may be spread over one, two or three years the payments represented by expenditure remain fairly stable.

A more realistic picture of the fluctuations in the volume of building is revealed by the figures in Tables 7 and 8. These show approvals given each year and reflect the ups and downs of the financial situation. In 1956 approvals for some types of building came almost to a standstill and almost all were greatly reduced. It is recognized by departments that with so many changes in the volume of approvals authorities almost ceased to plan their own programmes for such buildings, and lived more or less from

51

TABLE 7

BUILDING PROJECTS APPROVED BY HOME OFFICE FOR POLICE AND FIRE SERVICES[1]

	1954/55		1955/56		1956/57		1957/58		1958/59	
	No. of projects	Estimated cost £'000	No. of projects	Estimated cost £'000	No. of projects	Estimated cost £'000	No. of projects	Estimated cost £'000	No. of projects	Estimated cost £'000
POLICE SERVICE										
1. Over £5,000 each	53	1,356	35	1,300	11	465	36	1,419	42	1,349
2. Under £5,000 each	—	194	—	161	—	91	—	163	—	213
FIRE SERVICE										
3. Over £5,000 each	38	841	35	821	9	233	55	1,057	53	1,499
4. Under £5,000 each	—	104	—	26	—	15	—	48	—	24
Total of 1 and 3	91	2,197	70	2,121	20	698	91	2,476	95	2,848
Grand Total		2,495		2,308		804		2,687		3,085

[1] Excludes housing which is included in Table 5.

hand to mouth. Both sides know this is no way to plan local authority services.

With the relaxation of the restrictions on local authority spending, which started in 1958 and led to a greater volume of approvals in the year 1959–60, there were welcome signs that a better system of programming was being introduced, and that the lessons of the methods of the Ministry of Education were being applied elsewhere. In September 1959 authorities were for the first time asked by the Ministry of Health[1] to submit a tentative programme for the financial year 1961–62 as well as a firm programme for the year 1960–61, that is two years ahead instead of one. It remained to be seen if the tentative programme would be given a real measure of support by central government and allowed to be a genuine indication of works to be approved. If so, and authorities can plan their schemes in greater confidence, this change will prove to be an important step forward.

There are also schemes which in the last fifteen years have been approved too infrequently to make for any continuous level of building. So far decisions have been made individually for such schemes as and when requests come in. Most of the miscellaneous buildings controlled by the Ministry of Housing and Local Government are in this category. The Ministry is at present considering how to introduce some method of programming for them. This is no easy task, since only a minority of authorities are planning any such buildings at any one time, and resources are too limited to make it advisable to ask all authorities to submit programmes for all their requirements. To stimulate a rush for new swimming baths or town halls would only raise false hopes.

CONTROL OF STANDARDS

The second main way of controlling capital expenditure is through a close check on standards. Buildings on which public money is to be used must achieve acceptable standards of quality and suitability for their purpose. They must give good value for the money spent on them. Government departments have a responsibility, clearer for some buildings than for others,

[1] Circular 25/59.

TABLE 8

BUILDING PROJECTS APPROVED BY MINISTRY OF HEALTH
FOR LOCAL HEALTH SERVICES[1]

Type	1954		1955		1956		1957		1958	
	No. of projects	Estimated cost £000	No. of projects	Estimated cost £000	No. of projects	Estimated cost £000	No. of projects	Estimated cost £000	No. of projects	Estimated cost £000
1. Health centres	1	36	4	87	—	—	2	22	3	73
2. Maternity and child welfare clinics	24	245	44	505	6	68	34	461	42	566
3. Day nurseries	2	22	4	60	1	6	2	10	1	5
4. Ambulance stations	29	388	28	495	2	13	13	187	28	336
5. Accommodation for care and after-care	5	30	1	10	—	—	1	2	4	26
6. Training centres and hostels for the mentally disordered	16	247	13	117	21	293	26	462	28	674
7. Accommodation for home nurses and midwives	53	168	48	131	50	150	56	184	34	103
Total	130	1,136	142	1,405	80	530	134	1,328	140	1,783
Total excluding 7	77		94		30		78		106	

[1] Source: Ministry of Health. *Annual Report 1958*.

for seeing that these standards are met before loan sanction is given. Some are clearly defined minimum standards, which the building must meet before approval can be given. Others are objectives rather than minima. Some buildings are controlled by published standards. Others are dealt with almost 'ad hoc' and the standards are set for a particular scheme in consultation with the department concerned.

The two departments who control the largest local building programmes have each published standards. The machinery of controlling the large number of housing and education schemes would be impossible if authorities did not know in advance what standards would be acceptable. The methods of determining and administering these standards reveal interesting differences between the Ministries of Housing and Education. Apart from schools and housing, there is at present little comparable information which is generally available to authorities. Advice on design and accommodation has been published for various types of buildings, but the definition of standards is less clear.

Schools

The Ministry of Education has a statutory responsibility for fixing the standards of schools. These are embodied in Building Regulations, and are in effect minimum standards backed by statutory authority. These regulations first took their present form in 1945 as the result of the 1944 Education Act. Since 1945 they have been revised three times, in 1951, 1954 and 1959. They cover such things as the amount of teaching accommodation for different numbers of pupils, the size of playgrounds and playing fields, space standards for meals, lighting and heating standards and sanitary arrangements.

Three of the most interesting features of these regulations are their frequent revision, progressive simplification, and the ability of the Ministry to make the necessary changes administratively rather than through the machinery of advisory committees.

The first edition of the building regulations was a fairly short but complicated document. The intention was to raise standards, and to set them out clearly so that authorities knew exactly what they had to achieve. Any such attempt raises a corresponding difficulty. The clearer and more specific the standards are the greater the assurance they will be achieved, but also the less the scope for experiment and improvement. This is a difficulty with which architects are already familiar in the housing bye-laws.

The Ministry of Education, therefore, set itself the task of revising its building regulations at short intervals and of making them progressively simpler. With each revision there has been a gradual reduction of the detail and the omission of certain items which local authorities were considered to be able to decide for themselves. Each revision has also enabled the Ministry to take account of educational and technical changes.

The difference between the 1945 and the 1959 regulations is striking, both in content and in language. The 1959 regulations reflect the greater experience both of the Ministry and of authorities, and the greater confidence which the Ministry has in authorities' skill. The standards are reduced to the essentials and leave the authorities a much larger measure of discretion. This discretion gives them more freedom than in the past to work out their own solutions, and to meet the problem of costs in a wider variety of ways. Without this progressive freeing of authorities from detailed requirements the Ministry would have found it far harder to keep down costs. Greater freedom has permitted greater ingenuity.

The methods used to revise the regulations are also an example of the Ministry's first-hand knowledge of the needs of the schools. It does not rely on outside committees for advice on school standards. The revisions are drafted in the Architects and Building Branch of the Ministry, which is responsible for all its building controls. The Ministry is in constant contact with education authorities through the Inspectorate. The Architects and Building Branch is also in regular contact with authorities on their buiding programmes and on individual schemes. New educational problems and their solution in physical terms are thus constantly under discussion between authorities and the Ministry and inside the Ministry itself.

The Architects and Building Branch is an unusual organization. It is jointly headed by an administrator and an architect and has a similar pairing of architectural and administrative posts down the line. This has meant that the views of architects and administrators are closely aligned, they speak each other's language and share each other's problems. This organization was until very recently quite unlike that of any other government department. Elsewhere the technical staff are almost always in a separate division, act in an advisory rather than an executive capacity and have much looser links with administrative problems. In the Ministry of Education's organization administrative, architectural and financial issues are kept closely aligned, because those who are controlling them are working in close contact.

The Architects and Building Branch also has another asset which was unique until very recently. Attached to it there is a development group consisting of administrators, architects, engineers, quantity surveyors and other technical experts, who are responsible for exploratory work on school building and the design and erection of a small number of schools on behalf of local authorities. The work of this group makes it possible for the Ministry to have first-hand experience of the problems of school buildings and of their costs. This work is described more fully in the chapter on research and development. Here it is only necessary to emphasize that the existence of this development group gives the Ministry of Education's technical advice an exceptional authority. The Ministry's officers are regarded as experts to a degree which other departments cannot rival.

The Ministry has also issued a comprehensive series of Building Bulletins to make available to authorities the experience which the Ministry has gathered. Some cover the design of primary and secondary schools in general; others cover particular aspects, such as playing fields, kitchens or fire protection. Among the most interesting are those which give accounts of the experience of the Ministry's own development group in building schools for local authorities. These have the authority of first-hand experience and so carry conviction. Local authorities have spoken in the highest terms of the value of these bulletins. In them the minimum standards embodied in the building regulations come to life.

The Ministry of Education's success in controlling standards is thus based on three factors:

clear definitions of standards published in the Building Regulations;

an internal organization which closely integrates administrative policy and architectural experience; and

a large investment of effort in building development which enables its officers to be acknowledged experts.

No other department exerts so undisputed an authority or so confident a control. In spite of this, or perhaps because of it, the Ministry's control of building is subject to much less criticism from local authorities than that of other departments.

Housing

The Ministry of Housing and Local Government has evolved its standards by different means. It has relied mainly on the advice of committees and has not usually fixed housing standards independently.

There are three main reasons for this difference. In the first place the Ministry has no housing inspectorate, no organization comparable with the Architects and Building Branch of the Ministry of Education, and until very recently no development group. It has a large staff of architects who have been scrutinizing local authority schemes for years, but this is not the same thing as first-hand experience of the problems of building design and management. It is, therefore, more natural for the Ministry to seek the support of outside advisers.

Secondly, school design is accepted as the field of the expert. It can change with the development of educational methods without the layman feeling closely involved: the children must accept what they are given. Housing design in contrast is a matter on which every housewife and every housing committee has strong views. Changes in housing standards and design have to face the challenge of public criticism and a strong traditionalism.

Thirdly, the standards of housing are closely related to the rents which people are prepared to pay. If higher standards mean higher costs the tenants' reaction to rents must be considered. Both the Ministry of Housing and Local Government and local authorities are acutely sensitive to these reactions. The Ministry of Education's work on costs and standards is not complicated by this anxiety in the same way.

In fixing its standards for housing, the Ministry has usually worked from the recommendations of the Central Housing Advisory Committee and its various sub-committees. Of these, the most influential was the sub-committee which met under the chairmanship of the Earl of Dudley during the war. Its report, *Design of Dwellings*, which was published in 1944, set the standard for the design, planning, layout, construction and equipment of all public housing after the war.

The basic standards have remained almost unaltered since that time, though financial economies after 1951 necessitated reductions in some of the more generous allowances of space both inside and outside the individual home. A new sub-committee of the Central Housing Advisory Committee, under the chairmanship of Sir Parker Morris, was appointed in 1959 to review these housing standards and to suggest modifications of them in the light of changes in building techniques and social habits since 1944. The report was expected in 1960.

Between 1944 and 1959 a number of other sub-committees of the Central Housing Advisory Committee advised the Minister on other matters connected with housing design and management, while a number of special committees investigated the costs of house building and maintenance. In all there have been some twenty reports during these years which are the work of committees appointed by the Ministry to advise on housing standards, costs and management.

While the standards introduced by the Dudley Committee remain the backbone of the Ministry's control of standards, the interpretation of these has been modified in the light of experience and the pressure of rising costs. In 1949 the Ministry published its second Housing Manual which explained in greater detail the Dudley Committee's proposals and worked out their application for various kinds of houses, flats and maisonettes. This first manual and its technical appendices reflected a more optimistic attitude towards housing design and costs than has been possible since. In terms of space, inside and outside the home, housing authorities have never again had such latitude.

After 1951 the changed economic and political climate brought about a sharp alteration of view on standards. While the most essential standards remained, the Ministry was charged with responsibilities for pruning housing costs severely. Two supplements to the Housing Manual were published in 1952 and 1953. The first was a handbook designed to help housing authorities to build more houses from a limited supply of materials, labour, and capital. The second described methods for the more economical use of land, the reduction of expenditure on roads and services and the general tightening up of densities and house plans to save space. The supplement was liberally illustrated with layout and house-type plans to show how these could be designed to save space and therefore costs.

It is a matter of definition how far the two supplements *Houses 1952* and *Houses 1953* affected the standards as proposed by the Dudley Committee and set out in the 1949 Housing Manual. The standards of construction and room areas have remained unaltered. But the pressure to reduce costs squeezed out open space outside and circulation space inside the home and extinguished many comforts and amenities. To the layman, the general standards, as opposed to the technical standards of the houses built to conform with the new suggestions, were visibly lower. They were, however, successful in saving scarce materials such as timber, limiting the rise in costs and in producing more houses for a given expenditure. And the most important standards of the Dudley Committee were retained.

These conflicting definitions of standards make for confusion in any discussion of the Ministry of Housing's methods. The suggestions in the two supplements of 1952 and 1953 were not rigidly enforced. Authorities whose architects were exceptionally ingenious or exceptionally efficient could avoid their full rigour, at least for a time. The ultimate sanction was cost. The suggestions were designed to save costs and only to the extent that an authority could keep costs down without reducing these space standards could it escape. As soon as a scheme exceeded the current level of costs the Ministry could reject it, and justify its rejection on the ground that the authority was not using the most economical designs.

The Ministry has always made free use of layout and house-type plans to explain its suggestions. To do this, the Ministry's architects have drawn on existing schemes and have also worked out their own improvements and modifications. These plans are an essential element in the Ministry's methods of persuasion and

60

education. It has been argued that they offer housing architects too easy a solution, and stultify fresh thinking. Instead of thinking things out for themselves, authorities are inclined to adopt the Ministry's designs. This method is contrasted with that of the Ministry of Education which has made less use of lay-out and type-plans, and which relies more on stimulating the ingenuity of authorities' architects.

There is some truth in the view that these plans diminish local authority initiative. But it must be remembered that the Ministry of Housing is dealing with nearly ten times as many authorities as the Ministry of Education and that many of them are small and inexperienced. The task of persuading some 1,400 housing authorities requires different methods from those for persuading about 140 education authorities. A large part of the Ministry of Housing's efforts are directed to helping the smaller authorities and are geared to their needs.

During most of the post-war period housing schemes have been liable to close examination by the Ministry's architects. In the early days this scrutiny was designed mainly to ensure that minimum building standards were achieved and to help the less experienced authorities with their designs. When costs became of greater importance schemes were even more closely examined. Authorities have often been restive about the very detailed scrutiny their schemes received, and of the conflict between standards and costs which frequently emerged. This more meticulous examination of plans was really an aspect of cost control, which is discussed later in this chapter. It is, however, inseparable from the control of standards. The very fact that housing 'standards' are subject to two interpretations has made this examination of plans by the Ministry particularly difficult. This difficulty has been enhanced by the separation of the architects and the administrators. Technical advice on standards has sometimes seemed to conflict with administrative action on costs.

More recently the change in the trend of building costs and the shift in emphasis to slum clearance and flat schemes has lifted the pressure from two-storey housing. The Ministry is now concentrating its attention on flats. Schemes for houses are no longer examined in such detail. If an authority can certify that minimum standards have been complied with and the cost of the scheme seems to the Ministry to be reasonable there will be little, if any, further scrutiny. When the new committee on standards reports, the Ministry will presumably publish a new Housing Manual and will have for a time to watch schemes more closely.

Standards for Other Buildings

The housing and school building programmes were of a size to compel some kind of standardization of standards. It would have been impossible to control them without a system of working rules. Other buildings have not enjoyed so great a concentration of effort, but a good deal of advice on standards, though of varying quality, has been issued.

Departments which are approving a succession of similar buildings each year have an excellent opportunity to set standards and to give advice on designs. Experience of examining twenty, thirty, or forty schemes a year of the same kind provides the raw material for assessing the essential requirements (Tables 7 and 8). The quality of the advice and the efficiency of the standards rests, however, largely on the ability of departments to sort and analyse this raw material and to distil its essence. Departments have been very differently equipped to carry out the processes of sorting, analysis and distillation.

The Ministry of Education was exceptionally well equipped to turn the resources it had available for schools to other kinds of educational building. The results have been correspondingly successful. This is particularly true for the colleges of further education. The training colleges for teachers have been dealt with by different and more direct methods.

The Ministry of Education issued its first building bulletin on colleges of further education in 1951 as the result of a preliminary examination of requirements.[1] Further investigations followed and a second edition was published in 1955. A third edition was almost ready at the end of 1959. The advice given in this bulletin enables each authority to review its own proposals in the light of the Ministry's suggestions and to draw up schedules of accommodation based on the standards in the bulletin. These schedules can then be discussed and agreed with the Ministry before any design work is started. The frequent revision

[1] Bulletin No. 5.

of the bulletin to keep pace with new ideas enables authorities to keep in touch with new developments and to gauge the type and scale of accommodation likely to meet the Ministry's approval without narrowly restricting the authority's freedom to meet its problems in its own way. It is, however, fundamental to the Ministry of Education's methods that standards, schedules of accommodation and costs should be agreed before the authority starts to plan the college in detail. This is in line with their methods of controlling school building.

The resources of the Home Office are more limited. Its Architects' Branch is too small to undertake detailed research. The department has, however, issued two sets of memoranda to give authorities help. One such was issued for fire stations in 1949. It was the result of the work of a committee which reported in 1946. The circular was accompanied by type-plans showing different designs. The report contained detailed suggestions on the sizes and requirements of rooms and equipment. An even more detailed memorandum was issued in 1955 on the design and construction of police stations. It contained few sketch plans but gave definite advice on the sizes of rooms and their equipment. Neither of these documents even distantly approaches the quality of the building bulletins of the Ministry of Education. Both approach the problems of design too rigidly to be a stimulus to authorities.

So far the Ministry of Health has published little on standards, and what it has published has been on a very modest scale. In 1949 the Ministry issued a memorandum about occupation centres for the mentally sub-normal. In 1950 it published a circular containing some notes about the siting and planning of ambulance stations. And in 1955 it published a circular, accompanied by drawings, which set some standards for homes for old people. None of these documents was more than a very modest attempt to advise and help local authorities.

In 1960 the Ministry was to try a new system. Leaflets were being prepared in consultation with the local authority associations, about the standards of accommodation to be provided in various types of new building. It is expected that these will also indicate the sort of cost authorities ought to aim at, per place or square foot. The first leaflets are expected to cover maternity and child welfare clinics, old people's homes, ambulance stations and training centres for junior and adult mentally sub-normal people.

The quality of these leaflets cannot be judged until they are issued. To be of real value both the standards and costs will have to be regularly revised to take account of experience. It is to be hoped that the Ministry of Health will have learned from the experience of the Ministry of Education how to avoid making the standards too specific lest they hamper the initiative of authorities. As a general approach to the problem of how to help and control local authorities the new leaflets are to be welcomed. Any system which gives them a clearer picture of what the Ministry is aiming at before they start to design is a step in the right direction. It should reduce the detailed control by the Ministry and avoid last minute changes in design.

The Ministry of Housing and Local Government's published guidance on special buildings is confined to a manual on 'Housing for Special Purposes'. It was issued in 1951 as the result of the work of the Housing Manual sub-committee. It contains recommendations for standards of accommodation for old people, students, nurses, midwives and for middle-class housing. For municipal office buildings the Ministry applies, as far as is practicable, the standards of the Ministry of Works for government office building and authorities can obtain advice if they seek it. This does not, however, help them with the more specialized parts of a town hall building. Set standards for other kinds of building are not available although the Ministry has engineers who have acquired an exceptional knowledge of swimming bath requirements and can give valuable advice.

With all these buildings the problem for authorities is to know in advance what standards are desirable and acceptable to the Ministry concerned. The most satisfactory are those which are simple minima, related to the least possible number of items and regularly revised and available in a form which can be handed to the authority before they start to consider a design. Much of the advice they are offered falls short of these perfections. The imperfections arise mainly because departments have not been able to devote sufficient time and attention to these problems. Simplification is usually achieved only after concentrated effort of a high order. Up to now only the Ministry of Education has been able to make this concentrated effort.

CONTROL OF COSTS

This is the most rigorous of the controls because the most specific. Whatever guidance or consultation there may have been earlier on programmes or standards, all building schemes must be submitted for approval to the department concerned, with plans and information on costs. Approval is conditional on the costs being reasonable or within whatever limits the department has already laid down.

There is in this control a great difference between the various types of building. There are those of which both departments and authorities have a wide and continuing experience. There are those for which departments, in their coverage of all authorities, have much more experience than individual authorities. And there are those which are built too infrequently for either side to have much experience. Housing and schools are in the first category; buildings such as technical colleges, fire stations and police stations are in the second; town halls, concert halls, covered markets and various special buildings come within the third.

Schools

The Ministry of Education has evolved a method for controlling the costs of school building which differs from that of all other departments. It alone has been able to fix cost limits which are known in advance and apply to the whole country. It is a system which has been of the utmost benefit to education authorities because it tells them, before they start to design, what costs will be approved. In doing so it reduces the necessity for much of the consultation and adjustment which characterizes the control of costs of so many other kinds of local authority building.

Since 1950 the Minister of Education has published from time to time cost limits applicable to schools of different kinds. These are revised to take account of changes in building costs and of experience of new methods, but authorities always know the cost limits in advance of starting their projects. The costs are calculated on the basis of the maximum capital cost for each school place. At present the ceiling or limit per place is £264 for secondary schools and £154 for primary schools. The maximum

c   65

BUILDING BY LOCAL AUTHORITIES

cost of a school can thus be calculated by multiplying the number of children, for which it is designed, by the ceiling cost per place. Certain site costs, which are highly variable, are excluded from the calculation. The system is clear, it gives authorities all the advance notice they require, and if authorities keep within the ceiling it avoids those last minute adjustments to reduce cost which can be so damaging to the design and standards of construction of the building as well as to the human relations between department and authority. This ceiling cost per place is the basis of all the cost controls by the Ministry over schools. Its existence simplifies the Ministry's task.

It is clear that such a system of cost control lays two great responsibilities upon the Ministry of Education. It must ensure that the ceiling is not too high to permit authorities to be extravagant. This is the bogey of central government. It must equally make certain that the ceiling is not so low as to prevent authorities from designing satisfactory buildings. There can be no absolute standard of success for either. No one would, however, seriously claim that the cost limits are too high. In 1950 school building was undoubtedly unnecessarily costly. The first cost limit imposed a reduction of $12\frac{1}{2}$ per cent with a further $12\frac{1}{2}$ per cent reduction the following year. After 1953 there were gradual increases to take account of rising building costs. The present limits were fixed for the 1955–56 programme. They would almost certainly have been revised upward in 1958 but for the check in the rise in building costs. Any system which squeezed excess costs out so effectively at the outset, and held them against rising building costs later, cannot be regarded as extravagant.

There will always be authorities who, because of their zeal for better schools or the lesser skill and ingenuity of their architects, find the cost limits too low. A ceiling would have no meaning if this were not so. But both the Ministry's own development group and many authorities have demonstrated too often that good schools can be built within the cost limits for there to be any doubt that they are generally reasonable.

For those authorities who face special difficulties concessions can be made. To those who are inexperienced the Ministry is able to offer help through the publication of its building bulletins and by direct advice. Authorities and private architects, who have had cause to come to the Ministry for advice, speak highly of the quality of the help they have received. The close-knit building organization within the Ministry helps its architects and administrators to speak with a single voice. And the fact that the Ministry possesses teams of architects, who are designing schools for local authorities, enables the department to advise with first-hand experience. Criticisms and suggestions for reducing costs are more acceptable from a department where the architects not only vet other people's schemes, but design their own.

The freedom which authorities enjoy within this system is considerable. Between the minimum standards laid down by the building regulations and the maximum cost per place there is a wide margin of discretion. Some authorities choose to provide more space in the school and to save on the quality of the accommodation. Others prefer higher quality and less space. They are free to adjust the balance between the different types of accommodation, provided the basic minima for each is maintained. And with a limit of cost fixed before design starts they are able to plan with confidence in the final approval of the costs of the scheme and with the greatest incentive to obtain good value for money. Since 1950 the Ministry has been ready to approve any project which was within an agreed programme, below the cost limits and up to the minimum standards. This approval can be transmitted to an authority within three weeks of receiving the final plans, provided these three conditions are met. No other government department can offer this certainty and speed of approval. Its benefits in building efficiency and in administrative simplicity are very great.

Housing

The Ministry of Housing has been at least as much concerned with costs as the Ministry of Education. But there are no cost limits fixed in advance for housing as there are for schools, and authorities do not know with certainty what costs will be approved.

The general level of costs which the Ministry has recently been approving in a region is usually known. This, it is argued, gives authorities sufficient guidance in submitting schemes, but enables the Ministry to maintain enough flexibility to meet local difficulties and prevents contractors from assuming that any tender just below the cost ceiling will be acceptable. It is claimed that by keeping a relentless pressure on authorities about costs, by the advice given in the housing manuals, and by suggesting economies when schemes are submitted for approval, the rise in housing costs has been much less than it might otherwise have been.

There can be no doubt about the relentlessness of the pressure or the devotion of the Ministry. No effort has been spared to help authorities to keep down their costs. Authorities have learned under this pressure to build more economically, and housing costs have not risen proportionally with the general rise in building costs. Over the years more houses have been built for an equal expenditure of public money and for this the Ministry must claim much of the credit. What is at issue is whether even better results could have been achieved by other means or the same results by simpler means.

The Ministry's main objections to the publication of cost limits are three:

that the publication of such limits would drive up all estimates and tenders to this level and thus increase costs;

that there are regional and local differences in building costs which would make a national limit impracticable; and

that it is much more difficult to find a common unit, such as cost per school place, which could be applied to houses.

The experience of the Ministry of Education does not suggest that there is much validity in the first objection. The Ministry of Education has been notably successful, first in bringing down the cost of school building, and then in keeping the rise in costs to a minimum. Schools now cost about 20 per cent less than they did in 1949 in spite of the rise in building costs. It is true that school building was unnecessarily extravagant in 1949 and gave scope for economies, but there is nothing at all to suggest that the imposition of cost limits has added to costs. The contrary is the case.

The circumstances of housing vary. But the difference in costs of basically similar houses and still more of flats are too wide to suggest that the Ministry of Housing's control of costs has been as effective as that of the Ministry of Education's.[1] Still less do these differences suggest that the use of cost limits for housing would have increased costs.

Secondly the Ministry of Housing and Local Government and local housing authorities stress the regional and local differences in building costs and fear lest cost limits covering the whole country would cause local hardship. It may be that the greater volume of house building in the cities, its spread into more scattered areas and the use of more small contractors presents greater difficulties than for education authorities, although this seems a little doubtful. Pleas for special treatment must be examined warily. If, however, there are special regional or local difficulties which necessitate an adjustment of cost limits, it is much more satisfactory for such differences to be written into the cost limit before design starts, than to be argued when the plans are ready for tender. At that late stage cuts cannot be satisfactorily adjusted.

The third objection is the least tenable of the three. The best known cost limits used by the Ministry of Education are those of cost per place. But the Ministry uses other kinds of cost limit, based on cost per square foot for technical colleges and colleges for training teachers. These it has worked out for different types of accommodation. The Ministry of Housing and Local Government has itself made frequent use of the yardstick of cost per square foot in considering housing costs.

There is little doubt that some such method of measurement could have been worked out for fixing cost limits for housing. The problem is not easy, but the difficulties tend to be exaggerated by those who are not familiar with the Ministry of Education's techniques. Housing, particularly two-storey housing, is more standardized than most people recognize. Failure to evolve cost limits is attributable less to the basic difficulties of this problem than to the Ministry's lack of confidence in itself. Without an organization comparable to the Architects and Building Branch of the Ministry of Education, and without the first-hand experience of building housing through a development group, the Ministry has not so far been well equipped to

[1] See Chapter 9.

69

take the initiative in fixing cost limits. It is likely to be better equipped in the future.

The penalties for the failure to evolve better methods have been high. The nation is probably paying more for its two-storey housing and certainly more for its municipal flats than it ought to be doing. In spite of all the strenuous efforts made by authorities and the Ministry to keep down costs, the Ministry has done little systematic cost research. Some has been done by the Building Research Station,[1] but this has had little impact on the approach to costs or cost planning in the Ministry of Housing, and even less among local housing authorities. Housing costs have not been the subject of prolonged, intensive and systematic cost research, as the costs of schools have been.

Not only has the absence of cost limits made housing more expensive. It has also made house building less efficient and the administrative control more elaborate. There are great technical, administrative and psychological advantages in fixing definite cost limits before an authority starts to design. These advantages are not secured by a general knowledge of what costs the Ministry has been approving recently.

While the general level of costs likely to be approved has usually been known, it is sufficiently uncertain to encourage hope that particular schemes will secure approval even if slightly above this general level. Against a background of rising costs or a committee eager to maintain housing standards and amenities, architects are irresistibly tempted to try to secure approval for schemes even if the costs are on the high side. They are equally tempted to leave it to the Ministry to impose the discipline of cutting costs after the scheme is complete rather than to impose it on themselves from the start of the design. Many competent architect's offices resist these temptations, but in many cases their lure is too great to be withstood.

It has for a long time been customary for housing schemes not to come to the Ministry until they were ready for tender. More recently they have not been submitted until tenders were received. Under either system a scheme has long passed the stage when adjustments to the design to reduce costs can be made at all easily. If the scheme is too expensive there ensues a painful

[1] See Chapter 9.

70

struggle to devise means of introducing savings without radical alterations of the design. Time is lost, the intervention of the Ministry is liable to be resented and the pruning can only touch those features or specifications which are capable of alteration at so late a stage. These cuts are rarely those which would have been selected at the outset of the scheme. In the end the changes usually achieve only modest savings in cost and mean much delay. They may also seriously increase maintenance costs in years to come.

The control of flat costs by the present methods is even more difficult. With the growth of slum clearance the proportion of flats built by local authorities is increasing rapidly. Between 1945 and 1955 it was 17·7 per cent. By 1958 it had risen to 35·5 per cent and it is still rising. Flats are more costly than houses and tall blocks of flats much more costly. It is, therefore, particularly important that costs should be efficiently controlled, and that authorities should be given all possible guidance before design starts.

The Ministry has made great efforts to give advice on flat design and published a large manual on this subject in 1958.[1] This manual brings out clearly the relationship between height and costs, and the heavy penalties in cost to be paid for multi-storey flats. Authorities may take the lessons to heart. But the absence of cost limits robs the Ministry of any really effective control over authorities. At present flats providing similar accommodation may differ by as much as £1,000 a flat. The manual suggests reasons why such discrepancies arise. It does not solve the problem of how to reduce the number of more expensive schemes.

Under the existing system flat schemes, like housing schemes, usually come to the Ministry for approval when they are ready for tender. At this stage no major reductions in cost are practicable. Nothing but outright rejection would have any effect, and in the middle of a slum clearance scheme, with tenants urgently in need of accommodation, no Minister would face the public outcry. At this stage the Ministry can have no real influence on costs, but only tinker with small economies. This is because the costs of flats are affected mainly by early decisions on heights, densities, methods of construction and types of

[1] *Flats and Houses 1958.*

71

accommodation. Once these decisions are taken the main issues of costs are settled beyond remedy.

If there was general agreement that flat costs were to be tackled systematically authorities would have to consult the Ministry at a much earlier stage, before the design work started, and agree a cost target for the scheme as a whole depending on what types of dwelling and structure were to be provided. The Ministry of Education controls the costs of colleges for further education in this way with great success. In the case of such colleges each scheme is dealt with separately, and the schedules of accommodation for, say, science, art or workshop teaching are agreed between the Ministry and the authority. Each type of accommodation has its own cost limit, calculated as so much per square foot. The total cost limit for a college is therefore the sum of the costs for each kind of accommodation. Once the limit is agreed authorities may design freely within the ceiling.

Flat schemes present a similar problem. If the Ministry could fix cost limits for different types of accommodation in houses, low flats, tall flats or maisonettes, it would be possible to agree with an authority a total cost limit for each scheme based on the amount of accommodation of each kind to be provided. Having agreed this ceiling, and with the housing standards which already exist, authorities would have freedom to design and certainty about the final approval. Costs would almost certainly be reduced.

Success would depend on the willingness of authorities to co-operate, or the sanctions the Ministry was ready to use to secure early consultation. This has been a difficulty so far. It would also depend on the ability of the Ministry to fix satisfactory cost limits. A new development group is being set up within the Ministry, and it is to be hoped that it will have the resources to carry out the necessary cost investigations.

Other Buildings

There are no publicly known ceiling costs for other types of building. Nor is the number of buildings of any one kind large enough for there to be a general level of costs which is clear to authorities. For this reason authorities have neither the yardstick of known cost limits, as for schools, nor a general fund of

72

experience on which they may be able to draw, as for housing.

In such cases departments encourage authorities to consult them at an early stage and to discuss with them the preliminary plans and estimates of costs. This reduces the danger that major amendments in design and costs will be necessary at a late stage. The procedure of the Home Office on police stations, which is set out at the end of this chapter, is typical of the aims and methods of this kind of cost control. Such preliminary consultation is valuable, and where the department is concerned with thirty to fifty buildings of a similar kind each year, it should be able to give some fairly definite information about the costs it is likely to approve. Nevertheless, local authorities still find that they cannot plan with sufficient confidence in the level of costs which will be acceptable, and there is still liable to be last minute pruning by a Ministry at the final stage.

Most departments have in the past been opposed to any system of fixing ceiling costs for reasons similar to those argued for housing. They have laid stress on the variety of local requirements which may affect each individual design. It is difficult to be convinced by these objections in the face of the experience of the Ministry of Education. More recently the Ministry of Works and the Post Office have been using the Ministry of Education's techniques for Post Office buildings, and have also found it possible to fix cost limits. This provides further evidence that it is possible to devise cost limits if a department has or can be given the resources to make a proper investigation of design and costs.

It is, therefore, the more encouraging that the Ministry of Health is to make a start with devising cost limits for the various local authority health buildings which come under its control. It is to be hoped that the Ministry has been able to carry out a full enough investigation of user requirements, and design and building costs for these cost limits to be realistic, and that it will be able to revise them systematically as circumstances may demand.

In looking at the whole problem of the control of costs by central government there can be no doubt of the advantages of fixing cost limits in advance. The advantages are recognized by those who have experienced both methods. The inquiry of the Royal Institute of Public Administration revealed a widespread

73

appreciation of the methods of applying cost limits by the Ministry of Education. A questionnaire sent out by the Royal Institution of Chartered Surveyors found a similar reaction.[1] Seventy per cent of those who replied to the Institution's questionnaire in 1957 considered that the publication of ceiling costs had a beneficial effect upon design.

Those who fear that the use of cost limits would cramp an authority's independence or the architect's freedom are usually those who have not experienced this method. In practice the opposite seems to be the case. The fixing of cost limits sets alight a chain of reactions which diminishes interference from Whitehall. Self-discipline replaces an external discipline.

The Future

At its best, and therefore its simplest, the control by departments over authorities is three-dimensional. The programme determines the walls, minimum standards the floor and cost limits the ceiling. Within this space authorities can, and for some kinds of buildings do, have freedom of manoeuvre. The clearer the decisions on the outer dimensions the greater the liberty to move at will within them. The more definite the objectives, the less will government departments have to interfere with local authorities in their attainment.

The Ministry of Education has set out its objectives with clarity.[2]

. . . the partnership between central and local government has rested primarily on the general principle that the Minister's approval will be given to any project in an approved programme which complies with the requirements of building regulations and does not exceed the appropriate limit of cost per place. The Ministry's responsibility is thus to set reasonable and practical standards and limits of cost, while local authorities have both the freedom and incentive to secure, according to their skill and preferences, the highest standards they can within the limits of cost laid down.

It has been the avowed intention of successive Governments to reduce the amount of detailed control over local government. This aim was reaffirmed during the debates on the Local

[1] Chapter 9.
[2] *The Story of Post-war School Building,* Pamphlet 33.

74

Government Bill in 1958. Since the war much of the control of local authority building has been extremely detailed. This kind of control is not only irritating, it is time-wasting, and as a means of reducing costs relatively ineffective.

The methods used by the Ministry of Education have shown that it is possible for central government to retain the essential sanctions without detailed control; that greater local independence is compatible with central responsibility for public investments, standards and costs. The demonstration of the efficacy of these methods is slowly persuading the Treasury and other departments to follow the Ministry of Education's lead. It is unfortunate that the process of persuasion should have been so slow. If it goes far enough local authorities could look forward to a significant change in their relations with central government and a big opportunity to make their own building organizations more efficient.

SUMMARY AND RECOMMENDATIONS

1. It is the Government of the day which determines in broad outline the total volume of capital expenditure on building by local authorities and its distribution between the various services. It is for government departments to control programmes and priorities, standards and costs within this broad framework.

2. Total expenditure on buildings by local authorities increased steadily up to 1954. Since that time expenditure on housing has declined and is still declining owing to changes in Government policy and the less acute demand for housing for general needs. Expenditure on education rose consistently until 1959 but is near its peak. Numbers in the schools will soon be declining. Expenditure on buildings other than housing and education has been very small, but increased in 1958 and 1959.

3. The methods of control by government departments over building by local authorities vary greatly and reflect the consistency of the political support given by the Government to a particular service, the number and size of authorities concerned and the resources the department has been able to devote to investigating building requirements and costs.

4. The Ministry of Education has enjoyed three advantages:

high priority for school building; consistent political support; and the concentration of educational building in the hands of comparatively few and large authorities. These advantages have enabled it to develop methods of control which have been exceptionally successful.

5. The central administration of housing has had to face a radical change in Government policy, which has left it with a less positive role, particularly in the control of programmes. It has also to deal with a much larger number of authorities. Many of these are small and inexperienced. Both the political and the administrative problems are therefore more complicated than for education.

6. Other programmes have enjoyed no political support and have suffered constant interruptions from the succession of financial crises. Their total cost is small compared with housing and schools, but they have borne the brunt of the cuts.

7. The Ministry of Education's control of local authority building is based on an intensive study of costs and standards and first-hand experience of building. Coupled with its system of programming it has been able to give authorities an increasing amount of discretion on design and certainty on costs and timing. Control is exercised through:

programmes fixed two to three years in advance;

minimum standards, published and frequently revised;

cost limits fixed before design starts.

This system reduces administrative controls. If authorities submit schemes which are in agreed programmes and within the minimum standards and maximum costs, they can be certain of immediate approval.

8. A limited programming system for housing is in existence. Authorities are required to submit their requests in December for the calendar year immediately ahead. This is too short a period to enable them to plan their building operations efficiently. At least two years' notice is needed if the various stages are to be properly spaced, plans completed before tender and extra capital charges avoided.

9. Authorities are appreciative of the guidance given by the Ministry in its housing manuals on design and standards. They have been critical, however, of the control of costs. There are no cost limits for housing, fixed in advance. Control is exercised when schemes come in their final form to the Ministry of Housing for approval. Authorities are usually aware of the general level of costs the Ministry is likely to approve, but this does not induce sufficient self-discipline. Economies introduced in the final stages are usually ineffective and may have undesirable long-term effects.

10. The political and administrative difficulties of the Ministry of Housing and Local Government have been enhanced by lack of first-hand experience of building. Insufficient resources have been devoted to systematic and continuing investigations of design and costs. These would have enabled it to fix cost limits and to investigate building methods and standards more intensively. Steps now being taken to carry out some of this investigation are to be warmly welcomed.

11. In fixing cost limits for housing there would have to be limits for different sizes and types of dwelling. Authorities who designed within these limits and to the minimum standards could be confident of immediate approval. The target cost for large flat schemes, with multi-storey development, could be determined by special agreement on the lines now used by the Ministry of Education for colleges of further education.

12. So far programming for other buildings has at best been on an annual basis, and subject to frequent cuts. Some advice on design has been issued by the Ministry of Health and the Home Office for different types of building, but on a modest scale. No cost limits have been fixed. The Ministry of Health is now planning to give more advice on standards and costs in a series of leaflets.

13. Central government should aim to give local authorities the greatest possible continuity with the least interference. To do this it should:

give authorities a reasonable degree of certainty about their programmes two to three years in advance, and limit such cuts as become necessary to as few authorities as possible;

77

devote resources to ascertaining and revising the essential minimum standards for different kinds of building;

devise limits of cost adapted to the particular kind of building and revise these as necessary.

Both standards and cost limits should be published or made known to authorities before design work starts.

14. If the experience of the Ministry of Education is any guide such arrangements should result in:

simplified administrative control by central government;

greater freedom for local authorities;

more efficient design;

more economical buildings.

Annex

MEMORANDUM ON THE DESIGN AND CONSTRUCTION
OF POLICE STATIONS
issued by the Home Office in 1955.

Extract covering the procedure for obtaining approval
for schemes for police buildings.

Approval in Principle

Each police authority is invited in the autumn of each year to submit for the consideration of the Secretary of State a building programme itemized in respect of all new works which it is proposed to start in the ensuing financial year. (For the purpose of these programmes 'new works' means major works of construction, reconstruction or alteration of buildings or of any other fixed works of construction or civil engineering, including a road.) In the case of the largest projects, which may require more than eighteen months' consideration in the planning stage, proposals will have been discussed before they are formally entered in the annual programme. The programmes submitted by police authorities are considered in the light of the needs of the police force concerned as reported to the Secretary of State by Her Majesty's Inspector of Constabulary and of any relevant financial or other considerations. The Secretary of

78

State's approval in principle, or alternatively his inability to give such approval, is thereupon conveyed to each authority in respect of each project in their programme.

Informal Consultations

Where the Secretary of State's approval in principle has been given to a particular scheme, the chief constable should arrange to discuss with Her Majesty's Inspector of Constabulary the operational needs which the new building is to meet including the number of staff, uniformed and civilian, to be provided for. From this point of departure the way is then clear for the architect to prepare sketch plans, taking into account local requirements and the general guidance given in later chapters of this Memorandum. It is at this stage that much time and expense can often be saved by consultation with technical officers in the Home Office. Moreover the Department's architects will always make themselves available for the discussion of sketch plans with an architect, accompanied if desired by the chief constable, as soon as the architect has begun to evolve his proposals for meeting the stated requirements on the site selected. Such discussions are entirely without prejudice to the eventual formal approval of the plans by the Secretary of State, but they undoubtedly minimize the risk of drastic comment at a later stage which may involve the re-drawing of the plans.

Formal submission of plans for which the police authority wishes to invite tenders

The next stage is formal, and the police authority is required to submit to the Department:

(*a*) Sketch plans, elevations and sections sufficiently developed to reveal the lay-out and prospective uses of the various parts of the building and the method of construction . . .

(*b*) the best possible estimate of the cost of the project;

(*c*) an outline specification showing what is included in the estimate of cost under (*b*); and

(*d*) an indication of the date on which the police authority would be able to start the work and of its probable duration.

If the Secretary of State is able to approve the project either as submitted or with modifications, he will so inform the police authority, which will then be free to advertise for tenders on the basis of this communication. A tender can then be accepted without further reference to the Home Office, provided that it does not exceed the amount of the approved estimate by more than 10 per cent for projects costing up to £50,000 or by 5 per cent for projects costing more than that figure. Any proposal to accept a tender on any other footing should be submitted to the Home Office, together with a statement of the reasons which are considered to justify its acceptance.

The Department should be informed in due course of the amount of any tender accepted and assured by a responsible officer of the authority that the work is proceeding on the basis of the plans originally approved, or with only minor modifications. A copy of the final plans should at the same time be sent to the Home Office for purposes of record.

CHAPTER 3

CONTROL OF BUILDING
BY COUNCIL COMMITTEES

Pattern of committees—central, client and common service committees—dominating position of Housing and Education committees—long-term programmes and priorities—control of architectural services—Works committees—abortive work—examination of plans.

THIS chapter deals with the role of elected members in initiating building operations and in controlling the efficiency of their execution. It is their responsibility to determine needs, to settle priorities and programmes, to call forth the financial resources to meet the costs, and to ensure that the administrative organization is competent to oversee the design, erection and maintenance of all buildings.

To ascertain how building operations were controlled by elected members, authorities were asked to supply information on:

the general pattern of committees with responsibilities for buildings;

how programmes and priorities were determined;

how closely members controlled the architectural services and the execution of building operations;

in how much detail members examined plans and whether they were responsible for abortive work.

The control of maintenance is dealt with in a later chapter.

MAIN COMMITTEE ORGANIZATION

Much of the internal structure of local authorities is determined

81

by the committee system, and the pattern of their organizations is largely fixed by the distribution of powers and responsibilities between committees. These committees fall into three groups.

Firstly, there are the committees which oversee all the operations of the Council from the top and are, to a large extent, the General Staff or the Cabinet of the Council, taking a bird's eye view. The Finance committee is pre-eminently of this kind, and may be the main policy-making body, supreme over all others except the Council itself. In some authorities there are also other senior policy-making committees with general authority over the work of the Council, such as the General Purposes committee.

Secondly, there are the committees who are directly responsible for particular services, such as education, housing, public health, welfare of old people or children, libraries, parks, open spaces and highways. These committees are the clients, who require building services. They vary from authority to authority according to the range of responsibilities of the type of authority, its size and the particular allocation of responsibilities it chooses to adopt. Some committees, such as the Education committee, are statutory. But for many services it is a matter of local choice and convenience whether each shall have a separate committee or whether the volume of business is small enough to justify bringing separate functions, such as highways and parks, or the welfare of old people and young children, under one committee. Large authorities have main committees for each service. Smaller authorities will have sub-committees under a main committee with dual or triple responsibilities.

Thirdly, there are the committees which control common services for other departments. These include Supplies, Works and less commonly Architectural Services committees. Their role is generally of a more practical kind, and, without disrespect, might be said to take the worm's eye view of the Council's business.

It has already been shown how housing and education are the two major responsibilities of local government today. Both are associated with large building programmes and it is, therefore, inevitable that local authority building organization should be influenced mainly by the demands of these two services. In county councils[1] it is the Education committee which calls the tune; in county boroughs both the Housing and Education committees are influential. In the non-county boroughs and the urban and rural districts the Housing committee is usually alone in having any substantial building responsibilities. It is, therefore, the policies of these major committees, endorsed or modified by the Finance committee and the Council, which largely determine the size and character of a council's building organization.

This dominance of the building programmes of the Housing and Education committees was underlined by information provided by authorities about their capital expenditure on housing, schools and other types of building. This has been set out in Table 9. Among county councils 80 to 90 per cent of the capital expenditure on building schemes has of recent years been on schools. In the county boroughs, housing claimed 50 to 80 per cent of the capital expenditure, and education 15 to 20 per cent. In the non-county boroughs and districts housing was almost the only building activity and the district authorities covered by the inquiry reported hardly any other single building of any size up to the end of 1957. Since that date there has been an increase in other types of building and a decrease in housing construction. These changes came too late, however, to be included in the information given by authorities.

The concentration of effort on one or two dominant kinds of building activity influences the kind of building organization each type of authority creates. Indeed, other building needs tended to be pushed aside by the two great leviathans, a result made the easier by the corresponding pressures from central government. Every national economic crisis resulted in approvals for fire stations, community centres, town halls and various other local authority buildings being delayed, while the school and housing programmes emerged scorched, but not scotched. Repeated experience of the prior claims of these two services over the years gave the other service committees a pessimistic view of their expectations.

Building projects originate with the service committees. The following list of committees responsible for building works for

[1] With the exception of the London County Council which is also a housing authority on a large scale. The organization is described at the end of the chapter.

TABLE 9

DISTRIBUTION OF CAPITAL EXPENDITURE

Average annual expenditure[1]

	Dwellings[2] £000	Education £000	Other £000
Counties			
Bedfordshire	70	600	75
Derbyshire	110	1,365	205
Devon	27	600	50
East Suffolk	26	244	18
Glamorgan	—	950	70
Hampshire	73	870	110
Hertfordshire	90	2,234	Not given
Leicestershire	42	751	104
London	17,000	3,300	1,500
County Boroughs			
Birmingham	7,000	3,200	3,500
Burnley	339	114	89
Chester	562	103	37
Eastbourne	270	100	70
East Ham	620	160	52
Ipswich	567	89	6
Leeds	2,650	450	165
Liverpool	5,140	1,400	3,080
Middlesbrough	1,275	340	40
Preston	500	200	35
Reading	566	229	270
Stockport	500	150	100
Sunderland	1,498	193	28
Non-County Boroughs and Districts			
Bexhill Borough	80	—	—
Harrogate Borough	228	—	—
Slough Borough	670	—	—
Worthing Borough (Excepted District)	109	98	26
Banstead U.D.C.	119	—	20
Beeston & Stapleford U.D.C.	310	—	Not given
Braintree R.D.C.	200	—	—
Chesterfield R.D.C.	840	—	4
Dorking U.D.C.	147	—	—
Harlow U.D.C.	150	—	30
Ilkley U.D.C.	81	—	4
Malvern U.D.C.	24	—	3
Wortley R.D.C.	272	—	1

[1] For most authorities the figure is the average expenditure of the five years up to 1957.

[2] Except for the County of London, most of the dwellings built by county councils are police houses.

Devon County Council shows their range and the buildings for which they are responsible. It is representative of the general run of county committees with interests in building operations.

Committee	*Buildings*
Education and its Sites and Building sub-committee	Education, including Kitchens and School Clinics
Standing Joint	Police Houses and Stations
Health	Nurses' Houses, Occupation Centres and Ambulance Stations
Welfare	Old People's Homes
Children	Children's Homes
Fire Brigade	Fire Stations
Small Holdings	Farm Buildings

In the large cities this list would be augmented by committees controlling certain services only to be found in urban centres such as public parks and places of entertainment, markets, baths and washhouses, museums, art galleries and civic restaurants. All these committees would have buildings to maintain and occasionally to renew or build. In addition there would be the powerful Housing committee which absorbs the largest share of every council's building resources.

In the smaller county boroughs many of these services are on too modest a scale to justify a separate committee for each, and the more important committees will absorb the less important. In the non-county boroughs and district councils the Housing committee is the only committee which is likely to have any continuing responsibility for building. The division of responsibilities between the other committees is so varied as to make it difficult to say which committees would be responsible for the proposals for, say, new council offices, a swimming bath, depot, crematorium or sports pavilion on the rare occasions when such schemes were required. The allocation of responsibilities between committees for such buildings differs from authority to authority.

PROGRAMMES AND PRIORITIES

The settling of building programmes and priorities falls into three categories:

decisions by individual committees. The drawing up of a long-term programme helps a committee to see the scale of its responsibilities, the direction in which it is moving and to decide which schemes it will put forward first for approval by the Council.

annual capital estimates for capital budgets. These decisions rest with the central committees and the Council;

co-ordinated long-term capital programmes. These are designed partly to estimate future capital commitments and their effect on future liabilities for interest charges and running costs including maintenances, partly to encourage committees to think ahead, and partly to guide the technical and other departments on site acquisition, provision of services and recruitment of technical staff.

Programming by Individual Committees

Service committees are normally responsible for drawing up their own priorities. In big authorities the major committees have a large degree of autonomy and the Council or Finance committee would only be concerned with the broad outlines of policy and with the total capital allocation to these committees for their building operations. In smaller authorities the general run of committee business is less complex and less highly specialized. While committees would settle policy and priorities in the first instance there can be more general discussion at meetings of the Finance committee and the Council.

Clearly in a council of twenty-four to thirty-six members and an authority of limited size and responsibilities more members are familiar with the projects and problems of all committees and can take a more active part in committee and council decisions. In the large authorities, where members tend to specialize and considerable experience is necessary before a member is familiar with a committee's business, few members have the knowledge or temerity to intervene in other committees' business and council meetings are more formal.

The incentives to plan ahead vary from committee to committee for reasons which depend partly on the nature of the service and partly on Government policy. The service committee must base its proposals on estimates of need. Need is an elastic term, but the waiting lists for slum clearance and the foreknowledge five years in advance of the demand for school places are more tangible evidence of need than those usually available to other committees.

Except in areas of new development with growing populations, such as the new towns, it is less easy to be categorical about the need for new fire stations, clinics, covered markets or municipal offices. Public opinion cannot be mobilized to support the need for a new police station in the way it can be mobilized for a new school. If the cells are grossly inadequate their inmates do not write letters of complaint to *The Times* or pester their Member of Parliament.

Even when committees are anxious to plan ahead their efforts can be nullified by the actions of central government. The inquiry of the Royal Institute of Public Administration produced abundant evidence that except for housing and schools, authorities had received so many disappointments that many were unwilling to make further attempts to work out long-term programmes. So many schemes had been delayed or held up at the last moment that it appeared useless to continue to draw up a county plan for fire stations or homes for old people or to try to co-ordinate the capital programmes of different services. Several authorities reported in 1958 that they had more or less abandoned such efforts. It is possible that if the more recent encouragement of more varied capital expenditure continues, interest in programming may revive.

Education and Housing committees are the only ones who are controlling continuing programmes. It has already been explained that the Ministry of Education requires authorities to submit programmes in February of each year covering a period

87

of some two-and-a-half to three years ahead. Birth rate figures give authorities advance warning of the school population and most education authorities have programmes for school building several years ahead. These are drawn on when preparing the list of schemes to be submitted to the Ministry.

The five-year warning, the procedure used by the Ministry of Education for programming and the general political climate in favour of school building provides Education committees with an excellent opportunity for planning their building programmes. Many councils expressed their appreciation of the programming system used by the Ministry. There was, however, some evidence that some education authorities did not take advantage of the full span of time over which the Ministry of Education's approvals run. These authorities did not differentiate in their own internal planning between the annual system of approvals provided by, say, the Home Office and the Ministry of Health and the longer period covered by those of the Ministry of Education for school programmes.

The information on programming procedure for housing was obtained by the Royal Institute of Public Administration early in 1958 when the effects of the subsidy changes had not had their full impact. At that time the larger authorities and most of the smaller ones covered by the inquiry had long-term housing programmes, on which they drew in making their applications to the Ministry. They had very recently been asked by the Ministry to make considerable cuts in their programmes, but had not digested the effects of these cuts. Authorities were well aware of the need for and value of their programmes in order to keep land acquisition and development in proper sequence. There was, however, so much evidence of crowded time-tables and schemes going incomplete to tender that it was clear that the paper programmes were often not effective.

It was not possible in the time available to find out what changes in programming procedure had come about as the result of the reduction in house building after 1957–58. Clearly some councils who had only small slum clearance programmes and had been building mainly with the financial support of the general needs subsidy must have altered their long-term programmes very considerably. Only a small part of the energies released from house-building can have been absorbed in the slightly larger programmes for other types of building. The building of houses has fallen much more than that of council offices or other buildings has risen.

Co-ordinated Capital Programmes

Authorities were asked how far they had co-ordinated long-term capital programmes and how they settled priorities between committees. The replies differed greatly according to the type of authority and threw an interesting light on the different role of the Finance committee in county councils and the other authorities.

Among the nine county councils who supplied information only two had any defined system of settling priorities between committees with a special committee to determine these co-ordinated long-term capital programmes. Even the function of the Finance committee as arbiter for this purpose was barely referred to. Indeed the question of settling priorities between committees hardly seemed to arise.

That county councils do so little in the way of settling general priorities or working out co-ordinated capital programmes is due mainly to the overwhelming importance of the school building programme and the dominant position of the Education committee. While responsibility for the Cinderella state of other building projects must rest largely with central government, it seems doubtful if county councils serve their own interests best in this way. There are risks, Government approvals apart, that the claims of other projects will be pressed with insufficient vigour if there is no machinery for fixing co-ordinated programmes or of weighing the importance of one kind of building against another. A system of settling priorities, as a question of central policy, gives members an opportunity to look across committee boundaries.

County boroughs have two major building programmes and two major committees competing for resources. It may be that this is the reason why the role of the Finance committee appeared to be much more important than in the county councils. Thirteen authorities replied and seven of these referred to the Finance committee as the arbiter of priorities. Three showed no priority system and three had special arrangements for the purpose outside the Finance committee.

Birmingham, where the proportion of expenditure other than on housing and schools is exceptionally large, introduced such a system fairly recently. Until 1955 there was no well defined system for determining building priorities nor until the cessation of building licences in 1954 was the need for such machinery fully apparent. In 1955, however, the General Purposes committee, which is the policy making committee of Birmingham City Council, took over the function of settling priorities. Its terms of reference require it:

to receive from the several committees of the council in September of each year, and at such times as may be necessary, particulars of all building and civil engineering schemes estimated to cost not less than £5,000 each for which consent is required to the raising of a loan for the carrying out of any such scheme in the next (or some other) financial year, to consider the schemes proposed, to decide the order of priority in which they should be submitted to the appropriate Ministry and to report their recommendations to the committees concerned.

The General Purposes committee also has charge of the City Architect's department and is responsible for making available the services of that department to all committees of the Council. The result of these arrangements is that policy making is separated from finance and a close link is set up between the committee which determines building priorities and the chief officer who is most closely concerned with their execution. The Finance committee thus retains its basic function of determining what the total resources are to be, but as far as building programmes are concerned the General Purposes committee decides which schemes are to go forward.

The dual functions can be illustrated by the procedure adopted to deal with the 1957 credit squeeze and the increase in bank rate. Committees were asked to divide their building projects into four categories:

(a) Contracts accepted beyond recall.
(b) Tenders called for and difficult to postpone.
(c) Urgent schemes of high priority.
(d) Schemes of lower priority.

90

The Finance committee then prepared a consolidated list set against the financial possibilities, and the General Purposes committee settled the priorities, and which schemes were to be postponed.

Any system of priorities whether determined by the Finance committee or elsewhere has the added advantage that it helps the Chief Architect or Engineer to determine the order of work for his own technical staff and to withstand pressure to carry out preliminary work on schemes which are not likely to be approved by the Council or the Ministry. Committees flushed by enthusiasm for some new project are apt to demand sketch plans and estimates without closely assessing the prospects of obtaining Government approval. An officer must exercise considerable discretion in determining how much work is to be done on a scheme in advance of Council and Ministry agreement. If too much is done on a scheme which does not obtain the necessary approvals, not only will the work itself prove abortive, but it may hold up work on other schemes which are going forward. A priorities committee will serve to guide and protect the officer from such embarrassing demands.

Annual priorities are usually settled at the time when the capital estimates are agreed. Longer-term programming is less usual. Even among the county boroughs, only a minority had any arrangements for programming building on a co-ordinated basis for more than the year immediately ahead. Among the non-county boroughs and district authorities the concentration of effort on housing meant that there was little competition between different types of building, and long-term programmes were, almost always, limited to housing alone.

The findings of the Royal Institute of Public Administration's inquiry confirm those of an earlier investigation. In 1955 a research study carried out by the Institute of Municipal Treasurers and Accountants[1] revealed that only seventeen out of fifty local authorities covered by a questionnaire carried out annual capital estimates and only fourteen had long-term capital programmes. The proportions for England and Wales were as follows:

[1] *Local Authority Borrowing.*

Replies received	Annual capital estimates prepared	Capital programmes
15 Counties	10	4
15 County Boroughs	11	5
2 Metropolitan Boroughs	2	—
6 Boroughs	1	2
6 Urban Districts	2	1
6 Rural Districts	—	2
—	—	—
50	26	14
—	—	—

This table shows the low proportion of authorities who drew up co-ordinated long-term capital programmes. If anything the situation has deteriorated since 1955. Experience of the further cuts imposed during the crisis of 1957 discouraged authorities still more from attempting any long-term forecasts.

Throughout the whole of the post-war period almost all local authorities have consistently underspent on their programmes, and have wished to do more than Government restrictions have permitted them. Long-term capital budgeting would take on a greater importance if local government capital expenditure were to be increased or the proportion of building other than housing was to rise steeply. While it is clearly not the Government's intention to increase expenditure on municipal housing, there is at present a relaxation of the restrictions on other types of buildings which have been starved of money in the last fifteen years and this could affect the position. If there was any real prospect that the volume of this building was going to remain at a higher level, local authorities would be more disposed to renew or to start programming their capital budgets.

It must, however, be recognized that there are interests and pressures inside local authorities which militate against the co-ordination of long-term programmes, quite apart from any discouragements from central government. There is a strong centrifugal tendency among committees, and they are by no means eager to set in motion a system which highlights their competing claims for resources and gives to some superior committee the power to determine programmes and priorities.

This centrifugal force is due to a variety of causes. One is the part-time service of elected members. This makes it difficult for many of them to take an overall view. They can only interest themselves in the work of two or three committees, and the greater their interest the more eager their partisanship. Committees are jealous of their independence and resist infringements of their autonomy.

The desire for independence felt by committees is reinforced by the departmentalized structure of the various services, especially in the medium and large authorities. Chief officers have a status and responsibility for the services they administer quite different from those customary in business or the civil service. They are jealous of their independence and have no wish to see any central system of co-ordination encroaching on their departmental territory. However co-operative with their fellow chief officers their instincts are as centrigufal as those of their committees.

A third cause lies in the status and functions of the Finance committee. The Finance committee usually combines technical functions, closely associated with the raising and control of money, with policy functions. Whether these are ideally combined in one body or separated, as in Birmingham, between two committees is a matter of argument. But spending committees, who are more aware of the 'economies' forced by the Finance committee than of its attitudes on broad matters of policy, tend to fight shy of enhancing the powers of that committee by giving it still more influence over programmes and priorities.

There are those who consider that the reluctance to encourage co-ordinated planning and the discussion of priorities between different services would be reduced by giving these responsibilities to say the General Purposes committee. Others argue that, as the Finance committee usually has the chairmen of the service committees on it, it is already well equipped to do this work.

Equipped or not, it is clear that Finance committees do not as a rule use long-term capital programmes for deciding building priorities between the different services. Central government has been advocating the forward planning of capital expenditure by local authorities ever since 1929. It is clear that little progress has been made in this direction. Responsibility for the failure lies at least as much with central as with local government, but it is none the less disappointing.

CONTROL OF ARCHITECTURAL SERVICES

It was explained earlier that building operations could be controlled by members at three levels: by the service committees over their own buildings, by the control of programmes and priorities through senior committees, and by a more immediate supervision of architectural services and of a direct labour organization, if this existed. The architectural organization and the works organization generally provide common services for all departments, although some authorities have a separate architectural organization for housing or a divided maintenance organization. For present purposes it is of value to look at these services as common to all departments.

The majority of authorities leave to the appropriate chief officer, the Architect or the Engineer, the responsibility for organizing the architectural services, with very little regular supervision. Requests for staff are brought to the Establishment committee. There will be consultation over the appointment of private architects or on matters of particular difficulty, but the operation of the Architect's department or section remains almost entirely a departmental matter and members will not hear much about it, and certainly not regularly.

A minority of authorities appoint an Architect's committee or sub-committee with the express purpose of exercising regular control, month by month or quarter by quarter, over the policy questions which arise in the course of carrying out a large volume of architectural work.

It must be recognized that the Chief Architect or Engineer is always under pressure from committees and other chief officers to produce buildings quickly, and if possible to give preference to the pet scheme of one committee as against that of another. Unless the authority makes use freely of private architects, the Architect or Engineer will often not have enough architectural staff to meet all the demands, and he must use some system of priorities, formal or informal, to decide how the demands are to be dealt with. Where the Council has an effective method of settling programmes and priorities between committees, this will help the Architect or Engineer. This is, however, exceptional and would in any event rarely determine priorities between schemes approved for the same year.

There are many chief officers who carry this burden successfully, and there are many more, who would resist any encroachment on their independence. The inquiry of the Royal Institute of Public Administration, however, evoked so many complaints by architects that committees were unreasonable in the timetables they demanded and revealed so many difficulties due to compressed schedules for design that it was clear that architects were often unsuccessful in keeping the client committees at bay.

There are many reasons why the architect's work is so rarely complete when schemes go to tender. One is that it is difficult for elected members to understand the complicated processes of design and the penalties in cost and inefficiency on the site to be paid for lack of time during the preparatory stages. It may be that part of the architect's difficulties is due to members' lack of contact with his work and his problems.

A few authorities, most of whom have large architectural programmes, have set up special committees or sub-committees to oversee the architectural services and to help the Chief Architect to apportion the resources at his command. Authorities with arrangements of this kind include Derbyshire County Council, Birmingham, Bristol and Leeds. The arrangements vary in detail but in broad terms their object is to:

give one committee the power to adjudicate between the competing claims of service committees if the Architect cannot meet all the claims simultaneously;

advise on staff requirements;

give a group of members a clearer insight into the work of the Architect's department, and thus foster an understanding of the time required for the preparation of plans and the costs of additional work by builder and quantity surveyor if the plans are not ready;

give service committees a place to lodge complaints about delays or inefficiencies. Without this, they may find themselves in an invidious and baffling situation when the claims of committees conflict or put too great demands on the Architect's department.

95

The duties of the Architectural Services committee or sub-committee vary from authority to authority, but most of them cover the following responsibilities:

appointment and management of the staff of the City Architect's department within the framework agreed by the Establishment committee;

settling of priorities between requests by service committees for the services of the Architect's department;

recommendations on the use of private architects either as long-term policy or to relieve sudden pressures on the Architect's department;

consideration of regular progress reports.

There is always the danger with a committee of this kind that the members may interfere with the internal work of the department, which must remain the chief officer's responsibility. In smaller authorities with only a moderate amount of architectural work this could be a real difficulty. In the larger authorities the volume of work in the Architect's department and the policy issues to which it gives rise are sufficient to prevent this.

Where, as in the majority of authorities, no such special committee exists, the Architect or Engineer should still be responsible to one committee for the operations of his department, even if there is no regular reporting on progress. In this way he can seek the advice and support of the chairman if committees are too pressing in their demands. Some officers can withstand such pressure single-handed. But there are too many examples of rushed design work or of private architects commissioned at too late a stage to suggest that Architects and Engineers are as successful in their independence as they would like to be.

WORKS COMMITTEES FOR BUILDING

All Works committees are associated with the activities of Works departments and have a direct labour organization. Direct Labour is the subject of a separate chapter, and at this stage it is appropriate to discuss the Works committees mainly in relation to the other committees. Authorities, covered by this part of the inquiry (Table 9), were asked to give details of the size of their direct labour organization for building and to say whether they had a separate Works committee and by what officer this committee was principally advised. They were also asked to say if the functions of the Works committee could be kept sufficiently distinct from those of the service committees whose building requirements it was meeting.

A Works committee of this kind only exists where the local authority has a separate Works department for building. The obverse is not, however, true. Not all authorities with a large direct labour organization have such a Works committee. In these circumstances the Chief Architect or Engineer runs the department administratively without the organization being under the supervision of any particular committee. It did however appear that wherever the size of the organization and the authority's enthusiasm for direct labour justified the appointment of a Building or Works Manager as a chief officer, there was also a Works committee. A senior Works or Building Manager and a Works committee always went hand in hand.

Among the county councils covered by this part of the inquiry (Table 9) only three, Derbyshire, Glamorgan and the London County Council, have direct labour organizations, and only Derbyshire has a separate Works committee. Its main function is 'to ensure that the Works department is efficient and provides good service to the executive committees'. Both Derbyshire and Glamorgan have a direct labour force of some 600 men, employed mainly on maintenance, but in Glamorgan there is no Works committee and the organization is just part of the County Architect's department. Outwardly similar circumstances are, therefore, met by dissimilar solutions. The London County Council also has no Works committee, and the greater part of the work is commissioned by the Housing committee and is under its control.

Practice is equally diverse among the county boroughs. Six out of the thirteen authorities investigated had separate Works committees but there was no clearly defined pattern which seemed to determine the presence or absence of such a committee. Politics, the interests of members, the separation of the

D

building works organization from other departments and the calibre of the chief officer in charge were all contributory factors.

The functions of the Works committee are to run the direct labour organization and to see that the requirements of the service committees for maintenance or new building are met efficiently. Among the medium-sized authorities the most clear-cut definition of the functions of a Public Works committee came from Sunderland.

There is a Public Works committee, whose only concern is to deal with matters arising from the Public Works department. The Public Works department is a contracting department, dealing with civil engineering as well as building, and the Council have laid it down quite specifically that this department must be treated precisely in the same way as any other contractor doing corporation work. It is therefore not the function of the Public Works committee or the Public Works department to do anything more than carry out work decided by other committees and the Council.

All building maintenance work costing up to £200 per item has been specificially allocated to the Public Works department by the Council and all work above that figure must go out to public tender. The actual work to be done is decided by the appropriate committee and the Council and/or Technical Officer, and it is the duty of the latter to see that the Public Works department, if they are doing the work, carry it out satisfactorily in strict accordance with the specification. The work of the committee is largely concerned with detailed labour questions and obtaining supplies, the sort of work with which any contractor would be concerned, and the committee is therefore advised for the most part by the Public Works Manager.

The relationship between committee, chief officer and direct labour organization appeared very variable among the other county boroughs. Works committees were serviced by the Borough Architect, the Borough Engineer or the Works Manager according to local circumstances. One difficulty had been pointed out in advance: the danger of the committee interfering in the day-to-day organization of the Works department. Authorities were asked to comment on this. Only one authority reported this as being a source of friction, but during discussions it appeared that unless the committee's business was carefully arranged, meetings were short or the committee had other responsibilities for supplies, civil engineering services and so on, lack of sufficient business could lead to difficulties.

Among the non-county boroughs and district councils only a small minority had such a committee. At this level the problem of giving it enough to do and of separating its functions from those of other committees can be more delicate, and consequently the advantages to be derived from a separate committee will be marginal. One borough reported that the functions of the Housing and the Works committees overlapped so much that it had become difficult to keep their business distinct. In contrast Chesterfield Rural District, with a labour force of 150 men, uses its Public Works committee as a contracting organization on much the same lines as Sunderland and also with responsibilities for civil engineering works.

It has succeeded in keeping the business of the Housing and Works Committees separate.

The Council have a Public Works committee to manage the Public Works department. Its functions are in effect to manage the department as a contracting organization in much the same way as a board of directors might manage a limited company, but subject to the overriding jurisdiction of the Council and its standing orders.

The committee's principal adviser is the Public Works Manager, but it is also serviced by the Clerk and the Treasurer in the same way as other committees. No other chief officers are allowed to attend meetings of the Public Works committee and the Public Works Manager does not attend meetings of any other committees. He is responsible only to the Public Works committee and through it to the Council.

The Public Works committee has sole jurisdiction over its manual employees. Staff matters are dealt with by the Establishment committee, but only on the recommendation of the Public Works committee. The committee deals with sub-contracting arrangements, apprenticeship matters, bonus schemes, work progress, purchase of plant, authorization of the acceptance of new contracts, and other such matters.

ABORTIVE WORK AND EXAMINATION OF PLANS

It had been suggested at the outset of the inquiry that committees were responsible for much abortive work at the design stage of new buildings. Authorities were therefore asked in what detail

99

members examined plans and whether there was often a loss of time and effort because committees asked for revisions. The replies revealed no widespread difficulties on this score. Few authorities complained of abortive work. Where committees suggested changes they appeared to be made at sketch plan stage. Officers complained much more of the impatience of committees to get work started too soon, and of the alterations in designs or abortive work due to changes in central government policies or delays in approvals.

The detail with which members consider plans varies from committee to committee and also according to the scale of building operations. Designs for schools are fairly complicated for the lay member and tend to be accepted without close inspection. Housing designs are more comprehensible and in the small authorities may be examined in considerable detail. In authorities with large housing programmes, members' suggestions for improvements are more often made during the annual inspections of new property than at the planning stage. Individual schemes such as a project for a new concert hall can evoke great interest. Similarly, committees which only rarely have a building to supervise may relish any opportunity that is provided and examine the plans with special interest.

LONDON COUNTY COUNCIL

The London County Council has been excluded from the earlier review of the county councils because its responsibilities and therefore its organization does not correspond with those of the other counties. London is a major housing authority as well as an education authority and these dual responsibilities, in addition to the other services usually administered by a county, give its committee organization and its departmental administration a different character. Since the war its building output has been double that of any other housing authority and larger than that of most other local education authorities.

Committees

The following service committees deal with building operations:

Housing   Children's   Rivers and Drainage

100

Education	Health	Supplies
Welfare	Establishment	Town Planning
Fire Brigade	Parks	Public Control
	General Purposes	

There is no Works committee, although there is a direct labour force of over 7,000 men divided between the Director of Housing and the Architect. Some 800 are also employed on new building for the Housing department.

Programming and Priorities

Each committee works out its own building programme on the advice of the chief officers concerned, including the Comptroller of the Council. This is subject to any directions received from government departments and any limitations thus imposed. In each year, the estimated capital costs of work on all projects under construction or to be started during the year are brought together by the Finance committee for the purpose of determining the Council's capital budget and borrowing requirements and these form the content of an annual Money Bill promoted by decision of the Council at its Budget meeting.

Before these estimates go to committees for consideration and then on to the Finance committee, the total extent of the suggested capital expenditure is carefully examined by the Comptroller of the Council. If, as often happens, the total of the provision suggested by the heads of the service departments exceeds what the Comptroller would advise that the Council could have reasonable hopes of raising by loan, he will so advise the Chairman of the Finance committee. Then by a process of informal consultation as between chairmen of committees the estimates of one or more committees will be pruned, so that the total capital programme is reduced to dimensions within the ability of the Council to finance. In times of difficulty, such as have frequently occurred since the war, the Finance committee has also to take into account the willingness of the Treasury to sanction the total capital sum. Subject to compliance with the broad directions of the Treasury in this respect, the Council then obtains its authority to raise money directly from Parliament by the annual Money Bill, and does not have to seek loan sanction from each individual government department for individual projects as the year proceeds.

Detailed programming is done on an annual basis. There are, in addition, two ways in which a longer conspectus is taken with the object of securing an orderly programme of capital investment and an avoidance, or at least a mitigation, of the uncertainties which impair the efficiency of a building programme which looks forward no further than one year.

In the first place, there are reasonably firm longer-term programmes for each of the major services taken individually, such as housing and education. Secondly, there is the twenty-year forecast of capital expenditure on all services, being the sum of separate figures for each service, which forms part of the Development Plan for the County of London prepared under the Town and Country Planning Act. This twenty-year forecast is in two parts, one relating to the first five years, and the other to the last fifteen. Its value as a guide to the size of the individual programmes was increased when the Council on February 18, 1958 decided to review its capital commitments under the Plan at each of the quinquennial reviews required under the Act. As part of the first of these reviews a revised figure of £30 million a year was adopted for the twelve-year period 1960–72. Each service's share in this comprehensive figure is accepted by the committee responsible for that service as the basis of its detailed planning year by year.

SUMMARY AND RECOMMENDATIONS

1. In broad terms committee control of building falls into three groups:

overall policy decisions on programmes and priorities by Finance and General Purposes committees;

decisions on building requirements for particular services by the individual client committees;

oversight of common services for the design or execution of building by Architectural Services or Public Works committees.

Many councils have no committees in the third group.

2. Individual client committees fix their own building pro-grammes and priorities subject to Council approval. Arrange-ments for determining co-ordinated long-term programmes and priorities between committees and services are exceptional. The majority of councils have no such arrangements. Some have abandoned them in the face of recurrent cuts in capital pro-grammes by central government.

3. The Housing and Education committees are the dominant client committees. Their requirements overshadow all other building operations. In the county councils (except the London County Council) it is the Education committee which uses the major part of the building resources. In the county boroughs both the Housing and Education committees make large de-mands. In the non-county boroughs and districts the Housing committee has, until recently, been the only committee with any significant demand for building. The control of building is strongly influenced by the dominant position of a few client committees.

4. Part of the failure to prepare co-ordinated long-term pro-grammes has been due to the repeated adjustments or cuts in programmes by central government. But part of the failure is caused by the centrifugal attitudes of committees and the sharply departmentalized authority of chief officers. Commit-tees and chief officers are inclined to pull away from any cen-tralized system of settling programmes and priorities.

5. Some authorities consider that this problem can be eased if responsibility for the co-ordination of programmes and the fix-ing of priorities is placed on a committee other than the Finance committee. Financial control is thus separated, at least partially, from policy control. Others regard such an arrangement as a duplication of functions.

6. Whatever the reasons for the failure, the absence of machin-ery for co-ordinating building programmes may adversely affect the efficiency of the building services. The advent of the new block grant and the more encouraging climate for capital ex-penditure which became apparent in 1958–59 made it all the more important that local authorities should review their pro-cedure for co-ordinating long-term programmes.

103

7.   A few authorities, mainly large ones, have an Architectural Services committee or sub-committee which oversees the work of the Architect's department, fixes priorities for the design services and acts as a buffer between the client committees and the Architect. These authorities report favourably on this method of keeping members in regular contact with the problems and responsibilities of the Chief Architect.

8.   Other authorities have no such committee and have no regular machinery for giving the Architect or Engineer support or advice on policy matters. It is recommended that all authorities should, if they have not already done so, arrange for the Architect or Engineer to be responsible to a particular committee for the operation of the building services in his charge. In this way he can turn to the chairman for advice or support if committees press their demands too hard.

9.   This part of the inquiry produced a large number of complaints from officers that committees pressed their demands too hard and allowed insufficient time for the preparation of plans, bills of quantities and tenders. These complaints appear to arise from members' unfamiliarity with the technical work involved and from insufficient confidence between officers and members. Such difficulties can be overcome by a fuller appreciation of each other's problems. The existence of an Architectural Services committee is one way of doing this.

10.   Works committees supervise the operations of separate Works departments. It is, however, common for authorities to have a large direct labour organization without such a Works department or committee. Generally, authorities with a Works Manager of chief officer status in charge of a separate department also have a separate committee.

11.   There is some risk that the Works committee in the smaller local authorities will not have enough business to keep it occupied. The duties of this committee are sometimes combined with supervision of engineering works or supplies. If they are not, care must be taken to avoid interference in the day-to-day work of the department.

12.   Authorities did not substantiate allegations sometimes made that committees are responsible for much abortive work. Members usually make their comments at sketch plan stage,

and there was little evidence of wasted effort due to changes of policy or plans demanded by members. Authorities were, however, disturbed by the delays and abortive work caused by changes in the policies of central government. This applied particularly to buildings other than housing and schools.

CHAPTER 4

CHIEF OFFICERS AND THE DIVISION OF FUNCTIONS

Division between client functions and building functions—
responsibilities for architectural services, maintenance and
direct labour in different types of authority—wide diversity
—examples—division of functions between Architect and
Engineer—reasons for joint and separate departments—
views of authorities—contribution of Housing Manager to
design and maintenance.

IT is the function of the chief officers to carry into effect the policies laid down by the Council and its committees. They are the executive and to them falls the administration of the council services. Building operations underpin many of these services and make them possible, and they account for the largest share of local authority capital expenditure.

Nearly all the service departments are responsible for commissioning buildings at one time or another. Some have continuing programmes; some only an occasional project. In all these departments the preparatory stages of a building and its maintenance and repair is only a means to an end. It is the buildings in use which are their main concern, and the occupants their principal interest, be they school children, tenants, old people, young delinquents, fire engines, library books or stacks of wellington boots.

Only in those departments which are responsible for the design and erection of new buildings and for their maintenance and repair will preoccupation with the problems of buildings be continuous. This chapter is concerned mainly with those officers and departments responsible for the design, erection and maintenance of buildings and only secondarily with those which require these buildings.

THE ROLES OF CHIEF OFFICERS

In exercising their responsibilities for building, the chief officers

106

have roles which correspond with those of the client, the architect and the contractor. Sometimes a chief officer only changes his hat as his responsibilities change within his own department, and so becomes a client, an architect or a contractor as the circumstances demand. This is particularly true of the Engineer's[1] department in a medium-sized or small authority. In other authorities, the client department, the Architect's department and the direct labour or contracting department are each quite separate under their own chief officers and memoranda may pass between them in the most formal manner, addressed to the Chief Education Officer, the City Architect or the Works Manager.

The permutations and combinations of these roles do not fall into a tidy pattern corresponding to the type of authority or its size. Some very broad generalizations are possible about the organization of the county councils and also about the district councils. With county boroughs the diversity is overwhelming: while some of the differences are due to their varying sizes, authorities of the same size and similar responsibilities often organize their departments in widely different ways. One authority may prefer, for the sake of easier co-ordination or lower salary costs, to have a few chief officers each with many responsibilities covering a wide variety of services; others regard it as a greater stimulus to individual enthusiasm to have more heads of departments and to split the organization into a greater number of separate units.

The number of chief officers which authorities are required to appoint by statute or direction is comparatively few and the larger authorities appoint many more than the legal minimum. County councils and county boroughs must appoint a Clerk, Treasurer, Medical Officer of Health, Surveyor, Education Officer, Children's Officer and Chief Constable, as well as some less senior officers. They may also choose to appoint a number of other chief officers according to the size of the authority and its internal organization. In the counties these may include an Architect, Planning Officer, Welfare Officer, Fire Officer[2] and

[1] This chief officer is variously named the Engineer, Surveyor or Engineer and Surveyor. For the sake of brevity 'Engineer' is used throughout this book to cover all these variations, except for the county councils where he is called the Surveyor.
[2] Local Government Act, 1933.

107

Chief Librarian. In the larger county boroughs the list would be extended and might also include a Housing Manager, Markets and Parks Superintendent, Valuation Officer, Transport Manager and others. In the smaller county boroughs many of these would not be chief officer posts.

The non-county boroughs and urban and rural districts are required by statute to appoint a Clerk, Treasurer, Surveyor, Medical Officer and Public Health Inspector. The range of additional chief officers which they are likely to appoint is much more limited. There are also a number of other statutory appointments, but the holders would not be of chief officer rank.

It is significant in the context of this inquiry that neither the Architect nor the Housing Manager are statutory posts and this fact accounts for many of the divergencies between authorities in their building organization. Since the control of architectural services and the commissioning of housing are two of the most important parts of the building organization and neither the Architect nor the Housing Manager has a universally accepted place among the senior appointments, the pattern has an almost kaleidoscopic variety. Each authority shakes the prism to reveal a different allocation of functions, the county boroughs being particularly versatile in their design. The variety embraces not only different groupings of departments with building requirements but various ways of placing the client and architect functions under a single chief officer.

As far as the building organization is concerned the key functions are those of the Engineer, the Architect, the Housing Manager and the Building Manager. Authorities vary from having only one chief officer, the Engineer, with the other three functions subordinated to him, to having two, three or four separate departments with independent chief officers.

The inquiry revealed that the division of functions between the Engineer and Architect was one of the changing frontiers in local authority organization and one to which many authorities were giving much thought. This question, which radically affects the building organization, is, therefore, dealt with very fully in this chapter. It affects particularly the medium and smaller county boroughs and the larger non-county boroughs and district councils, whose size and building responsibilities lie on this frontier. For them it is a matter of keen interest whether the architectural services should be divided from the engineering services and be placed under a Chief Architect, or remain under the Chief Engineer.

It is hoped that those authorities who are considering this problem will find this chapter helpful. It must not, however, be forgotten that if the majority of the large authorities have separate Architect's departments, only a very small number of the other authorities is at any one time contemplating a change or the appointment of a Chief Architect. The overwhelming majority of the non-county boroughs and districts are not considering any such an alteration of the traditional pattern. In these authorities the Engineer is and is likely to continue to be responsible for the architectural services, either through salaried architects or by the use of private architects.

County Councils

The county councils, excluding the London County Council, vary in size from 2·2 million inhabitants to 19,000, but the majority of the populations of the administrative counties are between a quarter of a million and three-quarters of a million. Only thirteen out of the sixty-one counties have populations of less than 100,000, and of these seven are in Wales. It is, therefore, natural to think of the county councils as large authorities. This impression is reinforced by their geographical size. Twenty-nine cover administrative areas of half a million to over a million and a half acres and the smallest, the Soke of Peterborough, covers an area larger than Birmingham, which is the most populous city in the country. Size, both in terms of population and area, has had important influences on the building organization of these authorities.

The wide range of functions carried out by the county councils has already been described. The main departments with building requirements are divided in much the same way as the main committees and include education, health, police, fire, welfare and children's departments each with their individual head, who is generally a chief officer. In the architect/client relationship these are all client departments and there is virtually no ambiguity about the dividing line between the functions of the client and those of the architect. Only in one county is there a Schools Architect attached to the Education department and entirely separate from the County Architect's department. The clear dividing line between the technical departments on the one hand and the client departments on the other is one of the most distinguishing features of county organization.

In 1937, forty-four counties had separate Architect's departments. In the rest the County Surveyor was usually responsible for architectural as well as engineering services. Now all the counties, with the exception of the Soke of Peterborough, have County Architects with separate departments. This change has come about partly because of the general change in the climate of opinion towards architecture, and because for historical reasons the County Surveyor has been associated with a less diverse range of functions than the Borough Engineer. It was immensely accelerated by the size and urgency of the school building programme which the county councils had to undertake at the end of the war. The counties have been well aware that schools for the post-war bulge rivalled housing in urgency and political importance and they therefore reorganized their architectural services, where they were not already in an independent department, to take the strain.

Among the county councils there is now a clear cut distinction between the Architect's department and the Surveyor's department, though co-operation between the two may have to be very close on schemes where the two services interlock. The county councils are the only type of authority in which the Architect has come to have undisputed responsibility for the architectural services.

The principal client of the County Architect is the Chief Education Officer and co-operation between their respective departments must be close and constant. Table 9 in Chapter 3 showed how in the county councils the educational building programmes overshadow all other types of building and this balance is reflected in the number of architects employed in the Architect's department on school building compared with the requirements of other client committees (see Diagram 1). The school development plans, which many counties have drawn up covering a five-year period, coupled with the Ministry of Education's arrangements for settling authorities' building programmes well in advance, make it possible for the County

Diagram I

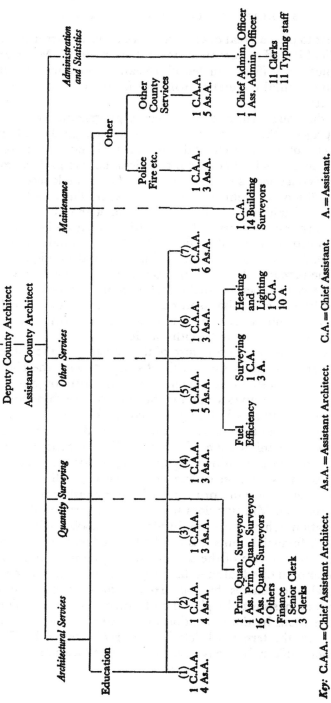

HERTFORDSHIRE

COUNTY ARCHITECT

Deputy County Architect

Assistant County Architect

Architectural Services	Quantity Surveying	Other Services	Maintenance	Administration and Statistics

Education

(1)
1 C.A.A.
4 As.A.

(2)
1 C.A.A.
4 As.A.

(3)
1 C.A.A.
3 As.A.

(4)
1 C.A.A.
3 As.A.

(5)
1 C.A.A.
5 As.A.

(6)
1 C.A.A.
3 As.A.

(7)
1 C.A.A.
6 As.A.

1 Prin. Quan. Surveyor
1 Ass. Prin. Quan. Surveyor
16 Ass. Quan. Surveyors
7 Others

Finance
1 Senior Clerk
3 Clerks

Fuel Efficiency

Surveying
1 C.A.
3 A.

Heating and Lighting
1 C.A.
10 A.

Maintenance
1 C.A.
14 Building Surveyors

Other

Police Fire etc.
1 C.A.A.
3 As.A.

Other County Services
1 C.A.A.
5 As.A.

1 Chief Admin. Officer
1 Ass. Admin. Officer

11 Clerks
11 Typing staff

Key: C.A.A.=Chief Assistant Architect.   As.A.=Assistant Architect.   C.A.=Chief Assistant.   A.=Assistant.

Hertfordshire is representative of the most usual county council organization in which the County Architect is responsible for the architectural services and for all maintenance, but without a direct labour organization.

Architect to plan a great deal of the work of his department and to predict his staff requirements several years ahead. Moreover, the Education Officer can tell him years in advance how the bulge in the child population will shift from one kind of school to another.

Into this long-term and fairly secure programme of educational projects the Architect can fit in the less predictable requirements of the other client departments. Unless there is some major scheme, such as new county offices, no one project from another department is likely to be larger than a single secondary school and most of them will be much smaller. The problem for these other buildings has been not so much the allocation of staff to carry out the design, but the risk that the design will be pigeon-holed at the last moment for lack of final Ministry approval. As every architect and client knows, the design taken out of the pigeon-hole twelve months later never looks so good and there is an expensive inclination to make changes. Having suffered from such set-backs in building police stations, health clinics or community centres, the Architect has learned to treat his other client's demands with caution.

Because of the size and nature of the demands of the Education department upon the Architect's department, the client/architect relationship can become a valuable form of joint collaboration, which gives scope for the evolution both of educational theory and new building techniques. Educational policy is reflected in the type of school buildings and the schools are the outward manifestation of the council's educational aims. The Ministry of Education's regulations provide for minimum standards and set a cost ceiling on capital expenditure. It is, however, an important principle of the English educational system that the Ministry does not directly determine the kind of education which goes on inside the schools. Within the Ministry's financial limits it is for the local education authority to decide on the size of the schools, their grouping on a large campus or on individual sites, the proportion of grammar school places, whether schools shall be mixed, or for boys or girls only, or what emphasis is to be placed on technical education. These policy decisions by the Education Committee have to be transformed into the terms of briefs for the architects by the Chief Education Officer. In the last ten years both educational theory and the buildings in which these theories are practised have changed a great deal and the Education Officer is able to influence these methods through the brief which he gives to the architects.

In spite of the complicated educational problems involved in determining the needs of new schools, those authorities which have large programmes of school building have also become expert in formulating their requirements to a standard, if also evolving, pattern. This may indeed reach so high a degree of mass production that each successive brief is no more than a modification of the one before or, like a box of children's bricks, disposes of the same units in different groups. A great deal of evolution is possible and a great deal of experience is amassed by authorities who have constructed 50–150 schools in a ten year period. Both building needs and teaching methods can be tried out and tested in such a large laboratory.

Such continuing programmes are not possible for other county council departments and the Children's Officer, the Welfare Officer, the Chief of Police or the Fire Officer are accustomed to drawing up their briefs in a very different context. Many of the buildings they require are only one of a kind due to the smaller demand or to limitations on capital expenditure, and neither the client nor the architect can have the same kind of experience as for schools. Contact between these departments and the Architect will not be of the continuing kind possible for the Education department. There is, indeed, a danger that there may be insufficient contact and joint consultation, and that in a busy Architect's department there will be neither the time nor the experience to give full study to the requirements of these less common buildings. This is a problem which the investigation came upon in many different forms and one to which possible solutions are offered later.

The responsibility for the maintenance of county buildings is also usually placed clearly upon the County Architect's shoulders. Sometimes another department has a small organization for minor urgent repairs, but generally speaking, the Architect acts for all departments. Usually he carries out maintenance through contractors. The geographical spread of the counties makes supervision of direct labour more difficult than in a compact town, and the political pressures in favour of the use of

113

direct labour are generally less strong. Large direct labour organizations are, therefore unusual, though the County Architect may control small teams of men for urgent work and there are some counties which employ their own force of painters.

A few counties have large direct labour organizations and where this is so there may be a separate Works department or the County Architect may be directly responsible. In Glamorgan, the County Architect controls a force of 600 men of which the greater part are employed on maintenance, and the Building Manager is a member of his staff. In Derbyshire, the direct labour force of similar size is also mainly employed on maintenance, but there is a Building Works department controlled by the Building Works Manager who is a chief officer. While these two authorities carry out the functions of maintenance contractors by direct labour, they have two quite different organizations for doing so. The contracting function in the client-architect-builder relationship is not, however, widely represented among the county councils and the execution of both new buildings and repairs is usually carried out by private builders and contractors while the County Architect has the responsibility for placing the orders and for supervising their execution.

Looking at the county building organization as a whole, the following common features stand out:

the clear distinction between the Architect on the one hand and the client departments on the other;

the undisputed responsibility of the Architect within the building field. The County Surveyor is concerned only with civil engineering services;

the overwhelming importance of the Education department as a client, and the size of its requirements;

the small amount of direct labour, and therefore the absence of contracting responsibilities.

The London County Council

The preceding account has excluded the London County Council for reasons which have already been explained. London is 'sui generis', both in size and scope of its responsibilities and therefore the functions of its chief officers differ from those of the other county councils and correspond more nearly to those of the large cities. Housing under the Director of Housing is the largest client department, though its overwhelming importance is now slightly diminishing with the shortage of undeveloped sites and the need to change over to the more laborious programmes of slum clearance. The Education Officer is also a client on a large scale.

The emphasis on these two services had until recently kept the claims of the other departments down to a low level. Of an average capital expenditure in recent years of about £25·4 million, £16·8 million has been spent on housing, £5·0 million on education and £3·6 million on other services. This has meant that, housing and education apart, the London County Council has constructed only about a dozen buildings costing more than £50,000 since the war. These include two session houses, four homes for the aged, a large health centre at Woodberry Down, the National Film Theatre and the Royal Festival Hall. The emphasis is now, however, beginning to change and departments other than Housing and Education will be receiving larger allocations.

The architectural services for these programmes are provided mainly by the Architect. The Architect is responsible for the design and construction of all schemes except:

housing schemes prepared by private architects;

education schemes prepared by private architects;

non-residential structures in parks such as lidos, refreshment houses, and shelters which are designed by the Chief Officer of the Parks department through architects on his staff and by private architects.

The volume of new building work carried out by the Architect is thus very large. In addition, he is responsible for the maintenance of all buildings other than housing and buildings in parks, and has a direct labour force of 600 for this purpose. The constructional side of the department employs about 1,400 technical officers (including clerks of works and other supervisory grades). The internal organization of the Architect's department is described in Chapter 5.

The Director of Housing, in addition to his responsibilities for managing nearly 200,000 dwellings, is responsible for:

the oversight of private architects;

the construction of new dwellings by direct labour. This organization has been increased to over 800 men;

the maintenance of all housing and part of the school painting programme with a force of nearly 6,500 men.

The direct labour force engaged on new building is supervised directly from headquarters by the Works division. The day-to-day control of the maintenance organization is entrusted to ten district officers.

The Education Officer has the oversight of schools designed by private architects and the Chief Officer of the Parks department of park buildings designed privately. The Architect thus has no oversight over the private architects employed in the largest fields of the council's work, housing and schools. It is an arrangement which permits very close liasion between the client department and the private architect. Whether it may also make it difficult for the private architect to exchange experience or ideas with the official architects and also to fit in with the various routines is discussed more fully later. This segregation of the private architect from the official architect is a practice also used by other authorities and is of general interest.

The distribution of functions between the various chief officers in the London County Council corresponds fairly closely to that of a number of other large county boroughs, except that the scale of operations is larger. The similarities are due to their common responsibilities for housing. Indeed, in the context of building operations and the organization of architectural services it is more appropriate to group the large cities and the London County Council together rather than to align London with the other county councils. As will be seen in what follows, the relationship between the chief officers in charge of client departments and the Architect, and the arrangements for maintenance by direct labour, resemble those of the larger county boroughs rather than those of the county councils.

County Boroughs

When we come to the organization of the county boroughs and the functions of their chief officers the comparative simplicity of the county council organization splinters into a confusing diversity. This is due partly to the differences in size and character and partly to the existence of the two major services, housing and education, instead of only one. It is also due to the absence of any uniformity in practice about the officer or officers on whom responsibility for housing management falls. Since the burden of this responsibility is heavy a great deal turns on this decision, and its effect on other departments.

The variety in the character of the county boroughs was described earlier. They range from populations of $1 \cdot 1$ million to 30,000 and from industrial towns in the north to seaside resorts in the south, or watering places and market towns on west and east. The interest in planning and architectural matters also varies greatly and can influence the distribution of duties between chief officers. Towns which have high architectural traditions to uphold and where the influence of historic buildings is strong are likely to stress the responsibilities of the Planning Officer and the Architect. Towns under the pall of industrial grime may have few aesthetic standards by which to judge their buildings and so pressing a need for more sanitary dwellings as to make the architectural merits of their work seem less important.

With so many varying circumstances the road taken to meet building requirements is highly individual. In the largest cities the scale of services provided calls for a wide range of separate departments. As the size of the authority decreases and the scale of the services diminishes, so will the number of separate departments and the chief officers at their head. The Libraries and Museums department may be absorbed by the Chief Education Officer, parks, markets and baths by the Engineer while the fire service may be run jointly with the county council. The absorption of one department by another may finish by blurring the clear line of division between the client and architect, so that

117

Diagram 2

BIRMINGHAM

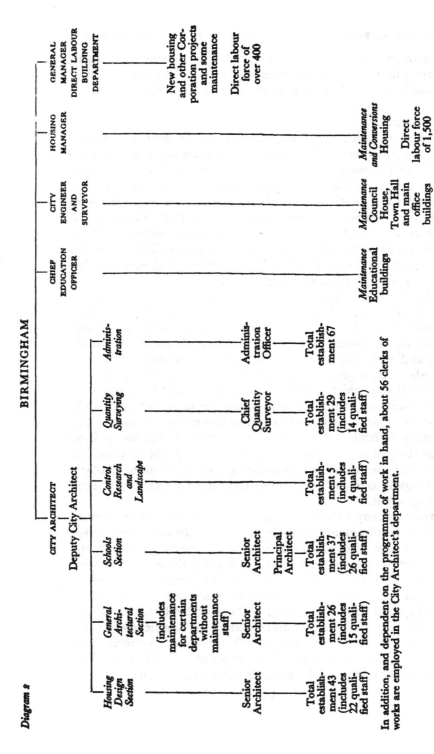

	GENERAL MANAGER DIRECT LABOUR BUILDING DEPARTMENT	HOUSING MANAGER	CITY ENGINEER AND SURVEYOR	CHIEF EDUCATION OFFICER
	New housing and other Corporation projects and some maintenance			
	Direct labour force of over 400			
		Maintenance and Conversions Housing	*Maintenance* Council House, Town Hall and main office buildings	*Maintenance* Educational buildings
		Direct labour force of 1,500		

CITY ARCHITECT

Deputy City Architect

Housing Design Section	*General Architectural Section*	*Schools Section*	*Control Research and Landscape*	*Quantity Surveying*	*Administration*
	(includes maintenance for certain departments without maintenance staff)				
Senior Architect	Senior Architect	Senior Architect / Principal Architect		Chief Quantity Surveyor	Administration Officer
Total establishment 43 (includes 22 qualified staff)	Total establishment 26 (includes 15 qualified staff)	Total establishment 37 (includes 26 qualified staff)	Total establishment 5 (includes 4 qualified staff)	Total establishment 29 (includes 14 qualified staff)	Total establishment 67

In addition, and dependent on the programme of work in hand, about 56 clerks of works are employed in the City Architect's department.

Birmingham has been selected as an example of a large authority where the City Architect is occupied almost exclusively with the architectural services. Other departments are responsible for most of the maintenance work, and there is a separate department for new building by direct labour. This will be taking over more of the maintenance services after 1960.

in the medium and small authorities not only may one chief officer be responsible for a number of services, but the roles of client and architect and contractor may end up in one department. The diversity is most marked of all in the allocation of functions for the design, maintenance and management of housing.

Some examples will make this clearer. Among the large cities, Birmingham, Manchester, Liverpool and Leeds have many common housing problems and ambitious housing programmes, yet the distribution of the housing functions in each of these authorities differs widely:

In *Birmingham* (Pop. 1·1 million) the City Architect is responsible for all architectural design, and the Housing Manager is a chief officer responsible to the Housing Management committee not only for the management of over 84,000 dwellings but for their maintenance by direct labour and by contract. The House Building committee's concern is to obtain the necessary land and to produce the new buildings. The City Architect is the officer principally concerned with this committee, but the Housing Manager attends all meetings. This is regarded as one of the means of keeping liaison between those producing houses and the client. There is a small but growing Works department mainly for new housing under its own chief officer. (See Diagram 2.)

In *Liverpool* (Pop. 762,000) the City Architect is also the Director of Housing, and apart from the collection of rents which is organized by the City Treasurer's department, he is responsible for housing management and maintenance, but not the maintenance of other buildings. He is also responsible for providing the architectural services for all the other client committees. The management of some 70,000 houses is thus combined with the oversight of building design to the value of £5·0 million to £6·0 million a year. (See Diagram 3.)

In *Manchester* (Pop. 676,000) the City Architect is responsible for the design of all buildings other than housing, and for the maintenance of all buildings other than the properties of the Housing, Transport, Waterworks, Cleansing, Highways,

119

Diagram 3

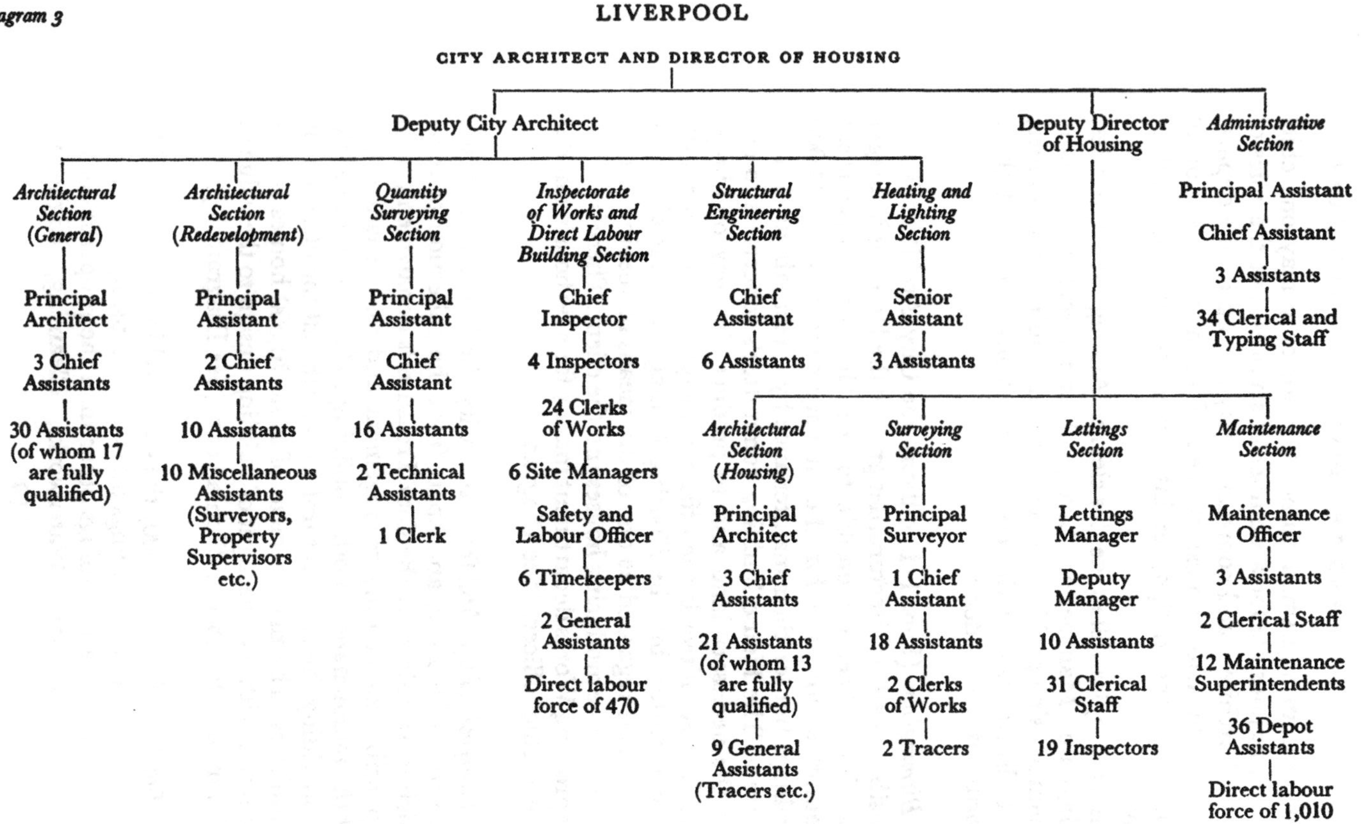

LIVERPOOL

CITY ARCHITECT AND DIRECTOR OF HOUSING

Deputy City Architect

Architectural Section (General)
- Principal Architect
- 3 Chief Assistants
- 30 Assistants (of whom 17 are fully qualified)

Architectural Section (Redevelopment)
- Principal Assistant
- 2 Chief Assistants
- 10 Assistants
- 10 Miscellaneous Assistants (Surveyors, Property Supervisors etc.)

Quantity Surveying Section
- Principal Assistant
- Chief Assistant
- 16 Assistants
- 2 Technical Assistants
- 1 Clerk

Inspectorate of Works and Direct Labour Building Section
- Chief Inspector
- 4 Inspectors
- 24 Clerks of Works
- 6 Site Managers
- Safety and Labour Officer
- 6 Timekeepers
- 2 General Assistants
- Direct labour force of 470

Structural Engineering Section
- Chief Assistant
- 6 Assistants

Heating and Lighting Section
- Senior Assistant
- 3 Assistants

Deputy Director of Housing

Administrative Section
- Principal Assistant
- Chief Assistant
- 3 Assistants
- 34 Clerical and Typing Staff

Maintenance Section
- Maintenance Officer
- 3 Assistants
- 2 Clerical Staff
- 12 Maintenance Superintendents
- 36 Depot Assistants
- Direct labour force of 1,010

Lettings Section
- Lettings Manager
- Deputy Manager
- 10 Assistants
- 31 Clerical Staff
- 19 Inspectors

Surveying Section
- Principal Surveyor
- 1 Chief Assistant
- 18 Assistants
- 2 Clerks of Works
- 2 Tracers

Architectural Section (Housing)
- Principal Architect
- 3 Chief Assistants
- 21 Assistants (of whom 13 are fully qualified)
- 9 General Assistants (Tracers etc.)

Liverpool is an example of an authority where the City Architect is also the Director of Housing, responsible for letting, housing maintenance and management. Rents are collected by the City Treasurer's department. The other main departments are responsible for their own maintenance organizations.

Rivers and Estates Management committees. The Director of Housing, who is an architect, is responsible for the design of all housing and ancillary buildings and for the management and maintenance of some 57,000 dwellings.

In *Leeds* (Pop. 511,000) the Housing Manager is responsible for housing management, the City Architect for design and the Director of Works for the maintenance of all council property, most of it by direct labour.

Among medium sized authorities some further examples illustrate the diversity:

In *Sunderland* (Pop. 185,000) there is a Borough Architect, Borough Engineer, Housing Manager and a Public Works Manager of chief officer status who is responsible for running the direct labour organization for both building and civil engineering. (See Diagram 5.)

In *Brighton* (Pop. 159,000) the Housing Manager is a chief officer, and the Borough Engineer, with a staff of seventeen qualified architects, is responsible for all the architectural services and the maintenance of all council property.

In *Blackpool* (Pop. 145,000) the Borough Engineer is responsible for architectural services and maintenance and the Borough Treasurer for housing management.

In *Lincoln* (Pop. 70,000) there is a City Architect; the Chief Housing Assistant is on the staff of the Treasurer and maintenance is divided between the Architect (housing), Chief Education Officer (schools) and City Engineer (other municipal buildings).

In *Eastbourne* (Pop. 58,000) the Borough Engineer is also the Architect and is responsible for all maintenance as well as housing management.

This list does not exhaust the variety of ways in which the responsibilities for housing design, management and mainten-

121

Diagram 4

STOCKPORT COUNTY BOROUGH

BOROUGH ARCHITECT
Deputy Borough Architect

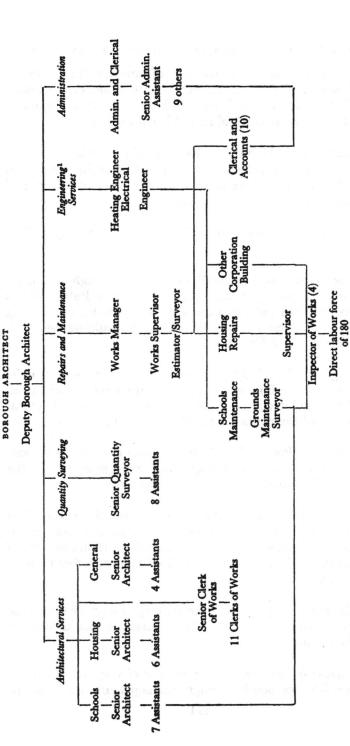

[1] In connection with building.

The example of *Stockport* is given to illustrate the type of building organization when the Borough Architect is responsible for the maintenance of all buildings, mainly by direct labour, as well as architectural design. Housing Management is the responsibility of another department.

ance can be divided, but it gives an impression of the diversity which is possible, and the differences of stress which authorities place on the importance of an independent Architect or Housing Manager, or on co-ordination by the Engineer.

The inter-relation between separate Housing, Architect and Engineering departments emerged very clearly among the medium and smaller authorities where the authority may be on the margin of decision about having one or two, or two or three chief officers. If the main objective is to obtain better architectural standards, the appointment of a Chief Architect may be combined with responsibilities for housing management. If better housing management is the council's chief concern, a separate appointment may be made and the architectural services may be kept within the Engineer's department.

No such ambivalence surrounds the Chief Education Officer. As far as his responsibilities for strictly educational services are concerned there can be no division of functions. The Education committee with its statutory functions and the Education Officer have an undisputed field. Usually the Chief Education Officer uses the services of the Chief Architect or Engineer for school building and has no architects on his own staff. In large authorities the programmes of the Education department may be the most interesting part of the Architect's work and, though second to housing in volume, may be the centre of a more than proportionate interest and attention. Schools have been the subject of much investigation of design and costs, and a close integration between the client and the Architect is necessary. As a result some authorities have placed school building directly under the control of the Education Officer with his own architectural staff. Alternatively, they may employ private architects for this work, who are briefed and supervised by the Education Officer.

Within the scope of the authorities covered by the inquiry, these alternative arrangements were only found in authorities where there was no separate Architect's department and the Borough Engineer was responsible for architectural work as well as, very often, the direct labour organization for maintenance and repair. In Middlesbrough, for example, where the other architectural services are under the Engineer, there is an Architect's and Building section under an Education Architect

123

Diagram 5

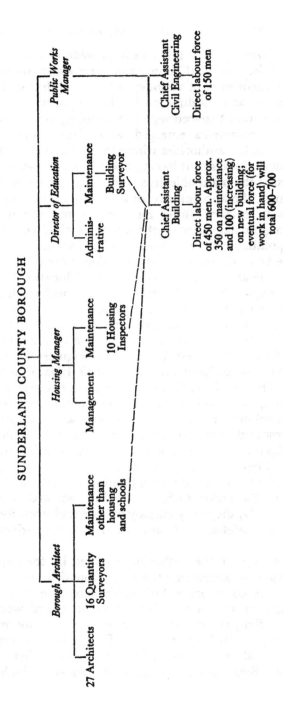

SUNDERLAND COUNTY BOROUGH

Borough Architect
- 27 Architects
- 16 Quantity Surveyors
- Maintenance other than housing and schools

Housing Manager
- Management
- Maintenance
  - 10 Housing Inspectors

Director of Education
- Adminis-trative
- Maintenance
  - Building Surveyor

Public Works Manager
- Chief Assistant Building
  - Direct labour force of 450 men. Approx. 350 on maintenance and 100 (increasing) on new building; eventual force (for work in hand) will total 600–700
- Chief Assistant Civil Engineering
  - Direct labour force of 150 men

Sunderland is an example of an authority which has a separate Works department under its own chief officer. The Works department operates as a contracting organization for other departments. It is unusual in that it carries out both building and civil engineering work. The dotted lines on the diagram indicate the source of instruction for building work.

as an integral part of the departmental organization for education. The Architect is responsible for the design and maintenance of all school buildings. There is a staff of fourteen architects, and private architects are also used as required.

An example of the alternative system is to be found in Ipswich. Ipswich uses the services of a single firm of private architects for all its school building. They are controlled by the Director of Education. By using one firm it becomes almost an extended arm of the Education department, and the architects become familiar with the council's procedures and requirements, more so than when the authority draws on a panel of architects, which is the more usual pattern. In Ipswich the school building programme will not continue indefinitely on its present scale and it was thought more economical to use private architects than to set up an organization with permanent staff who might become redundant. These two authorities show alternative methods of solving the two problems of overloading the Borough Engineer and of putting architects to work under an Engineer.

In determining the pattern of responsibility for the maintenance of schools considerations arise different from those for the maintenance of housing. With housing there is a close relationship between landlord and tenant and the wishes as well as the needs of the tenant exert a strong influence. Furthermore, housing management is to some extent a trading concern and rent policy is intimately bound up with repairs policy. These two factors demand very close contact between the Housing Manager and the maintenance organization, and affect in their own way the decision about keeping housing management and maintenance within the same department.

The Education department's problems concerning maintenance are different. The needs of the children are all important, but not their wishes and the relationship between head teachers and the Education department is not that of landlord and tenant. Nor do Education departments have to make the education accounts balance as a trading account in the same way as the housing account. Economy is just as necessary, but the day-to-day control is exercised by other means. The Education department has so many other educational links with the schools that the links on maintenance are of secondary importance.

125

Diagram 6

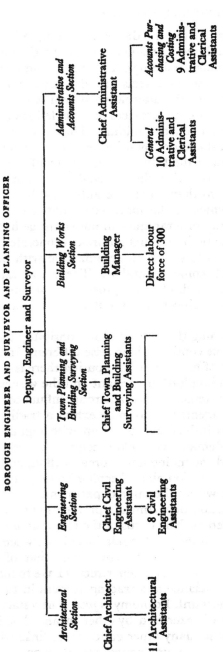

Tottenham is an example of an authority where the Engineer and Surveyor is responsible for architectural as well as engineering services, and for building maintenance and repair. The Housing Manager is a chief officer with a separate department.

School maintenance has its own problems. These are discussed more fully in the chapter on Maintenance.

Direct labour for maintenance is widespread among county boroughs and many carry out considerable new building programmes by this method. It is, therefore, fairly common to have separate Works departments with the Works Manager in charge. Some of these are chief officers; others heads of departments. The Works department acts as a contracting organization, and some authorities are at pains to underline the separate and contractual relationship. There appears to be no particular pattern which suggests that authorities have any common basis for deciding on a separate department or for placing responsibility for direct labour on the Chief Engineer, Architect or Housing Manager or, indeed, on more than one officer. Sometimes there may be a special enthusiasm for direct labour and this prompts the council to set up a separate department under a Works Manager controlled by a Works committee. But there are other councils equally emphatic in their support for direct labour, who place the organization within the framework of existing departments. The variety of practice is very wide, and will be covered more fully in the chapter on Direct Labour.

The survey showed that the county boroughs have divided the responsibilities for building in so many different ways that they defy any sort of generalization. The client committees do not, as in the county councils, necessarily find any counterpart in the departments, since the administration of several services may be under one chief officer. Nor is there any clear line of demarcation between the officers who are responsible for drawing up the brief and those responsible for design and construction. The trend, however, is towards more separate Housing departments and a clearer line of division between the engineering and architectural functions. The advantages and disadvantages of these arrangements are discussed later.

Non-County Boroughs and District Councils

Once we move into the territory of the non-county boroughs and the urban and rural districts we leave behind almost all the responsibilities for educational building, and most of those for health, fire, police, children and the like. The energies of the non-county boroughs and districts are concentrated heavily on

127

housing, and their building organization is, therefore, directed almost single-mindedly towards this objective. Occasionally, these authorities may have schemes to build council offices, a library, civic restaurant, municipal depot, market, swimming bath or other sports buildings, and these buildings will then stimulate exceptional interest. But, broadly speaking, there is not the dispersal of effort as between two major client committees, and no regular demands from other committees. The only important exception is to be found in those municipal boroughs which are also Excepted Districts for education purposes and may have authority delegated by the county council to design and erect schools.

This narrowing of functions has two main effects. Firstly, the number of chief officers and heads of departments is reduced and the Clerk, Treasurer, Engineer and, where he exists, the Architect, take under their wings a wider range of services. As the longest established technical officer, the Engineer is the natural repository for other technical or semi-technical services. He may also control parks and open spaces, burial grounds and crematoria, and often housing management as well.

Secondly, the client-architect relationship becomes more restricted, since housing is the principal building activity and housing management and housing design are frequently within the same department, either both under the Engineer or both under the Architect. Thus, in the inevitable process of reducing the number of chief officers and increasing the variety of their responsibilities, it is possible to travel to a position exactly opposite to that of the County Architect who serves a number of separate client departments and is responsible for the architectural services only. Among many of the non-county boroughs and districts the Engineer has functions which combine the responsibilities of the client, the architect and the contractor all within one department.

As with the county boroughs, the distribution of the functions related to housing is a key factor in each authority's organization. The responsibilities for housing management are combined or divided nearly as diversely among the non-county boroughs and districts as in the larger authorities, and the senior officer responsible for executing the Housing committee's requirements can appear in many guises. He or she can, as Housing Manager, be a chief officer with independent status: alternatively, the housing section can be a part of the Treasurer's, or more rarely, the Clerk's department. Or the Borough Engineer may double the responsibilities for management and design and thus combine the functions of client and architect. Or the council may appoint a Chief Architect with responsibilities for housing management as well, again combining architect and client in one person.

The following examples illustrate this variety. They deal first with the non-county boroughs:

In *Ealing* Borough (Pop. 183,000) the Borough Engineer and Surveyor with a staff of seven architects is responsible for all architectural services, as well as for housing management and all maintenance with a direct labour force of 200. (See Diagram 7.)

In *Hendon* Borough (Pop. 153,000) the Borough Engineer and Surveyor is responsible for all the architectural services and for the maintenance of all buildings other than housing. The Borough Housing Officer is responsible for the management and maintenance of housing. (See Diagram 8.)

In *Luton* Borough (Pop. 118,000) the Borough Architect with a staff of fourteen architects is responsible for the design of all buildings, including schools, and for maintenance other than housing and the Director of Housing, as the head of a department, is responsible for the management and maintenance of housing with a direct labour force of fifty-seven.

In *Paddington* Metropolitan Borough (Pop. 116,000) the Director of Housing and Borough Architect controls all the architectural services, housing management and maintenance.

In *Barking* Borough (Pop. 75,000) there is a Borough Architect with a staff of four architects, a Re-Housing Officer responsible for management, a Works Manager, with a direct labour force of 200, responsible for the erection and maintenance of houses, while the Borough Engineer is responsible

E   129

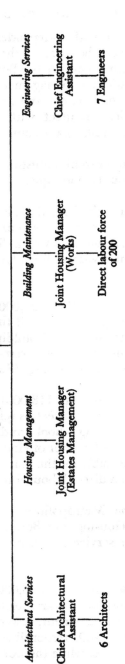

Diagram 7

EALING NON-COUNTY BOROUGH

BOROUGH ENGINEER AND SURVEYOR

Deputy Borough Engineer and Surveyor

Architectural Services	*Housing Management*	*Building Maintenance*	*Engineering Services*
Chief Architectural Assistant	Joint Housing Manager (Estates Management)	Joint Housing Manager (Works)	Chief Engineering Assistant
6 Architects		Direct labour force of 200	7 Engineers

Ealing is an example of an authority where the Engineer and Surveyor is responsible for the whole building organization and for housing management.

for the maintenance other than housing. Both the Re-Housing Officer and the Works Manager are principal officers.

In *Watford* Borough (Pop. 73,000) the Borough Engineer and Surveyor is responsible for architectural services and maintenance and the Housing Officer is on the staff of the Borough Treasurer.

The metropolitan boroughs make a particularly interesting study in this context. While they differ in size from populations of 21,000 to 337,000 and all have the London County Council building side by side with them as a rival or complementary housing authority, the distribution of functions among their chief officers differs widely.

Five out of the twenty-eight metropolitan boroughs have Borough Architects, four of whom are also Directors of Housing. This includes the very smallest, Holborn. The largest of the metropolitan boroughs is Wandsworth, which previously had a separate Architect's department, but now has all architectural services and housing management combined under the Borough Engineer and Surveyor, who is also a registered architect. Westminster has a Director of Housing who is an architect, but he is not the Borough Architect. One or two authorities, such as Bermondsey, have no separate Architect's department but a Director of Housing who is not an architect and a Building Manager of chief officer rank with a large direct labour organization.

The metropolitan boroughs illustrate very clearly the varying emphasis placed by the different authorities on the importance of architectural services, housing management and building management. With their restricted range of responsibilities, there are limits to the number of chief officers. Those who are specially interested in the architectural qualities of their buildings are inclined to bracket housing and architecture and to make an architect the head of the department. Those who rate the importance of housing management more highly make the Housing Manager a chief officer and leave the responsibilities for architecture with the Borough Engineer. Some place special emphasis on the leadership of the direct labour organization,

131

Diagram 8

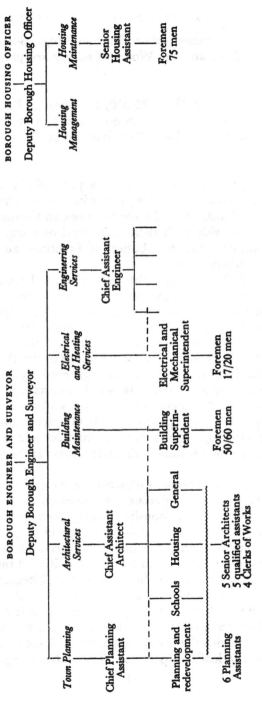

HENDON NON-COUNTY BOROUGH

BOROUGH ENGINEER AND SURVEYOR
Deputy Borough Engineer and Surveyor

Town Planning

Chief Planning Assistant

Planning and redevelopment

6 Planning Assistants

Schools   Housing   General

5 Senior Architects
5 qualified assistants
4 Clerks of Works

Architectural Services

Chief Assistant Architect

Building Maintenance

Building Superin-tendent

Foremen 50/60 men

Electrical and Heating Services

Electrical and Mechanical Superintendent

Foremen 17/20 men

Engineering Services

Chief Assistant Engineer

BOROUGH HOUSING OFFICER
Deputy Borough Housing Officer

Housing Management

Housing Maintenance

Senior Housing Assistant

Foremen 75 men

Hendon is an example of an authority where the Borough Engineer and Surveyor controls all the architectural and engineering services and the maintenance of buildings other than housing. The Borough Housing Officer, with a separate department, is responsible for housing maintenance and management.

and some prefer the more traditional role of the Engineer and Surveyor responsible for all these services combined.

Normally in the districts the responsibility for architectural services rests with the Engineer and Surveyor, and he is also responsible for maintenance and sometimes for housing management as well. For example:

> In *Harlow* Urban District Council (Pop. 40,000) the Engineer and Surveyor is responsible for architectural services, for housing management and for maintenance. He has three salaried architects on his staff. (See Diagram 9.)

Among district authorities the separate Architect's department is a rarity, but two examples show the variety within even this limited field:

> In *Huyton-with-Roby* Urban District Council (Pop. 61,000) the Architect is also the Director of Housing and has responsibility for all architectural work, for housing management and the maintenance of all council buildings. He has four architects on his staff and a direct labour force for new buildings and maintenance of seventy men.

> In *Pontypool* Urban District Council (Pop. 40,000) the Architect with one assistant is responsible for the design of housing and the Engineer and Surveyor for the design of other buildings. The Housing Manager is a chief officer and responsibility for the maintenance of housing is divided. The Engineer is responsible for all other maintenance.

A few of the smaller authorities retain a firm of private architects and employ them regularly for their architectural work instead of having architects on the staff.

The examples quoted reveal how wide the variations are between authorities of like size and responsibility. The variations should not, however, be allowed to obscure what are the most common patterns. The non-county boroughs and district authorities with their more limited responsibilities have comparatively few chief officers, often only the Clerk, the Treasurer,

Diagram 9

HARLOW URBAN DISTRICT COUNCIL

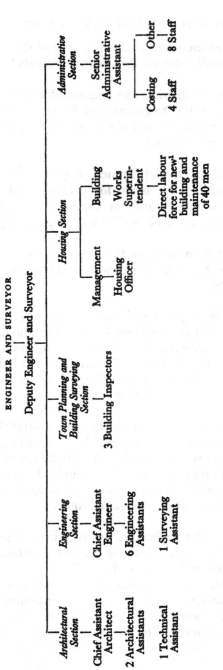

ENGINEER AND SURVEYOR

Deputy Engineer and Surveyor

Architectural Section
Chief Assistant Architect
2 Architectural Assistants
1 Technical Assistant

Engineering Section
Chief Assistant Engineer
6 Engineering Assistants
1 Surveying Assistant

Town Planning and Building Surveying Section
3 Building Inspectors

Housing Section
Management
Housing Officer

Building Works Superintendent
Direct labour force for new[1] building and maintenance of 40 men

Administrative Section
Senior Administrative Assistant
Costing 4 Staff
Other 8 Staff

[1] This also covers new building other than housing.

Harlow is a further example of an authority where the Engineer and Surveyor is responsible for all the building services and for housing management. Only private quantity surveyors are employed.

the Engineer and the Medical Officer of Health. When a committee requires a new building, it normally makes its request direct to the authority's only chief technical officer, the Engineer and Surveyor. Less than thirty non-county boroughs and districts have Chief Architects and against the background of 318 non-county boroughs and 564 urban and 474 rural districts this number is very small.

Where the Engineer is administratively in charge of the building services he may not have any architects on his staff, but may employ private architects either on some regular basis with a retaining fee, or more frequently, as and when the demand for architectural work requires it. The investigation showed, however, that among all but the smaller authorities it is extremely common for the Engineer to have architects on his staff. The reasons for the preference for the employment of official rather than private architects is discussed in Chapter 5. At this point it is necessary to grasp not only the diversity of practice between authorities but the widespread activities of the Engineer as the chief technical officer

Organization Charts

In order to clarify the various types of departmental organization, organization charts have been included in this chapter, covering Hertfordshire, Birmingham, Liverpool, Stockport, Sunderland, Tottenham, Ealing, Hendon and Harlow.

In examining the diagrams it should be remembered that, where the Engineer is responsible for architectural services as well as engineering services, the charts show the engineering services in skeleton form. Where there is a Chief Architect, details of the engineering service do not appear at all, as these are in a different department. It will also be observed that the diagrams do not go into any detail about the maintenance organization or direct labour, as these are covered by later chapters.

DIVISION OF FUNCTIONS BETWEEN THE ARCHITECT AND ENGINEER

It will be apparent by now that authorities vary greatly in the functions carried out by the Engineer and the Architect, and

135

that this is one of the most important differences in their building organization. A great change has indeed taken place in the
past twenty years, and authorities now employ a great many
more architects than they did before the war, and have appointed more Chief Architects as the heads of the architectural
services. The following table shows how the number of Chief
Architects has increased since 1937 to its present total of more
than twice the pre-war figure.

TABLE 10

NUMBER OF CHIEF ARCHITECTS[1]

	1937	1957	Total number of authorities
Counties	44	60	62
County Boroughs	14	47	83
Non-County Boroughs (excluding London area)	1	14	318
Metropolitan Boroughs		5	28
Urban Districts (20 largest)	1	4	564
Rural Districts (20 largest)	1	2	474
	61	132	1,529

This change reflects the greater volume of municipal building
since the war, particularly schools and houses, and the increasing realization of the contribution of the architect to good design.
If figures were available to show the change in the number of
architects at all levels in local government at these two dates,
the differences would probably be even more striking.

The change that is taking place is one aspect of an evolution
of local government which has been going on for many years.
Originally the functions of municipal authorities were conceived of mainly in terms of the protection of public health and
safety and the improvement of those services which reduce the
risks of epidemics and the ills associated with an unhealthy
environment. During the late nineteenth century, local authorities were heavily engaged in providing better and safer water

[1] These figures are derived mainly from the Municipal Year Book and are
based on the designation of officers given there. The status of the authority refers
to its status in 1957. Some of the authorities had not achieved this status in 1937,
but for the purposes of comparison the authorities are identical in the two lists.
Only the 20 largest district councils of both types were examined, as it was thought
that below this size the numbers of Chief Architects would be negligible.

supplies, drainage, sewerage, roads and street lighting, and in preventing by their bye-laws a repetition of the shocking housing standards of the industrial revolution. These years saw the rapid extension of civil engineering works in and around all the towns and the value of these services was amply shown by the dramatic improvements in public health and the reduction of diseases due to insanitary conditions.

During the period when the development of these public health services was proceeding so rapidly and was making so great a contribution to general welfare, municipal authorities needed men to work in partnership with the Medical Officer of Health, to design and maintain these civil engineering works and to inspect and control insanitary building conditions. As a result men with the kind of qualifications and experience now accepted as the hallmark of the Borough Engineer and Surveyor and Public Health Inspector established a firm foothold in local government and gradually came to be regarded as an indispensable part of the public health services. The process was slow, but it set a pattern which established the Engineer and Surveyor firmly in the saddle as far as the technical services of local authorities were concerned. They made him a natural magnet for many of the other technical or semi-technical developments which municipal authorities gradually undertook.

During these years the architect was called upon to design the prestige buildings of the authorities, the town hall, museum, public library or other monuments to civic self-confidence. To this end, he might be encouraged to produce something splendidly lavish by present standards and to commemorate in elaborate design the exuberance of his patrons. But he would generally be a private architect and his commissions would rarely extend to humbler buildings such as schools and housing. Many authorities considered the use of architects for dwellings for the working classes a quite unnecessary expense, and have indeed continued to do so until very recently.

It is thus the historical development of local enterprise and the early emphasis on civil engineering services which placed the Engineer and Surveyor in so strategic a position among local authority officers. Being first in the field and equipped with technical knowledge closely allied to that of the architect, it is small wonder that the role of the architect in local government

137

service, particularly as a chief officer, has not found an easy acceptance. It is, for example, interesting that there are few, if any, architects in charge of combined departments comprising both engineers and architects, though a few Chief Engineers have architectural qualifications and combine the two professions in one person. Where two separate departments are not thought to be justified, it is the Engineer who reigns supreme.

After 1919 house building by local authorities received a great thrust forward with the introduction of the housing subsidies and much greater interest began to be taken in the design of houses as well as of schools. Architects were increasingly employed, but many authorities still regarded the employment of an architect for housing as of doubtful value, particularly as they had an Engineer and Surveyor whose technical qualifications included a knowledge of building construction. Between 1919 and 1939 the number of salaried architects increased but, except among the county councils, few Chief Architects were appointed. Instead, the Chief Engineer and Surveyor reinforced his staff with architects, and when the importance of the building merited it, used private architects.

It took the Second World War and the expectation of major housing and school programmes to breach the Engineer's citadel and to bring about a more widespread division of the functions of the Engineer and Architect through the creation of separate departments. The division was in many cases made easier by the large civil engineering problems which faced the local authority Engineers as the back-log of the war years and as a result of shifts in population. While a considerable change has taken place, the pattern is still extremely fluid and there is so much divergence in practice between authorities as to make this an interesting and useful subject for investigation. There is no more lively centre of argument in the field of local authority building organization.

While the trend in the medium and large authorities is towards a separation of the architectural and engineering departments, there is also an opposite trend in the design of individual buildings. The larger buildings, such as schools, technical colleges and tall flats require an increasing collaboration between engineers and architects in their design. Many authorities use specialist engineering consultants, but it is important

138

that any separation of departments should not undermine co-operation between architects and engineers on the staff. Later parts of this book show how important teamwork of this kind can be.

Joint or Separate Departments?

The historical development of local government services and the strategic position held by the Engineer and Surveyor in local authority administration mean that the pressures have to be strong before a council will be prepared to cleave the Engineer's department into two and set up a separate Architect's department. The Engineer's long experience of house-building coupled with a council's natural conservatism and anxiety about additional administrative costs militate against a change. What then prompts an authority to change its building organization and to divide the architectural from the engineering services and to have two departments in the place of one? What reasons persuade an authority, having considered the dual organization, to continue with a single department under the Engineer? The decisions of an authority for or against a separate Architect's department must take into account:

the size of the authority and the range of its functions;

the size and continuity of the building programme;

special local circumstances which give particular prominence to building operations;

the scope of the Chief Engineer's other responsibilities and commitments, and the effect of the division of responsibilities on other departments such as Works or Housing;

the advantages of having a Chief Architect in charge of architects and the policy of the authority about employing private architects;

the problems of co-ordination;

the extra cost including another chief officer's salary, additional office staff, accommodation and plant.

139

Clearly the size of the authority and the type and variety of buildings for which it is responsible affect the decision very significantly. The county councils and the largest cities have separate Architects' departments, while few of the non-county boroughs have them and very few of the districts. Chief Architects are thick at the top and thin at the bottom of the population scale. This very broad generalization does not, however, take us very far in considering a broad band of authorities in the middle with populations ranging from about 180,000 at the top to 40,000 at the bottom, with only a few exceptions above and below those limits. Within this wide band, which includes county and non-county boroughs and urban and rural districts, both combined and separate departments are to be found. The variations work out as follows:

all but one of the county councils have made their choice in favour of separate departments and the County Architect's position is established beyond doubt;

county boroughs with populations of upwards of a quarter of a million all have Chief Architects, but both systems are common among authorities with populations of 80,000 to 200,000. Below populations of 80,000, the Chief Architects thin out rapidly, but they are to be found right down the scale to the smallest with a population of only 30,000;

most of the municipal boroughs in which there are Chief Architects have populations of over 100,000, but five with populations of 50,000 to 17,000 have separate Architect's departments under a Borough Architect. Nineteen authorities, mostly in or around London, with populations of 100,000 and over have combined departments under the Engineer and Surveyor;

among urban and rural districts the Engineer and Surveyor is usually responsible for the architectural services and a separate Architect's department is a rarity. Where it does occur it is not necessarily in the largest districts. Two districts with populations of some 40,000 have Chief Architects.

The size of the authority and its functions are, therefore, only an approximate indication of the reasons for the choice for and against the separation of departments. Many other considerations and influences affect the kind of organization.

Neither the size of an authority nor its range of functions accurately reflects its building programmes. Some authorities have much more pressing housing needs than others; in some the school population is growing particularly fast; in others the population of the city centre is diminishing. At the end of the war authorities were eager to push forward their programmes and to achieve an expansion unimpeded by avoidable bottlenecks within their internal organization. The separation of the Architect from the Engineer was as much an expression of their desire for singleness of purpose as of interest in the architectural qualities of their buildings. Time and again during the course of the inquiry authorities have stated that the appointment of a Chief Architect at the end of the war was an expression of the urgency of the task ahead and the wish to avoid delays. This view has been particularly stressed by some of the medium and smaller housing authorities in areas where waiting lists were exceptionally long; it was hoped by dividing the departments to give the new Chief Architect a clear field of operations unimpeded by preoccupations with other services. Conversely, authorities where the continuity or urgency of the building programme appeared less important have feared that the department might in a few years become redundant and the Chief Architect an embarrassment.

Apart from the size and continuity of the regular programmes for schools and houses some authorities have special problems which require the undivided attention of an Architect of first-rate quality. This has been particularly true of those towns which suffered severe bomb damage in their centres and where large schemes of reconstruction have been required. The destruction called for a major effort both architecturally and administratively, which could not be left to an architect in the second rank or to a department already overloaded with other cares.

Authorities have had to look not only at the scale of the strictly architectural services, but at the non-architectural responsibilities of the Engineer and the load he is already bearing, or is likely to bear in the future. Large building programmes mean large engineering programmes as well. Redevelopment of

141

the central area, either due to bomb damage or slum clearance, will call for complex revisions of the roads and services. A rapidly expanding population on the periphery will necessitate new roads and services and possibly an expansion of water and sewage installations, as well as an increase in the scale of day-to-day responsibilities for refuse collection, street cleansing and other services.

The central position held by the Engineer may mean that he is also responsible for a diverse collection of other services, such as housing management, maintenance of buildings, direct labour, parks and open spaces, burial grounds and baths. Too great a preoccupation with expanding engineering services or too diverse a responsibility for other non-engineering activities must hamper concentration of attention on the architectural services. Authorities, who have wished to set up separate architectural departments under a Chief Architect, have often been strengthened in their purpose by an appreciation of the Engineer's many other burdens.

Where the balance of advantage for either the combined or the separate departments is not so overwhelming as to quench all doubt, other arguments enter into consideration. Those who favour the combined department with the architects and engineers working in separate sections under one chief officer lay special stress on the advantages of co-ordination and economy. They argue that under one head co-ordination of committee work is easier, that members prefer to deal with one chief officer rather than with two, that the design of buildings, roads and services can be more easily dovetailed and that there can be a better system for settling priorities as between building and civil engineering work. They also claim lower administrative costs because offices, clerical staff and equipment can be shared, while there is the salary of only one chief officer to be paid instead of two. In addition, if the Engineer is responsible for maintenance and runs the Works department, he can keep in close touch with the effects of design on maintenance.

There are also those who argue that there are great advantages in detaching some of the semi-technical services such as refuse collection and disposal and for leaving the Engineer in charge of the professional services of architecture and engineering. A number of boroughs and districts give the responsibility for these technical services to a Cleansing Superintendent of chief officer status or to the Chief Public Health Inspector in order to relieve the Engineer of an excessive burden of work. By doing this they keep the professional services under the single control of the Engineer and take away some of the organizational responsibilities.

As against these arguments there is a strong body of opinion which holds that the best architectural results are not achieved when architects work under an Engineer, but that a much better quality of design is attained when they work under a Chief Architect and the two disciplines are kept separate. The two professions have different outlooks and attitudes which make them uneasy stable mates. Objections to the combined organization under an Engineer are based on the following arguments: that

the professions of architect and engineer are distinct and different and there are likely to be difficulties in putting the one profession in a subordinate position to the other;

a first-class architect of experience will not be attracted by posts of deputy or chief assistant to a Chief Engineer and that if this is the authority's senior post for an architect, a council cannot hope to obtain or retain an able man;

good junior staff are attracted by the prestige of a Chief Architect's name and are not so attracted to a combined department;

the general atmosphere and outlook in a combined department may cramp the architects, and lack of understanding of their work at the top will produce only mediocre results.

These arguments for and against combined departments are controversial and important in determining whether or not authorities should make a change in their organization. This is very much a live issue at the present time. Not only is the number of appointments of Chief Architect increasing gradually year by year, but it was found that many authorities were currently considering the reorganization of their technical departments, or had done so in the recent past. Since this is so disputed

143

a frontier in local authority organization and one which evokes so heated a partisanship from each of the professions concerned, it was decided to make it the subject of a specially detailed investigation.

As it was already clear that size alone, even in relation to authorities of similar functions, did not govern the combination or separation of the technical departments, an attempt was made to discover if there were any common factors which appeared to be decisive. A special investigation was made which covered ten of the largest county boroughs with combined departments, eight of them with populations of over 100,000, five of the smallest county boroughs with separate Architect's departments, six non-county boroughs with Chief Architects, seven of the largest non-county boroughs of over 100,000 population with combined departments and six urban and rural districts which were known to have separate departments.

By this selection it was hoped to cover authorities which were near the frontier, and therefore might be expected to have given the matter special consideration. They either had combined departments but were large enough to make a case for dividing off the architect, if they so wished, or they had separate departments but were small enough to suggest that the division of their organization denoted a special interest in, or responsibility for, architectural work. Two authorities, which were approached because they were large and were understood to have combined organizations, were found to have recently changed their organization and to have set up separate departments. This confirmed the impression that this was a growing-point in the administrative arrangements of local authorities, and indeed several authorities stated that they had been considering the matter.

The investigation was directed to finding out whether there was any indication that the single or dual organization existed because the Engineer had either exceptionally many or exceptionally few additional responsibilities. Did these make it important to relieve him of excessive burdens, or did they make it uneconomic to divide the architectural services from the rest? Were there any extra functions assumed by the Chief Architect which made the division easier? Or were the arrangements made by each authority peculiar to itself, in the sense that the reasons for having the joint or the separate organization was unrelated to the volume of engineering or architectural work?

The results were most interesting and authorities proved frank and informative about the reasons for their present organization and any changes that had been made. Extracts from their replies are quoted and give a valuable cross-section of opinion which confirms many of the general impressions obtained by less direct means earlier in the inquiry. Very broadly, the replies showed that just as there was no common pattern according to the size of population, so there was no common pattern according to the volume of work. Almost everywhere the capital cost of new building work exceeded the capital cost of new engineering works, but not more so in the authorities with separate organizations than in those without. Similarly, the cost of engineering maintenance generally slightly exceeded the cost of building maintenance, but neither more nor less in authorities with the combined departments.

Comparisons of the number of qualified architects and qualified engineers on the staff also showed no pattern which would indicate that the volume of architectural work necessarily influenced the decision. Indeed, one of the surprising results was the evidence that a number of combined departments employed as many as twelve to seventeen qualified architects and a similar number of qualified engineers. Conversely, separate departments in the districts sometimes had as few as two architects, while there were four or five engineers in a separate department. Neither the size of engineering and building programmes, nor the number of architects or engineers appears to be decisive.

Responsibility for housing management can be onerous and the officer who is responsible to the Housing committee must devote much time and attention to this service. It might have been expected that responsibility for housing management would affect the allocation of other responsibilities. As far as relieving the Engineer, the replies proved nothing. It is known that some Engineers have the housing management sections within their departments, but only three did so in this survey and each was also running the architectural services within the combined department in an authority of upwards of 100,000 population. Most of the Housing Managers were chief officers or heads of departments, though a few were under the Clerk or the Treasurer.

It could not, therefore, be argued that it was the burden of housing management on the shoulders of the Engineer which made it necessary to separate the architectural services. On the other hand, there was some confirmation of the fact already evident elsewhere, and particularly in the metropolitan boroughs, that the case for a separate Architect's department can be strengthened by adding housing management to the duties of the Chief Architect. Among the six district authorities covered by the inquiry three Chief Architects were also responsible for housing management. Another method of dividing responsibility for architectural services, by appointing a Schools Architect attached to the Education department, was used by the largest of the authorities.

While the general trend of change is towards setting up more separate Architect's departments, the movement is not without its hesitations. One or two authorities which have separate departments expressed a little anxiety lest the Architect should in time have too little to do. This applies most to authorities around London who are running out of land for housing and have little slum clearance for the architects to turn to, as well as to the very smallest authorities.

Even if many of the replies gave no guidance of general application for deciding for or against a separate Architect's department, the comments of authorities on their own organization were so interesting that a number are reproduced. They give in their own words the reasons for having the one kind of organization or the other far better than any report can do.

The following extracts are from authorities with combined organizations:

Croydon. County Borough. (Pop. 249,000)

It has always been the council's policy to keep the number of separate departments to the minimum. Functions are grouped so that the departments are as large as is consistent with adequate control and the similarity of the professions involved.

The council decided some years ago not to undertake new building work by direct labour, but most building maintenance is carried out by direct labour. Consideration was given to bringing together under one department the maintenance forces employed in three departments but the idea was abandoned. The three distinct types of property to be maintained would inevitably lead to sub-division in a combined labour force and no real advantage could be seen in disturbing the present arrangements which work satisfactorily. There is co-operation in the use of specialized items of plant and equipment.

The idea was also considered a few years ago of a Borough Architect's department to take over all architectural work from other departments, but this was abandoned. A number of factors led to this. There was the cost and the difficulty of providing suitable accommodation to bring a new department together under one roof. It was felt that the status of the appointment to control the amalgamated amount of work being undertaken at that time was unlikely to be justified by what was considered would be the normal volume of work after a few years. Even a combined organization, it was thought, could not adequately deal with the really major projects—new Technical College, Public Halls—and it would continue to be necessary to put out such work. The creation of a new department did not commend itself, therefore, as likely to promise improvements on the existing arrangements which work satisfactorily. The sections are staffed to the point necessary to undertake the amount of work which can be foreseen as the normal for the years to come, any excess required being usually put out to private architects.

This authority, with an average capital building programme of £1·6 million, employs twenty-one architects. Seven of these are in a separate Schools Section under the Schools Architect who is on the staff of the Chief Education Officer, but responsible directly to the Education committee. The maintenance organization is divided into three under the departments of the Borough Engineer, Housing Manager and Chief Education Officer. The Housing Manager is a chief officer.

Brighton. County Borough. (Pop. 159,000)

Prior to the war, general architectural work was carried out in the Borough Surveyor, Engineer and Planning Officer's department. Since the war, the school architectural work, previously done privately, has been added. The present combined arrangements, which include the Town Planning Section also, permit co-ordination of all schemes from their inception and additional administrative costs incurred by two or more separate departments do not arise.

147

The Borough Surveyor is responsible for maintenance and the Housing Manager is a chief officer with a separate department. There are seventeen architects.

Blackburn. County Borough. (Pop. 106,000)

The Architectural department, Housing department and Works department have always been under the control of the Borough Engineer. In addition, the Borough Engineer is also responsible for the Engineering, Town Planning, Estates and Valuation, Building Inspection, Highways, Cleansing, Lighting, Markets, Parks, Cemeteries and Sewage departments of the Corporation.

The combined organization of all these departments under the control of the Borough Engineer leads to much closer co-operation between departments and simplifies the programming of major schemes. Administrative and clerical services are centralized and all costing and the purchasing of materials are done by the Borough Engineer's department. There is much less inter-departmental correspondence under this system and it has worked efficiently.

Establishment: fifteen qualified architects.

Tottenham. Non-County Borough. (Pop. 119,000)

The Borough Engineer is, and always has been, responsible for the work of the architectural staff. The matter has been re-examined from time to time but the Council are satisfied that this is the best arrangement for their purposes on the grounds of policy of co-ordinating the engineering, surveying, planning, architectural and building work under one chief officer.

The Borough Engineer is responsible for all maintenance and the Housing Manager is a chief officer. There are twelve architects. (See Diagram 6.)

Watford. Non-County Borough. (Pop. 73,000)

Consideration was given in the immediate post-war years to the future responsibility for architectural work, and it was decided, in view of the volume of work expected, to strengthen the architectural staff, but to keep the administration of all the technical services under one departmental head.

The office of the Borough Engineer and Surveyor is divided below the position of the deputy, and the engineering and architectural sections each have a Chief Assistant.

There is no doubt that this policy of keeping a single department has been the right one, particularly during the last few years when shortages of staff have demanded the closest co-ordination of staff to achieve the best results. It is difficult at times to draw a clear dividing line between responsibilities on schemes, such as housing and town planning, where both engineering and architecture are involved and to have one departmental head responsible for both functions enormously simplifies administration. In committee work, too, there is the advantage that members need only look to one chief officer for advice on technical matters.

The Borough Engineer is responsible for all maintenance. The Housing Manager is on the staff of the Treasurer. There are four architects.

Those authorities with separate Engineers' and Architects' departments also contributed very interesting comments on the reasons for their arrangements. The name of the authority has been excluded in one or two cases.

Gloucester. County Borough. (Pop. 68,000)

The advantages of the present separate organization of Engineers' and Architects' departments are considered to be:
1. The probability of better designed buildings due to

> the responsible Chief Officer having specialized training in architectural design;

> the recruitment of higher quality staff than would be prepared to serve under an Engineer not architecturally trained. It is the aesthetic factor which normally attracts an architect into his profession. Assistant architects prefer to look to a chief officer skilled in the same professional techniques.

2. The probability of a lowering in cost of buildings due to the services etc., available to an Architect Chief Officer through the R.I.B.A., e.g. cost control and annual conferences, and discussions with fellow Architect Chief Officers; the City and Borough Architects Society; and regular liaison between members of the R.I.B.A., R.I.C.S., and N.F.B.T.E.

149

Design and cost control have brought major economies nationally in post-war school building initiated through the Ministry of Education, architects and quantity surveyors. The exercise of such professional skills is applicable to other buildings and it is advantageous that an Architect Chief Officer has access to the development of these techniques.

The Architect has a staff of thirteen architects. He is also the Estates Manager and has the oversight of all council property except housing. He controls a direct labour force for non-housing repairs. The Housing Manager is a head of department responsible to the Housing committee.

County Borough. (Pop. about 75,000)

Architectural work was carried out in the Borough Engineer's department until 1946. This was found to have some disadvantages, principally in the creation of bottle-necks, but also in the difficulty of retaining architects of experience and ability. Since the separation of the departments, the post of Borough Architect has been regarded as attractive and has been filled by high grade men. While it is thought that architectural work has been expedited, it is probable that the combined expense of the two departments is greater than would have been the case if the work had been kept within the Borough Engineer's department.

There is a staff of five architects.

Dewsbury. County Borough. (Pop. 53,006)

The advantages of the present separate organization which was set up in 1930 are that it is possible to have specialists at the head of each department with limited responsibilities permitting of maximum efficiency.

The Housing Manager is a chief officer. The Housing Manager and the Architect are responsible for ordering repairs etc., but the direct labour organization with one hundred men is controlled by the Borough Engineer and Surveyor. There are nine architects on the Chief Architect's staff.

150

Edmonton. Non-County Borough. (Pop. 96,000)

The separation into two departments was made in 1949. The Borough Engineer is responsible for highways, bridges, sewage, street cleansing, refuse collection and disposal, direct labour depots and workshops, parks, baths, building byelaws, administration and road safety. He controls some 430 manual employees and forty professional and technical staff. The Borough Architect is responsible for the design and erection by direct labour of all buildings provided by the Council, and is also Town Planning Officer. He controls some 450 manual employees and forty professional and technical staff, including eleven architects.

The Council has retained a joint administrative and clerical section, of some 12–14 staff serving both chief officers.

The range and extent of these functions fully justify division between two chief officers, in order to secure direct and responsible control by the chief officer, particularly of the direct labour organization for capital building work. The division secures a higher degree of specialization. It allows a closer relation between the functions of building development and town planning, in which this Council has pursued an active policy since the end of the war. The direct responsibility of each chief officer to the appropriate committees facilitates committee discussions and directions.

Whilst the Council has exhausted most of the new sites for housing, it is now engaged in an extensive redevelopment programme affecting some eighteen areas in the borough. Most of these areas are, or will, be redeveloped for housing, but some for open space and one for a civic centre. The Council is seeking to buy land outside the borough to erect additional dwellings.

The Housing Manager is a chief officer.

Non-County Borough. (Pop. about 120,000)

The Architectural department became a separate entity in 1956. By that time the volume of architectural work was such that it was no longer practicable for it to be handled by the Borough Engineer's department. Many of the schemes were of considerable financial magnitude and it was considered better that the direction of the work should be under the control of a qualified architect who could give his undivided attention to the work rather than leave matters with the Borough Engineer. With a great diversity of other work including valuation and town planning the Engineer could not give

151

the personal attention to building schemes, which is so desirable if the best is to be obtained from both the aesthetic and practical points of view.

The bulk of the architectural work is not confined to housing: schools and other building account for most of the staff's time. Even if no housing at all were handled, there would be more than enough work to justify the separate department.

There are fourteen architects.

Huyton-with-Roby. Urban District Council. (Pop. 61,000)

In 1945 it was felt to be desirable that an Architect, a man qualified to design and control the construction of buildings, should be in absolute control of architectural and building work. The Architect is also Director of Housing and has three architects and two quantity surveyors on his staff. He is responsible for the maintenance of all building and has a direct labour force of some forty for new building, and thirty for repair and maintenance.

Pontypool. Urban District Council. (Pop. 40,000)

The Architect's department was formed in 1947 to deal with the housing programme, and 2,113 houses have been built since then. The large volume of work involved in slum clearance, new house building and modernization necessitates a separate Architect's department.

There are two architects.

These comments confirm that, among authorities which lie on the borderline, the decision to maintain a single organization or to separate the architectural services and to place them under a Chief Architect depends on a council's estimates of the relative importance of three main arguments. The first concerns the advantages of co-ordination and economy under a single technical officer; the second rests on the advantages of freeing building services from engineering services, and of giving responsibility to a chief officer who can devote his attention single-mindedly to the production of housing, schools and other buildings; the third argument concerns the merits of placing the

152

architectural services under a chief officer who is a qualified architect. In this way the post itself may be a more senior one and attract more able men, thereby also making the department more attractive to junior architectural staff.

The advantages of co-ordination under a single chief depend on the scale of building and engineering programmes and the competence as an administrator of the head of the department. There are straightforward administrative advantages in having a single head, provided he is able and the department is not so large as to be unwieldy. Authorities have shown themselves to be well aware of these advantages and those with combined departments have stressed the simplifications in, for example, committee procedure, with advice from one technical officer instead of two, in the preparation of minutes and agenda, and the follow up of committee decisions. There are also advantages in the co-ordination of the work of allied services of planning, layout, design and engineering services when laying out, for example, new estates. Similar advantages derive from a single control of design and maintenance, though these need not necessarily be under the Engineer, but can be combined under the Architect.

These administrative advantages are often unconnected with the technical qualifications of the Engineer. They derive mainly from administrative skills and personality. The personality of chief officers plays a vital part in the decisions of authorities. Many councils have made their choice in the light of the character of their Chief Engineer and his interest or lack of interest in architectural design. A Chief Engineer who is approaching retirement or a man interested primarily in the engineering services may prompt an authority to seek a younger man to lead a separate and expanding Architect's department. Conversely, a Chief Engineer with drive and administrative skill can persuade his council that he is able to push forward the building programme with energy, and thus to leave him as undisputed master of the technical services. Some of the Chief Engineers holding these single posts in large authorities are evidence of the highly individualistic character of these appointments. A less vigorous successor might prompt a reorganization into two departments.

It is doubtful if the claims for the economies to be derived

153

from a combined department with joint clerical services and a single chief officer's salary are more than superficially relevant to the basic issue. No doubt some clerical costs and the extra costs of another chief officer's salary are saved. But if the buildings coming out of the separate Architect's department prove to be better designed and to meet user needs more efficiently, the extra clerical work or the additional salary of the Chief Architect should be repaid ten-fold. This is not to suggest that all Chief Architects live up to their opportunities. Nor is it suggested that administrative costs, including clerical services, are to be disregarded. A strict watch must be kept on these, many of which are equivalent to the fees charged by a private architect. But their importance must be kept in proportion and be compared with the benefits which may be derived from attracting more able architects.

Authorities have really to face two main issues: first, whether the volume of architectural work is sufficient to justify two chief officers and two departments and the greater administrative complications this must involve. Secondly, and closely associated with the first, whether they consider that such a department will result in better and more expeditious building. Some councils are not primarily interested in architectural quality; some consider that their Engineer is doing an excellent job already and see no need for change. Others see in the division of departments the opportunity to attract a more able architect and to give the architectural services an independence and *esprit de corps* which will improve the quality of their work.

Provided the volume of work justifies it, it can hardly be doubted that the quality of the architectural services will be improved if the professions of architect and engineer are kept separate at the top and that better architects will be attracted to lead and man a separate department. The more able architects will be attracted to the senior posts at the head of independent departments. Salary and prestige make this unavoidable. And it is well known that young architects aspire to work with the leaders of their profession.

Those authorities which set up the dual organization have been influenced by these advantages. The replies from authorities showed that among the medium and smaller councils, where the appointment of a Chief Architect is most controversial, it is

154

those authorities which are keenest on the architectural merits of their buildings which appoint Chief Architects. Conversely, the larger authorities frequently retain the single organization because of the personal qualities of their Chief Engineer and his skill in controlling the dual system. The personality of the individual officer is all important and influences the decision as much as other more abstract arguments.

It is sometimes argued that the difficulties which architects may meet in working under a Chief Engineer in a combined department could be overcome if the chief was an architect rather than an engineer. Why, it is asked, should the single chief officer of the combined services always be an engineer? Why not appoint an architect? If what is required is a competent administrator, would it matter whether the post was held by an architect or an engineer, or perhaps by a non-technical officer? There are indeed architects who argue in favour of appointing members of their profession as the heads of these combined departments and assume that the advantages of putting architects to work under an architect would be achieved by these means.

It is, however, doubtful if they fully appreciate the implications of this view. The benefits usually claimed from separating the Architect's section from the Engineer's department are based on a different interpretation of the architect's function. If the intention is to attract architects of ability and imagination and to give them singleness of purpose, a separate Architect's department serves this purpose much better than a combined department led by an architect. It is doubtful if architects with architectural, as opposed to administrative, ability would be anxious to run a combined department. If he was a first-rate administrator and ruled an empire which covered the maintenance of roads and buildings, engineering and building contracts and all the multifarious activities usually to be found in the Engineer's department, would he be the kind of architect authorities are asking for? This issue is, however, academic, though it may clear away a confusion of thought. Authorities show no sign of appointing Architects to oversee services which the Engineer has made his own. The live issue at the present time is whether to create a separate Architect's department and what functions, if any, to combine with those of architectural design.

155

The Housing Manager

The status of the Housing Manager and his role among the other officers has been evolving on lines rather similar to that of the Architect, although his emergence as the head of a separate department started rather earlier than that of the Architect among the medium-sized authorities. Like the Architect, the Housing Manager has no fixed station and is not a statutory officer. Like the Architect, his functions must be carved out of territory originally under the jurisdiction of other chief officers. Similarly, it is the great expansion of local authority house-building since 1945 which has forced many changes in departmental organization and made it necessary for those authorities with many council houses to regroup the responsibilities and to make more senior appointments for management.

Just as more Chief Architects are being appointed to enable building to be pursued with greater singleness of purpose, so Housing Managers are being appointed to strengthen and improve the contact between landlord and tenant. Authorities who own large numbers of houses can no longer expect chief officers loaded with other responsibilities to devote sufficient attention to management of this property or the needs of so large a number of tenants. Already local authorities in England and Wales own over 3·0 million dwellings and some 25 per cent of the population are local authority tenants. In these circumstances the growth in importance of the Housing Manager as a senior officer is inevitable.

Management is an elastic term, and many of the functions of the Housing Manager lie outside the scope of this book. The recent report *Councils and their Houses*[1] lists eight basic functions of housing management. These are:

advice at the planning stage on estate layout and house design;

administration of the waiting list;

letting the houses;

[1] *Eighth Report* of the Housing Management Sub-Committee of the Central Housing Advisory Committee, published by the Ministry of Housing and Local Government.

156

transfers and exchanges;

rent collection and advice on rent schemes;

maintenance and repairs, including responsibility for the operation of special services, e.g. central heating, lifts;

general care of estates and their amenities;

housing welfare, and liaison with the statutory and voluntary social services.

Of these, only advice at the planning stage and maintenance and repair relate strictly to building organization. In considering the role of the Housing Manager, this study is concerned with the contribution he can make to the planning of estates, the design of houses and their maintenance and repair. This contribution involves close collaboration with other officers and departments.

While it would generally be true to say that more Housing Managers are chief officers or heads of independent departments in large authorities than in small owing to the scale of management responsibilities and the need to relieve the Engineer, Treasurer or Clerk of these duties, the division of responsibilities does not at all accurately reflect size or the number of council houses. It reflects just as much the weight given by particular authorities to a variety of considerations, some of which have already been mentioned. Their individual solutions reflect their varying estimates of the value of combining design with management, design with maintenance, management with maintenance, or of giving different senior officers independent responsibility for each of the aspects of housing-design, construction, management and maintenance, in separate departments.

The following are the main variations in the pattern of responsibility to be found among housing authorities:

no Housing Manager or department. Responsibilities for design, maintenance, lettings and rent collection divided between the Engineer, Clerk and Treasurer;

157

a Housing Manager in a subordinate capacity in a department in which the chief officer assumes all responsibility to the Housing committee;

a Housing Manager with a housing section with direct responsibility to the Housing committee, but administratively under the control of the Engineer, Architect, Treasurer or Clerk;

a Housing Manager at the head of an independent department, but not a chief officer;

a Housing Manager as a chief officer at the head of a department;

a Director of Housing, who is an architect and responsible for architectural services as well as housing management.

The case for or against a separate Housing department with a Housing Manager at its head rests on arguments similar in many ways to those concerning a separate Architect's department. Housing management on any large scale is a recent development in local government compared with the older professions of architecture and engineering, but it is a separate function and disadvantages can arise from combining it with those of the Architect and the Engineer. Generally speaking, neither the Engineer nor the Architect is professionally adapted to oversee the more human problems of housing management. The Engineer has, in addition, too many other departmental preoccupations, while the good Architect, if he is an able man in his own profession and interested in creative design, may regard housing management as of secondary importance. If he is not an able architect, the extra functions of management can be useful in consolidating his position, but may not produce either good management or good architecture.

It is to avoid such situations that a growing number of authorities have either set up separate Housing departments, or where the number of council houses does not justify this, they have made the Housing Manager directly responsible to the Housing committee for matters connected with lettings, tenancies and programmes of repairs, while he remains administratively responsible to the head of the department, who may be the Clerk, Treasurer, Engineer or Architect. Clearly, the better managers will be attracted to the better paid and more independent positions. As with architects, only third and fourth rank officers are likely to stay in positions with third and fourth rank salaries.

While the Housing Manager is gradually gaining greater recognition among local authority officers, his professional status is not yet fully established. The various degrees and professional qualifications available for aspirants to the higher positions in housing management are of comparatively recent origin compared with those for solicitors, doctors, engineers, surveyors and architects. Many of the older Housing Managers date from a period when such professional qualifications were not required and when councils did not regard housing management as much more than the collection of rents by the Treasurer's department and the execution of the repairs by the Engineer's department. Against this background, the emergence of the Housing Manager as the head of an independent department with accepted professional status has been gradual. In these circumstances it is hardly surprising that the views of the Housing Manager on design and maintenance may not carry the weight they should.

It may be asked what formal qualifications the Housing Manager may have for giving advice on design or for controlling repairs, apart from the valuable qualifications of experience? For senior appointments most authorities now expect candidates to possess one of a variety of qualifications which range from a university degree in estate management to a Housing Manager's certificate awarded for an examination run on behalf of the Society of Housing Managers by the Royal Institution of Chartered Surveyors. The two qualifications most often held by Housing Managers, which give full professional status, are the final examinations of the Institute of Housing and of the Royal Institution of Chartered Surveyors. For the latter there is a special housing management division, though many candidates prefer to qualify in a division which offers wider prospects of employment, for example, the valuation section which covers similar ground.

159

A rough and ready measure of the Housing Manager's technical qualifications for collaborating with the architects on design or for controlling maintenance and repairs may be obtained from the examination syllabuses of the two main professional bodies in this field:

for the Institute of Housing's certificate the intermediate examination has six papers, one of which is on building construction; for the final examination there are seven papers, of which one is on the maintenance and repair of buildings and one on housing and planning law and procedure;

the syllabus for the housing management section of the Royal Institution of Chartered Surveyors' examination is similar. For the intermediate examination two out of eleven papers are on building construction and one on town and country planning law and procedure; for the final examination four out of eleven papers cover maintenance and repair, measurement of builders' work and estate development and site planning.

Such ground work coupled with practical experience should give Housing Managers who have passed these examinations a good knowledge of building construction. It is to be expected that an increasing number of young officers will take these examinations, since they are the gateway to many of the higher appointments.

Reference was made earlier to the authorities which had been the subject of a detailed investigation on the division of functions between Architect and Engineer. Information was also sought on the status of the Housing Manager and the officer to whom he was responsible when not the head of a department. As all the authorities were of medium size, with populations ranging mostly from 160,000 to 60,000 and including only four district councils, the responsibilities of the Housing Manager were on that frontier territory where authorities can argue in favour of specialization of functions with a separate Housing department, or of the economies of combined departments. Most of the authorities were neither so big nor so small as to make the case for a separate Housing department irrefutably strong or impossibly weak. The practice of these authorities is summarized below:

Housing Manager as chief officer	12
Housing Manager as head of department	6
Housing Manager responsible to Architect	3
Housing Manager responsible to Treasurer	7
Housing Manager responsible to Clerk	2
Housing Manager responsible to Engineer	3
Housing Manager responsible to Clerk and Treasurer	1
	—
	34
	—

This pattern does not of itself indicate what degree of responsibility the Housing Manager has for maintenance. It is possible on the one hand to place all maintenance operations for housing under an independent Housing Manager, to give the Housing Manager no responsibilities for maintenance, or to have some half-way house by which the Housing Manager orders but does not execute repairs. In the Ministry's inquiry, covered by *Councils and their Houses*, it was found that out of a sample of fifty-four authorities, forty-six had officers called a Housing Manager, though only twenty-seven of these were in charge of a separate department. In the forty-six authorities with Housing Managers, thirty-six were responsible for ordering repairs, but of these only eighteen were responsible for executing repairs. The details are set out in the Table below.

Applica-tions	Alloca-tions	Rent collection	Ordering repairs	Executing repairs	Super-vision of estates	Housing welfare
45	43	30	36	18[1]	45	42

[1] included in the 36 ordering repairs.

The Ministry's inquiry did not go into the ways in which responsibility for maintenance is allocated when this does not fall to the Housing Manager. The Royal Institute of Public Administration's inquiry showed that in terms of numbers of authorities, irrespective of size, the Engineer is most commonly in charge of the execution of housing maintenance, followed by the Housing Manager, the Architect and the Building Manager in descending order of frequency. Since Chief Architects and Building Managers in charge of separate departments are rare among the district authorities and the smaller non-county boroughs the Engineer, generally, and the Housing Manager, less frequently, has charge of maintenance. Among the larger authorities maintenance may be divided between departments. Or it may be given to the Architect and the Works Manager. These arrangements are discussed in greater detail in the chapters on Maintenance and Direct Labour. In those chapters the advantages and disadvantages of control of maintenance by the different chief officers are discussed fully.

While the report on *Councils and their Houses* did not recommend any particular system for general adoption, since circumstances and practice differ so much, it stressed two specially important points where responsibilities were divided. The first was the need for co-operation between the Housing Manager and the Surveyor or other technical officer. Secondly it recommended that:

the housing manager should be responsible for the co-ordination of requests for day-to-day repairs, for recommending their priority, for indenting on the surveyor for the work to be done, and for following up to see that it is properly done in reasonable time. Long-term maintenance work, its planning and co-ordination within the financial limits laid down by the council, is a large scale operation in which the human factor is less important, and here it is felt that the responsibility would rest more naturally with the surveyor. We would, however, expect that the housing manager's views as to the order in which the work should be carried out would be given due weight.[1]

The Housing Manager will only carry this weight if he is of the right calibre and has the right technical qualifications.

House building and housing maintenance are so prominent a part of most authorities' building responsibilities that the Housing Manager's functions in these two fields, either as client at the design stage or as ordering or executing repairs, deserve to be more highly regarded than they sometimes are. Change can only come slowly. If authorities do not expect men and women

[1] Page 21.

162

of the requisite ability and qualifications, entrants to the professions will not be of sufficiently high quality nor will enough struggle to acquire the more exacting qualifications. Conversely, if the candidates presenting themselves for the senior posts have insufficient weight and technical knowledge they cannot hope to establish for themselves the status and influence which the importance of their work demands. Supply and demand need to intersect well above their present level.

Whatever particular pattern of responsibility each authority adopts, there is no doubt that the sphere of influence of the Housing Manager is increasing fairly rapidly and will continue to do so. So long as local authorities continue to build over 100,000 new dwellings a year and to take over older houses for reconditioning, an increasing number of authorities will be obliged to revise their departmental organization and redistribute the responsibilities for housing management. In this process there are bound to be more Housing Managers in charge of separate departments. More senior appointments will lead to a greater participation in the preliminaries of design. Whether it will also lead to a more active responsibility for the execution of repairs is less easy to foresee.

The decision to have a separate Housing department depends mainly on the number of houses an authority owns, and this is a matter of fact. As will be seen later, there are a number of conflicting arguments in favour of placing responsibility for maintenance in the hands of the Engineer, the Architect, the Housing Manager and the Building Manager, and the basis for these are not factual but matters of opinion. The pattern of evolution for maintenance is thus far less clear.

Building Manager

The Building or Works Manager is in charge of a direct labour organization either in a separate department or under another chief officer. Direct labour is widely used for maintenance, and less widely for new building. The functions and status of the Works Manager and the organization of direct labour are discussed fully in Chapter 7.

The Clerk

The variety of services, committees and departments calls for

163

much co-ordination. In most authorities this is recognized to be the responsibility of the Clerk, but his role and powers are largely undefined. This whole question is of great importance and one on which widely differing views are held. The role of the Clerk and his powers and duties extend over the whole range of the work of the local authority and consideration of them cannot be limited to the smaller field of the organization of building construction and maintenance. In this book it is not appropriate to do more than call attention to the importance of the Clerk's functions. They may well be thought to merit a special study.

SUMMARY AND RECOMMENDATIONS

1. The county councils show the most clear-cut division of responsibilities. The County Architect now has an established position, and provides architectural services for all client departments. The Education department is much the most important client. The County Architect is also usually responsible for maintenance. The use of direct labour is exceptional, and the existence of a separate Works department rarer still.

2. The organization of the London County Council is allied more closely to the county boroughs than the county councils because of its responsibilities for housing. Apart from the oversight of private architects, the Architect is responsible for almost all architectural services, and all maintenance except for housing. A direct labour organization for new housing is being built up gradually.

3. The county boroughs defy generalization but the most interesting aspects of their building organization revolve around the division of functions between Engineer and Architect and the role of the Housing Manager. These are referred to below. The discussion of the place of the Works Manager or Building Manager is reserved until the chapter on Direct Labour.

4. Among non-county boroughs and districts the number of Chief Architects is small—not more than about twenty-five in all—and it is much more usual for the architectural services to be under the Engineer. A number of authorities have been impressed by the advantage of setting up a separate Architect's department in order to achieve greater singleness of purpose and

164

better design. It must not, however, be forgotten that in the majority of these authorities, who have built a large proportion of local authority housing, the Engineer has been the responsible officer.

5.   The division of functions between the Engineer and the Architect is a growing point in local authority organization. The number of Chief Architects is increasing, but not rapidly. The end of the war saw a considerable increase in such appointments, but a number of large authorities still have the engineering and architectural services combined in one department.

6.   A combined department simplifies co-ordination, but may adversely affect architectural quality. If the size of the authority and its building programmes justify it, there are advantages in separating the architectural from the engineering services and in appointing a Chief Architect. By this means more able architects and better junior staff are likely to be recruited. Such a team may be able to bring about improvements in the quality of the architectural work and in cost planning and research which could far outweigh the dis-economies due to having two departments. Authorities are urged to consider the setting up of separate Architect's departments under a Chief Architect if the volume of the architectural work would justify such an arrangement.

7.   The importance of the Housing Manager is increasing with the expansion of local authority house ownership and the growing recognition of the importance of management. In the context of this inquiry it is the contribution of the Housing Manager to housing layout, design and maintenance which is most significant.

8.   Authorities have evolved different solutions to the conflicting objectives of combining management with maintenance under a senior Housing Manager; of uniting maintenance with architectural services under the Engineer or Architect so as to bring home the effects of design on maintenance; or of providing a unified repair and maintenance service under a single departmental head.

9.   There are certainly some advantages in combining responsibility for design with responsibility for maintenance. But there are also differences of approach to the technical problems of maintenance and the human problems of tenants. It is not

necessarily in the best interests of the tenants to merge the functions of housing management with architectural design under a Director of Housing, who is an architect. Housing management and architectural design are different functions and there are merits in keeping them separate.

10.   It is important that the status of the Housing Manager should be such that he or she can contribute effectively to discussions on design and protect the tenants' interests on maintenance. Where the scale of council housing permits it there are great merits in making the Housing Manager directly answerable to a committee, so that the tenants' needs can have an effective spokesman. Whether or not the Housing Manager should be responsible for the execution of maintenance and repairs is discussed in the chapter on Maintenance.

CHAPTER 5

THE USE OF PRIVATE ARCHITECTS AND QUANTITY SURVEYORS

Reasons for using outside consultants—local authority use of private architects—advantages and disadvantages— briefing of private architect—contact with committees— quantity surveyors' functions, traditional and new—cost planning and control—use of salaried staff and private firms—stage when quantity surveyor brought in—teamwork with architects.

THIS book has so far dealt almost entirely with chief officers and their staffs who are on the regular pay-roll of local authorities. Councils do not, however, only employ full-time staff of their own. They also make use of the services of professional men and women in private practice to supplement and strengthen their permanent staff. The Health department may use private doctors and dentists on a sessional basis. Consultants may be brought in to advise on engineering projects. Expert legal advice may be sought by the Clerk. The use of professional people outside the local government service for councils' building programmes is widespread and varied. It includes the use of outstanding town planners or architects for major schemes and prestige buildings, the highly specialist advice of different kinds of engineers for structural work, acoustics or ventilation, and the widespread use of private architects and quantity surveyors to share in the regular building programme.

The inquiry sought to find out how much these consultants and private practitioners were used for building work, the various reasons for employing them and the advantages and disadvantages of so doing. Authorities were asked what was their policy about using private architects, what other outside consultants were employed and what use the councils made of private firms of quantity surveyors.

The replies from authorities and the supplementary information obtained from discussions with them provided much that was of interest about the use of private architects and quantity surveyors. The other professions were only briefly referred to by authorities and there was not time to pursue their use in any depth. This chapter deals, therefore, almost entirely with architects and quantity surveyors. The omission of the rest is no reflection on their importance.

Local authorities are responsible for so large a part of the building effort of the nation that their policies in employing or not employing firms in private practice can make a great difference to the volume of work available to these firms. Many firms of private architects or quantity surveyors would be hard put to it if they did not have local authorities as clients. Any strong trend away from the use of private practitioners would draw into official posts many of those now employed by private firms. The policy of local authorities has, therefore, widespread repercussions and more so in the professions related to building than in many others. The salaried doctor or dentist is in a minority: the bulk of these professions are employed outside local authorities. Similarly, a very high proportion of solicitors are in private practice unconnected with local authorities. But salaried architects employed by public authorities now outnumber private architects while a high proportion of private quantity surveyors are employed by local authorities. The future of the private sector of these two professions is, therefore, intimately bound up both with the size of the local authority building programmes and with the proportion of this work which is carried out by salaried staff or by private firms.

Broadly speaking, local authorities employ private firms of consultants and private practitioners for one or more of the following reasons:

because the volume of work is insufficient to warrant a full-time appointment on the staff;

because a scheme of outstanding importance needs a man of acknowledged standing or with special experience to design it;

to avoid building up a staff larger than the long-term requirements of the authority's building programme will justify;

to meet sudden and unexpected demands for increased work;

to introduce new ideas and to be a stimulus to the regular staff.

These reasons apply with different force to the different professions. No local authority could give full-time employment to a consultant in acoustics, and only the largest to ventilation or heating engineers. Eminent private architects are in demand for prestige buildings. Certain firms of architects have built up experience for special types of buildings such as swimming baths or public halls, and are called in for these. Many private architects are accustomed to come to the rescue of hard pressed local authority offices and to take some of the load. Their use generally also involves the employment of private quantity surveyors as well, but many authorities employ private quantity surveyors to help out their own architectural staff, whether they use private architects or not.

THE ROLE OF PRIVATE ARCHITECTS

Stress is laid in this chapter on the contribution which the private architect can make to the work of local authorities. It will be evident from the next few pages that most authorities are reluctant to use private architects except under the pressure of shortages of staff, and that this gives rise to difficulties on both sides. It is because authorities fail to take the best advantage of the services of the private architect that so much emphasis is laid on this problem here. Local authorities will continue to do the majority of their architectural work themselves, and the best of it will continue to be in the front rank of architectural work in this country. The discussion which follows applies a magnifying glass to matters which local authorities most easily overlook. Of these the contribution of the private architect to better design is one of the most important.

The dividing line between the two big groups in the architectural profession, those in salaried jobs and those in private practice as principals or assistants, has moved noticeably in the last quarter of a century. Salaried architects, once in danger of being treated as less important members of the profession, and needing a Salaried and Official Architect's committee at the Royal Institute of British Architects to protect their interests, now outnumber their colleagues in private offices. So great has been the change that attempts have been made to form a separate organization, as well as a new committee of the Royal Institute of British Architects, to speak for the new minority, the private architect.

The increase in the number of official architects is not confined to local authorities. Government departments, public boards and large private undertakings have increased the number of salaried architects on their staffs. With the change from the wealthy private client to public bodies and industrial and commercial concerns, many private architects look to local authorities for at least some part of their work and some firms have specialized in local authority work to the exclusion of other commissions. On the whole, however, private architects are not called in for local authority work as much as might have been expected. Nor indeed is two-storey housing, which constitutes the bulk of local authority building, financially or architecturally attractive enough to entice the leading architects, and the number of prestige buildings is very limited. While local authority housing forms an essential bread-and-butter line for private architects, and schools an interesting but rather specialized opening, the soufflés and plum puddings are sought elsewhere, on the South Bank, in the City, and in major redevelopment schemes in town centres.

The inquiry revealed an unexpectedly strong body of opinion against the use of private architects, and if anything this opinion grew stronger as the authorities diminished in size. Most authorities seem to use private architects from necessity rather than from choice, because the volume of work is too great for their own established staff. Very few, and those mainly the largest, were prepared to admit that the private architect might have something to offer which would add to the experience of the salaried architect or benefit the quality of local architecture. Between the one and quite common extreme of not employing private architects at all, and the other and very rare extreme of employing a regular pro-portion as a deliberate attempt to stimulate an interchange of new ideas, there are various intermediate points of view.

Some authorities aim deliberately to staff their Architect's or Engineer's department on the basis of long-term demand, or the numbers they think they can permanently employ, and use private architects for any work above this norm. This may mean that a third, a quarter or a tenth of the current programme is being designed by private architects according to the size of the bulge in the programme at any particular moment. Other authorities are less deliberate, and employ private architects as and when they cannot fill their permanent establishment or find the pressure of work beyond the capacity of their own staff. The first is a conscious policy to avoid redundancy in the future. The second is usually a question of expediency only, and very often a source of regret. The following quotations from four county councils reflect this more opportunist attitude:

The general policy of the county council is that if the County Architect's department is unable at any time to carry out the volume of work required by the council, private architects are employed.

The policy is to avoid the use of private architects, but the council has been compelled to employ them during the period of post-war development, and particularly because it has not been possible to recruit up to the authorized establishment.

Private architects are employed when it is considered that the County Architect's department cannot cope with any additional work.

Employed when there is a shortage of staff in the County Archi-tect's department.

These answers are characteristic of the policy of councils about the employment of private architects.

Because of the rather unusual features of school programmes, the specialist experience required and the size of County Archi-tect's departments, it is not altogether surprising that many county authorities should expect to carry out most of these pro-grammes themselves. It is much more surprising to find this attitude reflected in quite small authorities who build mainly houses. The majority of the non-county boroughs and district councils covered by this part of the inquiry stated that they did

171

not use private architects or had decided not to use them again. The following comments were typical:

The council have employed private architects, but now prefer to use their own staff. (Rural District)

At one time the council did employ private architects since they were unable to recruit sufficient staff of their own. They did not find that the employment of private architects increased the output in any way and are convinced that the employment of an adequate number of qualified architects on their own staff is the best method of making progress in housing development work. (Urban District)

Even in a rural district with a population of less than 20,000, which has completed about 500 houses since 1945, the same attitude prevails:

Private architects are not employed. The council consider that all work should be done within the department.

The preference for using only architects on the staff rather than private architects could not be stated more clearly.

Between the counties on the one hand with their dominant school programmes and the non-county and district authorities which build almost nothing but houses there is the variegated pattern of the county boroughs. Many of these have large architectural departments and ambitious programmes. All of them have been under severe pressure to produce houses and schools since the war, and some have been able to build a few important civic buildings. The following quotations give a cross section of the policies among the medium-sized authorities. They exclude the largest cities in which different attitudes are found.

It is fair to say that the council prefer all work to be done within the department, but if a sudden peak of activity occurs which cannot be in any way postponed, then private architects are employed.

Council prefer to use their own architectural staff. Work only placed outside when council's own staff have not been able to deal with a particular scheme which must be commenced by a stipulated starting date. In practice the council has commissioned private architects for schemes of substance—conference hall, school, training college—not just routine work.

172

Since end of last war council has engaged private architects for new schools and other educational projects because of shortage of staff. Policy is to have all architectural work done, if possible, by the Borough Architect (except such as might be the subject of an architectural competition).

Only employed in periods of excessive building activity when own technical staff is inadequate.

Only used when shortage of technical staff prevents the Architect's department from carrying out work. Very rarely required.

Employed where necessary to supplement insufficient internal staff and for very exceptional work.

It is natural and proper that authorities, having set up a large architectural section under the Chief Engineer or a department under a Chief Architect, should wish to carry out the greater part of their design work by their own staff. This is the object of the arrangement. But the fact that they prefer to use their own architects most of the time does not mean that the use of official architects is right for all schemes all of the time, even if the volume of work and the recruitment of staff could be kept level enough to make this possible.

The reasons for supplementing the work of the Architect's or Engineer's department by commissioning private architects were summarized at the beginning of the chapter. It is clear from the reasons given by authorities themselves that much the most important is the need to help out the Architect's department when the demands upon it are more than it can meet. No doubt it is implicit that they do not staff their departments to take the peak loads of work and a few authorities, when cross-examined, agreed that the limits on the number of established architects took long-term needs into account. It would, however, be more reassuring if the balance between long-term staff requirements and the use of private architects was a matter of explicit policy to even out the work rather than of an expediency of the moment. Too many authorities appear to be hoping for a utopian state where programmes and the numbers of architectural staff neatly fit. This can never really be so if the building programme is to fit local needs or the fluctuations of government policy rather than the availability of architectural staff.

It would be far more satisfactory if local authorities would

173

face up to the inevitable fluctuations in capital programmes and make use of the services of private architects on a long-term and considered basis, instead of in the hand to mouth way they are often used now. Private architects complain that too often they are called in at the last moment when an Architect's department has found itself in difficulties. They are then offered a commission on a time schedule which is unreasonably short with no option but to accept or reject it. Few private architects are in a position to turn down a commission, even if the time allowed for it is insufficient. Such a method of employing private architects can lead only to mistakes and mutual criticism, when in fact the two sides can be a valuable complement one to the other.

Emergencies there will always be, and there are occasions when both the official and the private architect will have to meet an unexpected dead-line. But if, as seems to be the case, private architects are used mainly for rush work and for schemes which have been delayed in the earlier stages, this is bound to place the private architect in a difficult position. When each side can be so valuable a complement to the other, it is a pity if authorities make it difficult for the private architect to make his best contribution. If a greater proportion of the work done by private architects was programmed in advance and commissioned at the proper time, many of these problems would be avoided. It is of some significance that those authorities who speak most highly of the use of private architects are those who commission them as a matter of long-term policy.

Authorities of small or medium size usually recognize the limitations of their own staff when it comes to prestige and specialist buildings such as municipal offices, public assembly halls, and technical colleges. Most authorities, who have not a big enough architectural department of their own, appoint an experienced private architect or use the device of an architectural competition. Among these authorities it is the method of employing private architects for housing schemes or new schools which is most open to criticism, and which in turn leads to the most criticism of private architects.

The Stimulus of the Private Architect

Quite apart from the practical value of the private architect

174

in helping to relieve the pressure on the staff and in undertaking special work on prestige buildings, the private architect has another function in a wider context. His greatest single contribution when serving local authorities is to help the official architect to break new ground. By the cross-fertilization of ideas between the official and the private architect better solutions may be found, which might have remained unexplored by either side working alone. This has been clearly expressed by a private architect:

The private practitioner is by the nature of his position as a free agent less fettered than the salaried man. He has not to live constantly in contact with committee chairmen and officials of other departments but goes away to his own office to evolve his schemes.

He lives, and expands his practice as his reputation for this class of work grows, by attempting to lift his work out of the common rut. He stamps it with the freshness arising from some ingenious new approach to the planning problem, some bold elevational treatment or the use of new materials. The healthy rivalry which exists between private architects serving the same authority stimulates them to great efforts to produce the best job and so secure the best of the new commissions handed out by the employing authority.

He goes on to say:

The raising of the private architects' standard of work inevitably has an effect upon that being produced by the official architects employed by the authority. Comparison by elected councillors of the finished product, where imagination has been exercised, with the more conventional work done departmentally, may create a demand for better work from the department and remove the restricting committee hand which has been holding back the Chief Architect when he has wanted, architecturally speaking, to forge ahead.

With the larger authority, particularly one with an outstanding Chief Architect who has gathered around him an adventurous staff, the flow of ideas is no longer in one direction, from the private architect to the salaried staff. In these cases a mutual gain is achieved from the exchange of ideas between the two offices. Where the highest standard has been set in the public office, particularly where, as in the London County Council, a team carries out research into new forms of constructional design and money is available not only to try experiments but to put right experimental work that fails, the private architect is more likely to be at the receiving end of new ideas.

Unfortunately, it is unusual for local authorities to realize that outside architects have a contribution of this kind to offer or if they do to commission them in such a way that this contribution can be forthcoming. Sometimes Chief Architects are not willing to apportion a share of the more interesting schemes to private architects. Often the conditions of the appointment, either in time or in the contact permitted between the private architect and the client committee, do not allow him the scope necessary for working out new ideas or the opportunity to explain them.

Fortunately, there are some authorities which take full advantage of the contribution the private architect has to offer, to the benefit of both the authority and the architectural profession. The London County Council is notable in this respect. Not only are private architects employed in the usual way to supplement the work of the staff directly employed by the Council, and to avoid redundancy if the volume of work is reduced, but it is the declared policy of the Council, irrespective of staff shortages, to entrust a part of its building programme to private architects. This is done deliberately to secure variety and new lines of approach, and the private architect's contacts are mainly with the client department and committee. There is no doubt that the London County Council's buildings have benefited from the cross-fertilization of ideas which this collaboration has produced, and that their architects have educated and been educated by private architects.

Birmingham is another authority which uses private architects as a matter of long-term policy, and gives them a share of the larger and more interesting schemes, as well as the routine work. It is the policy of the Council to maintain an Architect's department of moderate size in order to ensure continuity of work for established staff, and to keep the number of architects down to a level where more intimate personal relations can still be maintained. To secure both these objectives about 40 per cent of the work is carried out by private architects who practise locally. These architects have been responsible for about half of the new shopping centres and schools and have more recently been commissioned for housing schemes.

The benefits of the policy of using private architects are not only visible in local authority building. Some of the most outstanding examples of this stimulus and the cross-fertilization of ideas between private and official architects are to be found in some of the new towns, such as Basildon, Harlow and Stevenage, where 30 per cent or 40 per cent of the housing is designed by private architects. Most of the corporations have large architectural staffs of their own, and no doubt the peculiar circumstances of the new towns provided a special stimulus. But it is interesting that it is the new town corporations who have used private architects most persistently, who have given their own architects the greatest challenge and produced the most lively results. Local authorities could take a leaf from the new towns' book.

Reasons for Reluctance to use Private Architects

It may be asked why it is so rare for local authorities to employ private architects as a matter of deliberate policy instead of only to help out the Architect's department in an emergency or to do some of the hack work? The answers may be found in a complex mixture of motives, some of them based on a natural pride in the work of an authority's own staff, some on prejudice and others on the cost of fees or unfortunate experiences of the use of private architects. Most often the reason is a lack of appreciation of the benefits which may be derived from using private and official architects in collaboration to improve the quality of architecture.

With the tight limits of cost and the pressure for rapid output, it is easy for both selected representatives and officers to become so accustomed to the standard designs, particularly of housing, that they cease to realize how monotonous they have become. Having trained the architectural staff to meet the council's requirements, it is simpler to repeat the pattern quickly, efficiently, and economically. In such circumstances it is also natural to resent the intervention of a private architect, who is necessarily less expert than the official architects in carrying out the standard designs and routine procedures, and who may reopen questions which had seemed securely closed.

Yet it is here that the use of private architects can be most valuable, provided the local authority can call on men of the right kind. A national reputation is not necessary, only an ability on the part of the private architect to turn his particular circumstances to good account and present the authority and

177

the official architect with a fresh opportunity. It would be misleading to suggest that official architects can never do this themselves without prompting from outside. They can and do. It would be equally wrong to imply that private architects are all endowed with originality and capable of finding new solutions to old problems. There are good and indifferent on both sides, and no natural superiority on either. The advantage that the private architect enjoys is freedom. It is this freedom which can be the source of his special contribution to local authority work.

The value of this contribution would be more easily accepted if there was more understanding of the practical problems of using private architects and of the ways to overcome these. There are faults on both sides which need to be squarely faced.

Too many private architects do not try hard enough to meet authorities' cost and time limits, and are not business-like enough in preparing plans for committees. Councils constantly complain of delays, and say that their requirements have not been met. Committee procedure and the detailed arrangements for obtaining government sanctions can be very complicated to the architect new to this field. It is, indeed, so complicated and the number of people to consult and please so many that there are many private architects who refuse such commissions once their practices have become established. The effort to meet these procedures and to get plans approved by committees and officers is not considered financially worthwhile. This is particularly true of housing schemes.

On the other hand, many of the private architects' failures are the authorities' fault. All too often the brief is inadequate, there is insufficient guidance on costs, the time allowed as a condition of the commission is too short or the architect is not given enough information about procedures. Officers who have had decades of experience of the highly complex time-tables of committees and know to the last semi-colon how to approach a government department, are impatient with the private architect for making mistakes. They cannot expect the private architect to have the same administrative experience, and they cannot blame him for producing a more expensive scheme or for having put in the wrong details of design unless their own brief expressly explained the cost limits and the design requirements.

178

These objections to the use of private architects crystallize on two points. First, it is claimed that the extra time and effort needed to brief and steer private architects means that they are more trouble than they are worth. Secondly, it is argued that the level of fees payable to them makes their use more costly than the use of salaried staff. It is felt that this extra cost is particularly difficult to justify if there is any risk that the scheme may not be realized, so that the architect may have to be paid for abortive work.

Whether it is worth using a private architect depends on the reasons for employing him. If the aim is limited to the production of another scheme of more or less standardized design, it is only worth using a private architect if the salaried architects are too busy or there is a risk of future redundancy if more permanent staff are recruited. In terms of standardized designs, the private architect who is new to the authority's requirements cannot hope to produce plans as quickly or easily as the salaried architects who are preparing them regularly. On the analogy of the conveyor belt the private architect cannot achieve the same dexterity on one scheme as the official architects achieve on annual programmes. If, however, the aim is to introduce new ideas or stimulate a fresh approach, then the extra time spent talking over the scheme with the private architect and rethinking the standard requirements becomes worthwhile. The return is not necessarily immediately apparent. The fruits of the cross-fertilization of ideas may take some time to ripen.

On the question of fees it is difficult to say whether the private architect's fees work out more expensively than the comparable costs of schemes carried out by an authority's own staff. Authorities vary widely in efficiency and many private architects consider that the comparisons between the scale fees and the authority's own overheads are not fairly calculated, and that schemes done by the official architects do not bear the full costs of administrative overheads. They also argue that abortive work has to be paid for whoever does it, and that it is unrealistic to count only the fees payable to the private architect and to discount the work wasted in the authority's own office.

On the other hand, a firm of organization and management consultants who gave advice during the course of the inquiry held a contrary view. This firm has had a great deal of ex-

179

perience of local authorities and considered that an efficient local authority office ought to run at about two-thirds of the cost of the fees chargeable by private architects, mainly because it had a more even flow of work and fewer gaps between one commission and another.

Such a cost advantage, if it could really be secured, would be a powerful argument in favour of an authority doing the major part of its architectural work in its own office. It does not, however, invalidate the other arguments in favour of using private architects for a proportion of the schemes in large authorities and for the more important projects in the smaller authorities. Nor must it be assumed that all local authority offices achieve the higher levels of efficiency.

Method of Briefing the Private Architect

The methods used to brief private architects depend partly on the division of functions within an authority and partly on the nature of the building. Those authorities where the Education department or the Housing department has its own architectural staff will naturally arrange for the private architect to be briefed by that department.

Where, however, all the architectural services are centralized under the Chief Engineer or Chief Architect, it is a matter of some argument whether the private architect should be briefed by the client department or by the officer responsible for the main architectural services. The head of a client department may well prefer to have the private architect directly under his wing, so as to explain his ideas at first hand and to escape some of the restrictive effects of the more standardized methods. This arrangement gives the architect more freedom and if the object is to relieve the burden of work on official architects, the less they are asked to supervise the private architect the greater the measure of that relief. These arguments have served to keep some of the private architects outside the control of the Chief Architect and attached solely to the client department.

Where the authority is of small or medium size the private architect may well be a man of greater experience in his particular field of building than the authority. In that case, collaboration between the client department and the private architect is probably sufficient, without the intervention of the official

180

architects as a third party. In larger authorities where the Architect's or Engineer's department has a great deal of experience, the advantages of briefing by the client department are more doubtful. If little reference is made to the council's own architects, the private architect may find that he is not being well briefed and that much of the experience gathered over the years by the official architects is not available to him. Many of the failures of private architects are due to inadequate briefing and this risk is increased if he is cut off from the main centre of experience within the authority. In addition, the Chief Architect may be put in an awkward situation if he is responsible for the main building programme and yet is unaware about what is going on in that part of it which has been 'put out'.

It is necessary to find a compromise between leaving the private architect so detached from the Architect's department that he makes unnecessary mistakes or in such tight leading reins that he can make little original contribution to design. The London County Council, who make extensive use of private architects, arrange for the main contact between them and the Council to be through the client department. This is done partly to relieve the Architect's department of administrative work, and partly to foster direct contact between the private architect and the client department. The size of London County Council departments, and the ability of the large client departments to have large technical staffs of their own, cannot be repeated in small authorities. Nevertheless, the methods used by the London County Council may suggest adaptations of these methods elsewhere. They are as follows:

The Council maintains panels of private architects approved for use on Council schemes. The Council invites applications for inclusion on these panels by public advertisement from time to time.

For educational building the procedure is as follows:

First the Architect decides, in consultation with the Education Officer, which assignments shall be offered to private architects. A joint report is then submitted to the sub-committee concerned by the Architect and the Education Officer recommending that a particular job should be so offered, and indicating the name of the architect to whom it should be offered.

The sub-committee having decided to offer the assignment to a private architect, the Education Officer gets in touch with him and invites him for a preliminary briefing, at which he is given the accommodation required and any other information about the Council's practice and desires which the Education Officer thinks would be useful. Following this administrative briefing, the architect is introduced by the Education Officer to the head of the schools division of the Council's Architect's department for a technical briefing; he gives him such information about the Council's practices, ministerial requirements in respect of ceiling price, etc. as he thinks might be useful. Finally, the client department also introduces the private architect to those parts of the Architect's department which deal with planning and building control, so that in developing his plans he may keep in touch and avoid having to make modifications when they are at an advanced stage. The private architect then goes forward to produce his scheme and all contacts after this with the Council take place through the client department.

The practice of the Housing department is similar, except that the private architect is not introduced to the Council's Architect for a technical briefing:

This difference is accounted for by the fact that in the Education department the section which deals with private architects is staffed by administrative officers; the Housing Management department contains qualified surveyors and others who are fully versed in the technical requirements of the scheme, and have a knowledge of the practices of the Council's official Architect about which they can brief the private architect to the extent necessary. In their case, too, further contacts with the private architect are with the client department, but again they will put the architect in touch with the statutory side of the Architect's department so far as might be necessary to help him to ensure that his plans were acceptable as regards planning control and building regulations.

We find in practice that these methods are acceptable to the private architects, and that the technical guidance given in the two slightly different ways described above is found helpful but not intrusive.

The foregoing relates to our long-standing practice and will continue to cover the great bulk of the work which the Council entrusts to private architects. There is, however, beginning a new development due to pressure of work in the Architect's department, which makes it necessary to offer to private architects some work for com-

182

mittees other than Housing and Education. In these instances the private architects will not be responsible to the client departments concerned, but to the Council's Architect, thus forming an extension to the general division of his department. The private architects will have complete freedom architecturally; it is hoped, however, by giving them the same administrative service as is applied to schemes designed in our own office, to secure effective financial and procedural control.

The procedure used by the London County Council underlines the importance of giving the private architect considerable independence while at the same time securing the benefits of the Council's own experience. Even if this particular procedure is not applicable to other authorities its general objectives are of wide interest and deserve to be carefully considered. Authorities need to ask themselves whether their own methods permit private architects to give and to receive the best service.

It is not easy to steer between the two extremes of giving the private architect too little guidance and of giving him too much. The smaller authorities may employ an experienced private architect for schools, housing, or some exceptional type of building because they do not feel competent to tackle the scheme themselves. In these circumstances there will be no risk of keeping the private architect in leading reins, though there may be the other problem of how to prepare an adequate brief.

It is the medium and larger authorities who will be more tempted either to leave the private architect with insufficient guidance because they are too busy, or to control him too tightly because they have so much experience. The inquiry suggested that among the larger authorities it was becoming rarer for the client department to brief the private architect independently and control was being increasingly centralized in the Chief Architect's department. Where this is so, there is a greater danger that the private architect will become merely an extension of the drawing office staff, a convenient source of help in times of difficulty, but not a contributor to improved design.

Contact between Private Architect and Committee

The best way to preserve the independence of the private architect and to ensure that he can make his contribution is to arrange for him to explain his scheme to the client committee

183

and to present his sketch plans in person. This is particularly valuable for housing schemes, for which a fresh approach is often badly needed. If the private architect never meets the members, there is the risk that the new ideas which the committee would welcome will be strangled at birth 'as not the sort of thing the committee is likely to approve'.

Such strangling is not the result of malevolence. It is the unconscious result of working within a too familiar framework and in too regular contact with committees. Every objection can be foreseen before it is made. Repetition of accepted designs is so much easier than innovation, and the official architect may have already tried and failed to get accepted the ideas put forward afresh by the private architect.

It is, however, remarkable what the able and persuasive private architect can achieve. Committees will succumb to the charms of attractive perspective drawings and an eloquent explanation of the layout plans from the private architect which they would never accept from their own architects. It is indeed fortunate that they are vulnerable to such persuasion. Otherwise progress might be a great deal slower. Even if the official architect may find it galling to see the private architect breaking through the restrictions a committee had previously imposed, it can be a valuable alliance and bring greater freedom to the official architects for later schemes.

School building is different. The requirements are much more complicated than for housing. The average member of an Education committee usually has too little experience to follow the evolution of educational theory through the complicated plans of a school. Discussion of school plans means the discussion of teaching methods, the type of curriculum and the interpretation of the authority's own educational policies in technical terms. Having laid down the broad principles, most Education committees leave it to the Director of Education and the architects to work out the details, and examine the plans very cursorily. Similarly, most private architects would find themselves in deep educational waters if they were to present a school design to a committee.

The Smaller Authorities and Private Architects

Most of this chapter has been concerned with authorities who are large enough to have their own architectural staffs. These authorities use private architects, if at all, to supplement the work of the official staff. There are many smaller authorities with modest building programmes, however, who must decide whether it is worth employing an architect on the staff at all, or to use private architects only. The quotations given earlier in the chapter reveal a very strong preference for appointing a full-time officer if the volume of work can by any means justify this. As this is an issue which is facing a number of authorities, it may be useful to examine it further. During the course of the inquiry several authorities sought advice on this very point from the Royal Institute of Public Administration.

The two main reasons usually given in favour of appointing an architect to the staff of a small authority are:

the official architect's greater familiarity with the authority's standards, requirements and procedures;

the lower cost of salaries as compared with fees.

There is no doubt that a permanent officer can keep in closer touch with the methods and requirements of the authority. There are great conveniences in having an architect always at hand and in touch with council business. The difficulty is salary and status. Can the council offer a salary and a position which will attract as able or experienced an architect as the council would employ if they used a private architect? This depends on local circumstances, but generally speaking the smaller councils can only offer a post as assistant architect under the Engineer and Surveyor. This means a modest salary and junior status. Such posts are attractive mainly to young men who have had little experience and are not likely to stay long, or to older men without ambitions. It is for the council to decide if this restricted choice of candidates is better than the private architects they would otherwise employ.

In calculating the difference between the cost of the salaried architect and the private architect, authorities must also take into account the overhead costs of the salaried post. The salaried architect will require office accommodation, secretarial help, technical equipment and facilities for copying plans. These costs are covered by the private architect's fees. Such overheads must be added to the salary of the official architect before a true comparison of costs can be made. The total may well be no lower than the cost of fees.

As has already been explained, some of the difficulties of using private architects arise from inexperience in briefing them. Some of the small authorities overcome this problem by regularly employing one or two firms of private architects. These then become familiar with the council's methods and requirements and by regular contact become almost an outpost of the authority. This arrangement sometimes works very well, and puts at the authority's disposal experience it could not otherwise command.

The pros and cons of employing a salaried or a private architect can be resolved most easily by answering the following questions:

is the building programme large enough and continuous enough to justify the appointment of a salaried architect without risk of redundancy?

can the authority offer a salary and status which will attract as good a man as the authority would employ from private practice?

will salary and overheads be cheaper than fees?

can the deficiencies in the present arrangements for employing private architects be remedied by better briefing or by using one or two firms regularly?

ENGINEERING CONSULTANTS

Councils appeared from the inquiry to make regular use of experts in the various branches of engineering as circumstances demanded. The large authorities may employ their own electrical and heating engineers, but the medium and smaller authorities employ private firms as they need them. The specialists covered a wide range and no particular problems in their use were mentioned. This subject was not, however, pursued in

186

sufficient detail to reveal whether there were any difficulties in seeking or obtaining the necessary advice.

THE ROLE OF THE QUANTITY SURVEYOR

Quantity surveyors, as we know them, fulfil a function and occupy a position in the organization of building unique to Great Britain and to certain territories overseas, where British influence has been strong. Quantity surveyors of the same kind are not usually found in the United States of America nor in most European countries. In these countries the functions may be performed by the architect or the contractor, or may not be carried out in so elaborate a way. Even in this country the smaller firms of speculative builders often do not use quantity surveyors, or use them for a more restricted range of functions, while it is more common for engineers in the preparation of engineering schemes to draw up their own quantities without separate quantity surveying staff. These divergencies internationally and within the organization of building in this country account for some of the differences of practice and opinion about the quantity surveyor's role.

Traditionally the functions of the quantity surveyor are related closely to those of the builder. He is one of the main links between the architect and the contractor, but in training, outlook and experience he is usually orientated to the production rather than to the design side of building. This very definite orientation is now, however, showing signs of changing. The vast majority of the quantity surveyor's work is still with the builder, but he is beginning to move closer to the architect as well.

This change is due to two causes. First, the volume of building by public authorities has greatly increased since the war, and with it the public's interest in getting value for money. Secondly, the techniques of building are passing through a period of such rapid change that the architect has the utmost difficulty in keeping abreast of them. Pinioned between the client's interest in costs and the overwhelming choice of materials and techniques the architect can have a hard task. Gradually it is becoming more customary for the quantity surveyor to help the architect during the earlier stages of design to meet these two pressures.

187

In the account which follows, the role of the quantity surveyor is considered in three parts:

the traditional role, which begins when design ends;

a transitional role, in which the quantity surveyor takes a partial responsibility for the estimates of costs, but is not working closely with the architect;

full collaboration with the architect on cost planning and control from the outset of design.

In terms of the manpower the traditional functions of the quantity surveyor absorb by far the greater part of his time. Quantitatively the resources devoted to cost estimates and cost control are small. Qualitatively, the second and third aspects of the quantity surveyor's work are of great importance, and are closely bound up with the efficiency of building operations. It is for this reason that they are dealt with at greater length in this chapter than the quantity surveyor's more traditional and established functions.

Traditional Functions

The traditional functions fall into three stages. First, the quantity surveyor has to prepare the bill of quantities; secondly, he has to price and agree with the contractor the progress of work and the cost of variations in the contract as the contract proceeds, and thirdly, he has to settle the final accounts and in so doing to tie up the loose ends of the contract.

These functions are related closely to the operations of the builder and do not touch the architect during design. Only when the architect has prepared his design in detail, made the working drawings and drawn up his specifications of the materials to be used in all parts of the building, does the quantity surveyor prepare the bill of quantities, which shows the quantities of labour and materials which will be required. This bill, which can be a long and complex document covering every item in the building, is then sent to the contractor with the plans or other relevant information to assist him in making his tender.

188

During the course of the contract the contractor has to be paid at intervals. These interim payments are based on the amount of the work which has been completed. The quantity surveyor during the period of construction has to measure and agree with the contractor the progress of the work and the cost of any variations in the quantity of labour and materials, due to alterations in design or changes in specification. These changes may originate with the client and the architect, or they may arise because the contractor has not been able to obtain the materials specified. Strictly speaking all changes should be embodied in written instructions authorized by the client and sent by the architect to the contractor. In practice many of the changes are made verbally, and the quantity surveyor often has to find out what has been done and negotiate a price with the contractor on the basis of verbal instructions.

Finally, when the building is finished, there is a grand settlement of accounts, when the cost of every item changed during the course of building has to be added to or subtracted from the tender price, and hundreds of small sums covering these changes have to be agreed. This can be a long and laborious process, especially with a building for a local authority. The accounts will be scrutinized by the Treasurer's department and possibly by the district auditor, and every small item has to be agreed between the contractor and the quantity surveyor and carefully recorded for audit purposes. This process can be very prolonged; more prolonged than for many private clients, who have less elaborate financial regulations.

The exercise of these traditional responsibilities keeps the surveyor separate from the architect. Before the war the dividing line was plain and the quantity surveyor was involved mainly on routine tasks which saved the architect a great deal of time and trouble, but had no influence on design. His experience carried weight in negotiation with the contractor. It did not touch the architect closely.

This line of demarcation still governs the relationship between many architects and quantity surveyors. It is a line which simplifies the quantity surveyor's work and it leaves the architect completely independent during the gestation of his plans. But it is a line which has become blurred for two reasons. On the one hand, it is the exception rather than the rule for the

189

architect to have completed all his design work before the quantity surveyor is asked to start preparing the bills of quantities, so that the two operations may overlap. On the other hand, quantity surveyors are now often asked to collaborate with the architects in making the preliminary estimates of costs, and more rarely, to work with the architects on cost planning and cost control from the outset of the scheme. Where this collaboration has been most highly developed the two disciplines may work parallel to one another. Generally, however, the change is less thorough and represents an overlapping of functions rather than a re-alignment.

To appreciate how the quantity surveyor may be asked to collaborate with the architect during the earlier stages of design, it may be helpful to set out the sequence of operations prior to the sending out of the tender documents to contractors. The procedure in a local authority is generally as follows:

preparation of the brief by the client department;

discussion of the brief by the architect and officers in the client department and investigations of requirements;

preparation of layout plans and preliminary drawings;

approval of these preliminary drawings and estimates by the client committee;

preparation of the working drawings and specifications by the architect;

preparation of the bills of quantities and tender documents by the quantity surveyor;

despatch of tender documents to contractors.

Preliminary Estimates

Committees are well aware that once they have approved the preliminary plans and estimates a scheme passes out of their effective control. Later they will be asked to confirm the final estimates and the tender, but the scheme will then be too far

190

advanced to be recalled or fundamentally altered without much abortive work. It has, therefore, become fairly common for authorities to seek the quantity surveyor's help at an earlier stage and his confirmation of the preliminary estimates. This is an extra reassurance that final and preliminary estimates will be reasonably close. It is a natural act of self protection, and it can make possible a valuable co-operation between the architect and the quantity surveyor. But to be effective a number of conditions need to be satisfied.

There is little difficulty in giving a committee the necessary reassurance at the preliminary estimate stage, if the architects and quantity surveyors are both familiar with the type of building the council requires and with each other's methods. If the architects and quantity surveyors are both on the authority's own staff and are working on fairly standardized designs or components, as can be the case with housing or schools, they may be able to achieve a high degree of accuracy in the preliminary estimates. Similarly, if a few firms of private quantity surveyors are employed regularly to work with the authority's own architects, they will become familiar with the type of building and with each other's methods. With such an arrangement the private firm becomes almost an extended branch of the authority.

The same close understanding cannot readily be achieved when using a large panel of quantity surveying firms or when private architects and surveyors are new to one another. A panel system which gives an arbitrary pairing of quantity surveyor and private architect may serve well enough if only the traditional relationship is involved, and the quantity surveyor first comes in when the bills of quantities are needed. Any competent quantity surveyor can draw up a bill of quantities, if the architect has given him all the necessary drawings and other information at the proper time. The local authority is, however, seeking something more.

The reliable confirmation of the architect's preliminary estimates by the quantity surveyor demands an earlier and less routine kind of collaboration between the two than the preparation of the bill of quantities. And it assumes either that the quantity surveyor is already familiar with the architect's methods and approach, or, if the two are working together for

191

the first time, that a great deal of detailed work will be undertaken by both sides when the preliminary estimates are being prepared. This kind of joint effort cannot be turned on and off like a tap, regardless of the human element. It is less likely to be achieved if this is the first and probably the last time the two will work together.

It must be remembered that most private architects are working for many clients, and some firms of architects may have a dozen schemes on hand at the same time. If the private architect has to work with a different firm of quantity surveyors for each scheme this greatly reduces the probability of close collaboration between the two until the stage for preparing the bills of quantities is reached. This is too late for the control of estimated costs. As a result, it is all too common for the quantity surveyor to have to confirm the architect's preliminary estimates on the basis of inadequate knowledge of the architect's methods and ideas. His confirmation may be no more than an experienced guess at the architect's intentions. This is not at all what the client hoped for.

Cost Planning and Cost Control

If there is a need to bring the architect and the quantity surveyor into closer contact when preliminary estimates are being prepared, this is still more important if there is to be a systematic control of costs from the earliest stages of design. This demands a still closer partnership between the architect and quantity surveyor and a re-orientation of attitudes.

The fact that some buildings are so much better value for money than others with similar accommodation has prompted investigations into methods of improving the control of costs. These attempts to get better buildings for the same or even lower costs have inspired much of the most valuable work now being done in the field of cost planning and control. Where this has been carried out systematically quantity surveyors have taken an active part in the work. The Ministry of Education in its pioneer work on school building has brought in the quantity surveyor from the earliest stages of design, and those authorities and firms, who are most active in this field, are doing the same.

Costs are influenced far more significantly by early decisions on layout and on fundamental questions of height, foundations or methods of construction than can ever be rectified by economies called for when the design is nearing completion. It has been found that the best and most economical designs are produced when architects, engineers, quantity surveyors and other experts work together from the start of the design. The architect can then call for expert comparisons of costs and building techniques at a stage when the plans are still fluid. Adjustments can be made without costly changes in the drawings, and the quantity surveyor can put his experience of the building industry at the architect's disposal before, rather than after, the most important decisions have been made.

This joint work involves a different outlook on the part of the architect and the quantity surveyor from that required when the latter carries out only his traditional functions. It assumes that the architect is ready to be advised on costs during the preliminary stages. It assumes that the quantity surveyor can talk the architect's language and is interested in the problems of design. It assumes that he is well equipped to advise on costs. And it assumes that the building owner is prepared to appoint the quantity surveyor before design starts.

Some architects do not welcome the early intervention of the quantity surveyor, and do not wish to be hampered in their general conception of the design by considering the relative costs of different parts of their buildings. Some quantity surveyors are not anxious to enter this new field of work, which is more exacting and not immediately remunerative. Many clients are too unfamiliar with the methods of cost control to appreciate the importance of appointing the quantity surveyor as soon as the architect is ready to start work.

It will take time for these changes of outlook to come about. The work of the Ministry of Education is becoming more familiar and the Royal Institution of Chartered Surveyors and the Royal Institute of British Architects have been active in encouraging cost research and in bringing architects and quantity surveyors closer together.[1] There cannot be any doubt that this kind of collaboration between the different disciplines will increase and that it will be of great benefit to clients. The experience already available gives ample evidence that this joint

---

[1] See Chapter on Research and Development.

effort makes for a far more reliable control of costs and more economical buildings.

With this introduction to the traditional and new fields of work carried out by the quantity surveyor it is time to examine in more detail what use authorities make of quantity surveyors. The inquiry sought to find out whether authorities made regular use of quantity surveyors, how far they employed salaried staff or private firms, at what stage the quantity surveyors were brought in, and what particular problems were involved in making the best and most economical use of them.

Employment on Traditional Functions

The inquiry showed that local authorities made full use of quantity surveyors for all building schemes costing more than £3,000 or £4,000. The lower cost limits are agreed from time to time by the Royal Institution of Chartered Surveyors, the Royal Institute of British Architects, and the National Federation of Building Trades Employers. Local authorities are usually punctilious in adhering to the codes of professional practice, and it appeared that they were no less so for quantity surveyors than for the other professions.

In terms of manpower the traditional functions of quantity surveyors absorb the greatest time and effort. Even if the architects consult the quantity surveyors on questions of costs, or the authority seeks their confirmation of preliminary estimates, it is the bill of quantities, the contract and the post-contract work which will occupy most of the time of the quantity surveying staff. Even if these functions are, and are likely to remain, the quantity surveyor's main preoccupation, they usually take far more time and effort than they should. They are, in consequence, more costly than they need be to the client, but for reasons which lie largely outside the surveyor's control.

The quantity surveyor's work is intimately bound up with the time sequence of planning a building. The less time devoted to the plans and the less complete the designs and specifications when bills of quantities have to be prepared, the more time the

194

quantity surveyor must spend sorting out variations and final accounts. No single factor increases or decreases the efficiency of building as much as the increase or decrease in the time devoted to design. No single factor does so much to reduce or extend the work of the quantity surveyor after building has started.

A succession of government and other reports[1] has stressed and re-stressed the importance of completing all the preparatory stages of a scheme before going out to tender. To do this means having the scheme prepared in all its detail. The client and architect must agree everything first; what they have agreed must be embodied in the plans and then elaborated in the working drawings and specifications. Having done this, the quantity surveyor can measure all the quantities and the contractor can tender with full knowledge of the details. This procedure assists everyone involved in the scheme, and is the only way to ensure that the project is efficiently designed and built and that the final accounts can be settled quickly and without waste of effort.

In spite of all the advantages and the constant reiteration of its importance, this sequence of events is seldom achieved. The main reason is that the architect is rarely given the time to think out a scheme in all its detail and thus to prepare a complete set of drawings and specifications. Because he has failed to secure enough time and is compelled to go on to the next stage before the first is complete, a series of changes, adjustments, revisions and variations follow, all of which have to be chased, measured, and agreed between the quantity surveyor and contractor. As a result of the original failure to bring the scheme complete to the starting post, the contractor cannot plan his work efficiently and there is a trail of loose ends to hamper operations and eventually to be tidied and sorted out by the quantity surveyor.

This wasteful state of inefficiency continues through lack of programming and through lack of understanding of the intricate processes of design. On the one hand, delays in obtaining approval for schemes from government departments may mean that the design of a scheme has to be rushed to get started

[1]*Placing and Management of Building Contracts*, H.M.S.O., 1941. *Working Party Report on Building*, H.M.S.O., 1950. *Productivity Team Report on Building*, 1950. *Joint Report on Tendering Procedure*, R.I.B.A., R.I.C.S., N.F.B.T.E., 1954. *Building Contracts of Local Authorities*, Royal Institute of Public Administration, 1958.

within the programme year. Or the authority may not have drawn up its own programme effectively and finds itself short of design staff. On the other hand, elected members sometimes press for early starting dates without being aware of the consequences of their demands. They rarely understand the amount of time and work involved in preparing working drawings, specifications and bills of quantities, and do not appreciate the extra costs which will be incurred if there has not been time to prepare the scheme properly. As a result they are, unwittingly, unreasonable in the time schedules they demand.

The need for better programming both by central and local government is argued elsewhere. The inexperience of members can only be overcome if officers are firm. It is their duty to make clear to members the ill-effects of haste and the benefits to be derived from giving the technical staff sufficient time to complete their work. Haste in the early stages will increase the quantity surveyor's work later, and lead to extra costs all round.

Use of Salaried Staff or Private Quantity Surveyors

The use of salaried or private surveyors varied very much according to the size of the authority. The large authorities had many surveyors on the staff; the medium were divided between those who used mainly salaried staff and those who used mainly private firms. Nearly all had some salaried staff. The majority of the smaller authorities used only private firms, but some had staff of their own. There appeared to be no authorities who kept a single quantity surveyor on the staff to act as a liaison officer with private firms, a system used sometimes by commercial and industrial concerns.

Only a few authorities used entirely salaried staff. Some would have liked to do so, but had had insufficient staff to carry the work. A number used private firms regularly and expected to do so. The complaint that there was a shortage of salaried quantity surveyors was common, but it was not accompanied by any obvious objection to the use of private firms. Salaried staff and private quantity surveyors appeared to be interchangeable without difficulty.

The ready use of private quantity surveyors is in marked contrast to that of architects. It appeared to be taken as a matter of course and to raise no particular obstacles. This is

196

partly because one quantity surveyor can normally cover the work of several architects. A much larger volume of architectural work is necessary to justify the appointment of a quantity surveyor on the staff than of an architect. It is also because the more routine parts of the quantity surveyor's work do not require the same individual knowledge of a council's policy and procedures as are required of the architect. Authorities who employ quantity surveyors for the more traditional functions see less advantage in using salaried staff.

The shortage of quantity surveyors, of which many of the larger authorities complained, is only partly a product of the larger post-war building programmes of these authorities. It is also due to the higher prestige and earnings and the more varied range of work in private offices. Quantity surveyors enjoy a different status inside and outside local government service. Inside local authority offices they form part of the Engineer's or Architect's staff and there are very few who are paid more than £1,500 a year. The senior post is usually the head of a quantity surveyor's section with no prospects of promotion inside local government to chief officer or deputy chief officer status. As far as is known, there is only one authority, Dundee in Scotland, where the Chief Quantity Surveyor is the head of a department.

This situation means that able and ambitious quantity surveyors tend to gravitate to private practice or to government departments, and are regularly moving out of local government service. This not only increases the turnover but thins ability at the top. One by-product of this situation is that the local authority quantity surveyor is hardly ever represented on government and other committees, where the private or civil service quantity surveyor regularly finds a place.

No authority stated that use was made of private firms to avoid future redundancy, although this was stated in rare instances in the case of architects. Clearly, in terms of the volume of building work, redundancy can arise more quickly with quantity surveyors than with architects. On the other hand the impact of reductions in programmes is longer delayed for the quantity surveyor than for the architect. Cuts in capital programmes can reduce the architect's work at once; schemes in the pipeline can keep the quantity surveyor busy for years.

It is just as important for authorities to avoid redundancy in their quantity surveying as in their architectural staff. The volume of building work is bound to fluctuate with the programme of the authority and with the level of capital expenditure sanctioned by the Government. Local authorities who fix their establishments in relation to the long-term requirements of their programmes and use private firms to carry out work above this level, are likely to obtain a more economical quantity surveying service.

Private firms are not necessarily used to complete all the stages of a scheme. Either as a matter of policy or to relieve the pressure on the salaried staff, private firms may be asked to take over only part of the sequence of quantity surveying functions. In East Suffolk private firms deal with the bills of quantities in all major schemes, while the authority's own staff covers the subsequent operations. A similar procedure is used in Worthing. In the London County Council some three-quarters of the bills of quantities as against about one-tenth of the final accounts are dealt with by private firms.

Stage when the Quantity Surveyor is brought in

The use made of private firms or salaried staff is also bound up with the stage at which the quantity surveyor is normally brought in.

The inquiry showed that some authorities used the quantity surveyor only at a very late stage when the working drawings were nearing completion or the bills of quantities were required. The majority of the authorities brought in the quantity surveyor rather earlier, when the preliminary drawings and estimates had been approved by the committee and working drawings were about to start. A number of authorities referred rather loosely to consultation at the stage of preliminary planning without making it clear how full this consultation was. The number who carry out full cost planning techniques and ensure that the quantity surveyors work closely with the architects from the beginning of the design is still very small.

While there were some authorities who stated that private firms were brought in while the sketch plans were under discussion, there was a good deal of evidence that this early consultation was more usual when there were salaried quantity surveyors available. It was clear that authorities were hesitant

198

about appointing private firms of quantity surveyors until the preliminary plans had been approved by the committee. Until that stage the future of the scheme may still be uncertain and authorities do not wish to be committed to any outside firms or the payment of fees. Such difficulties do not arise when there are quantity surveyors on the staff. These are close at hand, and can readily be consulted without any problem of fees or commitment.

If authorities are sometimes nervous about appointing the quantity surveyor before the scheme has been approved by the committees, private quantity surveyors may also be nervous about participation while the scheme is still in its early stages. If the scheme should prove abortive in its early stages, the private quantity surveyor's position is far from clear. This ought not to be allowed to become a hindrance. Authorities who have experience of early collaboration with private firms have established the precedent that a modified fee is payable if, on rare occasions, a scheme does not go ahead. The cost advantages to be gained from the early collaboration of the architect and quantity surveyor are far greater than the small and exceptional loss on an abortive scheme.

The difficulty in which a private quantity surveyor can find himself if he is asked to confirm the preliminary estimates without previous contact with the architect has already been discussed. If an authority wishes to have confirmation of the architect's preliminary estimates by a private quantity surveyor it must facilitate understanding between the two by its method of appointment. This means making the appointment of the quantity surveyor in such a way that the private architect need work with only a limited number of firms, and making it early enough.

Sheffield is an example of an authority which gives the architect some freedom of choice in the appointment of the quantity surveyor, and recognizes the value of teamwork in controlling costs. When a private architect is appointed, he is invited to nominate the firm of quantity surveyors and other consultants. Provided the authority is satisfied that these nominated consultants are efficient and reliable, arrangements are made for them to be appointed by the Corporation. The quantity surveyor thus appointed is made directly responsible to the authority. But, to quote the authority's own words, 'by virtue of being nominated by the private architect he is also conscious of their joint responsibility to work as a team and to ensure that the scheme is produced within the cost ceiling laid down'. It is claimed that this arrangement works much better than when the quantity surveyor is appointed regardless of the views of the architect.

Cost Planning in Practice

There are at the present time less than thirty education authorities in the country who are attempting to do intensive work on cost planning through teamwork between architects, quantity surveyors and others. The majority are county councils, with only a small number of county boroughs. The number of housing authorities is not known, but is certainly much smaller.

This work is being done mainly by teams of salaried staff. Most of the large education authorities have a quantity surveyors' section, whose staff can conveniently be called upon to do this work and have much experience and full records of the costs of school building. There are those who consider that this teamwork is essentially a field for salaried staff, who can work in close and continuous contact, and that the private firm of quantity surveyors is unlikely to be brought in early enough or closely enough to achieve the same results.

There are, however, private firms who are developing a more elaborate cost service to meet the clients' demand for closer cost control. They can offer the architect much valuable advice in making his first and most important decisions provided the client has appointed the quantity surveyor in time. The most forward looking members of the profession see in these new cost techniques a valuable method of improving the efficiency of design and of reducing building costs. A shift in emphasis from the traditional functions to those associated with cost research and cost planning offers the quantity surveyor an enlarged responsibility and an opportunity to extend the advisory rather than the routine side of his work.

While the most elaborate forms of cost study and comparison, similar to those worked out by the Ministry of Education,[1] are still exceptional, there are many authorities who are deeply

[1] *Cost Study*, Building Bulletin No. 4.

concerned with these issues of costs and are moving more tentatively in the same direction. Much of the hesitation about extending the use of cost planning and control is due to anxiety lest these methods should prove expensive in time, salaries and fees to the authority and in costs to the private firm. Experience is still too limited to make any final judgment. But those authorities who have practised these methods for some time have found these fears unnecessary.

This has been the experience of Hertfordshire. There, it has been found that there is no increase in total production time. Whatever extra work is involved at the beginning is saved later. Careful control of design and costs at the outset saves reduction bills, re-designing and re-submission to the client. Fewer queries arise during the preparation of the bills because the quantity surveyor is already familiar with the design. The final settlement of accounts is simplified. In this office it has been found that the clerical work involved in keeping cost records is minimal. One clerk can keep track of cost information for a large staff of surveyors and undertake other work as well.

Small authorities cannot hope to achieve the methods of Hertfordshire. But the experience has its relevance to them also. The work that is being done on cost planning and cost control by the larger authorities emphasizes the importance of early contact between the architect and the quantity surveyor and of giving time for the preliminary stages of design. Both are matters which the small authority can arrange as well as the big. It is, indeed, possible for the architect and quantity surveyor in a small authority to control costs together most effectively, even if by less elaborate means.

Those who have employed these methods emphasize that the differences of attitude are much more important than the variations in the system of keeping cost records or the other office routines involved. To bring the architect and the quantity surveyor closer together poses more problems than to file the necessary information on costs. It takes much longer to educate architects to be cost conscious or quantity surveyors to be architecture conscious than to devise a new filing system. Many of the leaders of both professions are aware of the possibilities before them and are anxious to provide a better service to the public by this more systematic approach to costs.

Private Architects

1. The contribution of the private architect to local authority building falls into five parts:

> to provide a reservoir of manpower to be drawn on in emergency or in times of staff shortage;

> to be a regular supplement to local authority staffs, so that redundancy can be avoided and the fluctuations of programmes be evened out;

> to design prestige buildings beyond the experience of an authority's regular staff;

> to bring variety and the stimulus of fresh ideas and a new approach to familiar problems;

> to serve small authorities who would not be justified in making a salaried appointment.

2. Authorities make frequent use of private architects to supplement their staff in times of pressure. This can lead to difficulties if, as often happens, the private architect is given insufficient time to prepare his plans. Many of the criticisms of private architects by local authorities stem from too compressed a time-table.

3. It is recommended that authorities should plan their long-term staff requirements for architects in such a way that more of the work to be done by private architects is determined well ahead. Not only will this avoid risks of redundancy; it will give private architects the opportunity to do better work.

4. Emergencies there will always be. Both official and private architects must expect such calls from time to time, but with well planned programmes they should be exceptional.

5. The inquiry revealed a strong feeling among local authorities against the use of private architects. The fault lies partly

with those private architects who are unbusiness-like and who have done the reputation of their profession a disservice. Part of the fault lies with authorities themselves for making the private architect's task unnecessarily difficult. To get the best results the private architect should be given:

adequate time to prepare his plans;

clear instructions on procedure and the administrative arrangements;

a cost target;

a clear brief, which gives the council's essential requirements but is flexible enough for the architect to develop his own ideas;

direct access to the committee to explain his plans, unless it is a type of building in which members take little interest.

6. Only a few authorities recognize the value of the private architect in stimulating fresh thought on familiar problems. Local authority building, especially housing, can become monotonous under the pressures of low costs and high output. Those authorities who have made the most regular use of private architects to encourage a cross-fertilization of ideas have shown how fruitful this partnership can be.

7. It is recommended that large authorities should regularly give a proportion of their work to private architects, and that smaller authorities should commission them from time to time to provide the stimulus of fresh ideas. If the results are to be worthwhile, the architects must be carefully chosen and well briefed.

8. Small authorities, who are considering the appointment of a salaried architect for the first time, should consider very carefully the quality of the officer they are likely to attract and the overhead costs. These must be compared with the best methods of using a private architect, if the relative advantages of using a salaried or a private architect are to be fairly judged.

203

Quantity Surveyors

1. The quantity surveyor's functions can be divided into three parts:

the traditional functions starting with the bill of quantities;

assistance with preliminary estimates;

participation in cost planning and cost control.

2. The traditional functions occupy the greater part of the quantity surveyor's time. Local authorities appear to use surveyors for these purposes in accordance with the rules of professional practice.

3. The cost of salaries or fees for carrying out these traditional functions are greatly influenced by the efficiency and completeness of the design work. If the quantity surveyor receives the drawings and other information from the architects at the proper time and with the detail completed, his task is comparatively easy, and the extra costs for settling variations and negotiating final accounts can be avoided. If the scheme is incomplete when the bills of quantities are prepared and sent out for tender, much extra cost will be incurred.

4. The reason for this state of affairs is often lack of time during design. Rushed work may be due to late approvals by central government, inadequate programming by the authority itself, or to lack of knowledge among elected members. It is essential that authorities should do all in their power to give the designers adequate time fully to complete their schemes before going out to tender. Officers have a duty to make members and their own staff fully aware of the penalties paid for rushed work. If time is adequate they must be equally rigorous in insisting that designs are completed before tender.

5. Authorities also use quantity surveyors to confirm the architects' preliminary estimates of cost. This can readily be done when salaried architects and quantity surveyors work together. It is not so easy for private architects and quantity surveyors to do this unless the authority ensures that the arrangements for appointment facilitate collaboration. Authorities are urged to

examine their methods of appointing the private quantity surveyor, so that the architect and quantity surveyor may be encouraged to work closely together.

6. More exhaustive methods of cost planning and control demand an even closer integration of the various members of the building team. At present much of this work for local authorities is being carried out by salaried staffs, who are more easily accessible to one another. If private firms of quantity surveyors are to contribute their full share to this work they must be appointed early.

7. Not all architects or quantity surveyors are anxious for this re-alignment of functions. Authorities also are apprehensive lest the new work should be expensive in time, salaries or fees. Such experience as is available suggests that time spent at the beginning pays for itself directly during the latter stages of design and repays itself yet again during the building and settlement of the contract. This is quite apart from the likelihood that the whole scheme will be better designed and give better value for money.

8. The number of authorities with only salaried staff is limited. Either because of shortages of staff or of deliberate policy there is a widespread use of private firms. Their employment did not appear to present any particular difficulty, such as was found with the employment of private architects. Most large and medium authorities used both salaried staff and private firms. The majority of the smaller authorities employed private firms only, but quite a number had salaried staff.

9. If authorities aim to carry out a large proportion of their work by salaried staff, it is important that they should look to long-term demand. The quantity surveyor's section can be run most economically if fluctuations above the norm are carried by private firms.

10. The most important finding of the inquiry on the role of the quantity surveyor was the value of his contribution to the planning and control of costs, and the ultimate effect on building costs generally. Local authorities can do a great deal to extend this work and are urged to do so.

CHAPTER 6

MAINTENANCE

Importance of maintenance—capital value of building—control of maintenance by committees—pattern of departmental responsibilities—arguments for and against control by different chief officers—calibre of officer in charge—programming of repairs—reserve funds—cost control and work study—capital costs and maintenance costs.

THIS chapter and the next one on direct labour are closely interlocked, because a great deal of maintenance by local authorities is carried out by direct labour. On the other hand, direct labour is also used for new building, and this falls outside the scope of a chapter on maintenance. In order to keep the treatment of maintenance and direct labour related yet distinct, this chapter deals mainly with maintenance organization up to the point when the contractor or the direct labour organization takes over. The next chapter deals with both new building and maintenance when this is carried out by a council's own labour force.

A further clarification is necessary. Building operations are usually divided into major capital works, minor capital works, and maintenance and repair. The exact dividing lines in each authority are a matter of definition, but the broad distinctions are well understood. This chapter discusses only maintenance and repair.

The capital value of buildings owned by local authorities runs into thousands of millions of pounds. An authority, for example, owning 5,000 houses built since 1945 has an asset which cost some £7 million. Taking into account the 2 million houses built by local authorities since the war the cost must be of the order of £3,000 million. Similarly with schools; nearly £1,000 million has been spent on them since 1945. When to this is added pre-war housing and schools and all the libraries, fire stations, clinics, colleges, town halls and other buildings owned by local authorities the total is very large. Since 1948 local authorities have been adding to their stock of buildings at the rate of £300 million to £500 million a year.

All these buildings have to be maintained. Maintenance of this large volume of physical assets is a matter of great national, as well as local, importance, since the standards of maintenance greatly affect the life of these buildings and the balance between renewal and a continued useful life. Renewal can be postponed in some cases almost indefinitely by far-sighted maintenance policies.

New buildings create interest and sometimes excitement. They are built to meet pressing and immediate needs; to house families from the slums, to educate children who would otherwise run wild, to bring the fire or ambulance service within reach of flames or sickness, or to provide councillors and officers with fit surroundings for carrying out their duties. The erection of these buildings is of immediate interest to committees, architects and the public.

Once erected and in familiar use these buildings cease to demand that continuing interest and attention which their value may require. Their maintenance becomes a matter of routine administration, only occasionally ruffled by controversy. In periods of financial difficulty or labour or material shortage—standards of maintenance and programmes of modernization may be reduced. In times of rising rents, responsibilities for internal decoration or minor repairs of council houses may be transferred to the tenants to avoid rent increases. These decisions are taken in the light of the year-to-year commitments of local authorities, and the financial resources at their command. Whether they take fully into account the real values which have been created, or the effect on these values of short-term economies must depend on the vigour with which officers press the claims of maintenance and the willingness of committees to spend money on uninteresting and sometimes temptingly postponable items.

At a conference in 1955, Mr W. T. Jackson, A.R.I.B.A., then Director of Maintenance Services of the Ministry of Works, said:

Maintenance is not a job for the less efficient: it is an extremely exacting science, and the people responsible for it have demands made on them which are quite outside the sphere of the ordinary professional man. The maintenance officer needs to be a first class businessman, an accountant, a statistician, a lawyer, an industrial labour manager, and at the top level a very competent economist and an organizational and accounting expert. You do not get that calibre of man by sending odd-job men to do the work.

Mr Jackson was speaking of the large organization but the spirit of his remarks is applicable also to smaller organizations. Maintenance is a complex matter in terms of the financial issues it raises, the management of men and materials it demands, and the long-term effects it can have. This applies to the smaller district authorities as well as to the larger counties or cities. This is not to suggest that local authorities are poor property owners. On the contrary, their record as landlords of low rented houses is superior to that of many private landlords, while civic buildings are generally well maintained. But the magnitude of their responsibilities and the effect on the value of council property and on rents and rates means that maintenance is a matter of much greater importance than its sometimes hum-drum routine might suggest.

THE CONTROL OF MAINTENANCE BY COMMITTEES

Members control maintenance at three levels. First, there are the decisions of policy which determine, for example, how much maintenance is to be carried out by contract or by direct labour, and how the responsibilities for direct labour shall be combined or divided between committees. Secondly, there are the client functions of committees, who determine what maintenance and repair shall be carried out annually for the buildings in each committee's charge. Thirdly, there are the management functions, more clearly defined in some authorities than in others, by which committees oversee the organization of maintenance by direct labour.

The major policy decisions arise only occasionally, as the responsibilities of authorities increase, larger building programmes necessitate larger maintenance organizations, or changes in the political control of a council bring direct labour into greater or lesser prominence. Generally speaking the maintenance organization carries on without attracting much of the limelight.

Client committees are responsible for authorizing expenditure on maintenance. Most of this is dealt with as a matter of routine at the time of the annual estimates. Unexpected supplementary estimates may arouse discussion, but in the main the interest of members is limited to the more outstanding issues. For the Housing committee these can centre on matters such as the frequency of the external painting cycle, tenants' liabilities for internal decorations, programmes for structural maintenance and repairs and the renewal of fixed equipment. Beyond housing and perhaps the painting programmes for schools, libraries and other buildings used by the public, questions concerning maintenance are unlikely to evoke much discussion.

The management functions arise when an authority uses direct labour for maintenance on any scale. These will be discussed more fully in the next chapter. Here it is only necessary to explain that the most clear-cut form of management emerges when there is a separate Works committee or when some other committee is given clearly defined responsibilities for the direct labour organization. In most authorities the Engineer, Architect or Housing Manager controls the direct labour organization without any committee assuming active management functions.

To say that a service committee is 'responsible' for the maintenance of the buildings under its control can mean a variety of things according to each authority's type of organization. This can confuse any discussion of maintenance unless the type of organization is clear from the outset. For example, a Housing committee's responsibility for the maintenance and repair of houses can mean at least four different things:

it can decide annual programmes of repair and maintenance, and approve tenders knowing that the Engineer or Architect will give the necessary instructions to private contractors;

it can approve similar expenditure knowing that the execution will be controlled by a Works committee and the Building Manager;

209

it can authorize such expenditure knowing that the Engineer or Architect will supervise the execution by direct labour, but without any regular committee supervision of the direct labour organization;

it can approve such work knowing that its execution will be controlled directly by the Housing Manager either through direct labour or through contractors.

In all these cases the Housing committee, as the client, has a different relationship with those who are charged with ensuring the execution of the maintenance work. Similar variations in the pattern of responsibility can be found among Education committees and to a lesser extent among other committees.

DEPARTMENTAL RESPONSIBILITY FOR MAINTENANCE

In discussing the distribution of responsibilities for maintenance among departments, it is necessary to make the same distinction between client, technical and contracting functions as in discussing committee responsibilities. In the smaller authorities there may be only one department, the Engineer's department, with all these responsibilities combined under one officer. As the size of the authority grows, health, housing, education and other services become separate client departments which order maintenance work from the Engineer or Architect. A still greater volume of work, or a larger direct labour organization may lead to a separate Works department, or to client departments taking over responsibility for the execution as well as the ordering of maintenance and repairs. It is among the county boroughs that the greatest variety of organization occurs. Among the county councils there is usually a clear cut division between the client departments, who authorize maintenance work on buildings in their care, the County Architect who is responsible for ordering and supervising the work, and the private contractor who executes it.

The control of the building maintenance services by the Chief Engineer has the same background as his control of the architectural services. Since for many decades he was the only

210

technical officer he acquired responsibility for building maintenance in the same way as he acquired responsibility for building
design, and he continues to carry it in almost all the small
authorities and in a large number of those of medium size. The
Engineer is already accustomed to running a direct labour
organization for maintaining the roads, street lighting and
cleansing and other civil engineering works for which supplies
must be ordered, depots provided for storage, and transport
organized. From this it is a short step to a similar organization
for building.

So accepted is the system that it arouses little comment, and
the passions which flare over the divisions of functions between
Architect and Engineer on the architectural services are coun-
terbalanced by a considerable phlegm when it comes to maintenance. Many Architects feel only a secondary interest in maintenance compared with new building and may prefer to avoid
this responsibility unless it facilitates the establishment of a
separate department. And Engineers are so accustomed to
running such an organization that it may be taken for granted
that they do so. The only pressure groups are among those who
support a separate Works department under an independent
Works Manager, and consider that the whole maintenance
organization should be gathered under a chief officer who has
no other responsibilities to divide his energies, or those who
believe that the Housing Manager should be responsible for the
execution as well as the ordering of repairs within the Housing
department.

Once the Chief Engineer can no longer handle the technical
supervision of repairs or their execution, and an authority
decides to change or sub-divide the maintenance organization,
there are three main ways of doing so:

an authority can transfer the responsibilities for building
maintenance from the Engineer to the Architect, and leave
only civil engineering maintenance with the Engineer;

it can give to certain client departments responsibilities for
their own individual maintenance organizations;

it can set up a Public Works department to serve all departments.

211

Where there is a separate Public Works department it is common for the Architect to exercise some technical control over the ordering and inspection of work in much the same way as he would do with a private contractor. Some authorities arrange for all but day-to-day repairs to be routed through the Architect's department, to ensure that there is full architectural and technical supervision.

Some impression of the different types of organization can be gained from an examination of the diagrams which were given in Chapter 4:

Hertfordshire (Diagram 1) is typical of the county councils, where the County Architect is responsible for supervising maintenance for all the client departments, and there is no direct labour organization;

in *Stockport* (Diagram 4) the Borough Architect is responsible, on behalf of the client departments, for all maintenance, either by contract or by direct labour. The Works Manager is on his staff and runs separate sections for school, housing and other maintenance;

Birmingham (Diagram 2) is representative of some of the large authorities where the maintenance organization is split between several departments. Housing and education are two client departments with separate maintenance organizations;

in *Hendon* (Diagram 8) the Borough Housing Officer runs a separate maintenance organization for housing. All other maintenance is controlled by the Engineer.

in *Sunderland* (Diagram 5) the Public Works Manager runs a separate department and carries out the instructions of the client departments, either by direct labour or through contractors. He is advised by the Borough Architect, who is also responsible for protecting the interests of the client departments;

in *Tottenham* (Diagram 6) the Engineer is responsible for all maintenance and repairs. The Housing Manager runs a

separate department, but the Engineer carries out maintenance and repairs for the Housing department;

in *Ealing* and *Harlow* (Diagrams 7 and 9) the Engineer has
responsibilities as client, technical adviser and contractor,
since both housing management and the direct labour force
are under his control.

These examples show the main variations. The frequency
with which each version occurs in authorities of different kinds
and size is described below.

County Councils[1]

It has already been explained that the County Architect is
now accepted among county councils as the head of all the
architectural services, and that with one exception County Surveyors are concerned solely with the civil engineering services
for which county councils are responsible. As the only technical
officer responsible for building the Architect is also the natural
repository for maintenance responsibilities. The client departments normally look to the Architect for advice and the supervision of their repairs.

The maintenance problems of the county councils differ from
those of most other authorities. Both the character of the buildings and their wide geographical spread present some special features for the maintenance organization. County councils are not
concerned with housing maintenance on any large scale, and the
police houses in their charge are scattered in ones and twos.
They have, therefore, no compact and uniform maintenance
responsibilities which can be dealt with on a standardized basis.
Instead, the maintenance organization must cover a large territory containing a high proportion of big and diverse buildings
including schools, libraries, fire and police stations, which may
present fairly complex maintenance problems. The maintenance organization suitable for such demands is likely to be very
different from that of a compact borough, whose largest preoccupation is housing.

It is argued later that to give the Chief Architect charge of the
maintenance organization has certain objections, partly on the
ground that the professional training of architects and the usual

[1] Excluding the London County Council.

architect-builder relationship are not well adapted to the running of a maintenance organization in which direct labour plays a large part. These objections have less force with county councils, partly because county buildings can present the architects with more complex maintenance problems to which architectural knowledge can make a useful contribution, and partly because direct labour is the exception and most repair and maintenance is carried out by contract.

In the county councils the Architect can remain in his traditional role separate from the contracting organization, even although he may have a section dealing with maintenance headed by an architect whose full-time job this is. Such an arrangement seems to work well. It is one thing to select an assistant architect with special aptitudes in this direction out of a large staff, and to give him full-time responsibility for ordering maintenance work to be carried out by contractors, while others are concerned more directly with design. It is another to expect a Chief Architect in a smaller authority with many other preoccupations to give the organization of maintenance by direct labour the attention which it needs.

County Boroughs

The county boroughs have a much more varied division of responsibility due partly to the stronger tradition in favour of the Engineer, partly to the existence of the two dominant departments covering housing and schools, and partly because direct labour organizations are much commoner in the county boroughs than in the county councils. Out of twenty-seven county boroughs which supplied information for the inquiry of the Royal Institute of Public Administration, the division of responsibilities for maintenance was as follows:

Officer in Charge of Maintenance	*No. of Authorities*
Engineer	8
Architect	4
Works Manager	4
Responsibility divided between departments	11
Total	27

214

Among the eleven authorities with divided responsibilities there were six Housing Managers and seven Directors of Education responsible for maintenance and two Architects in charge of housing maintenance only.

From an examination of the information provided by authorities it is clear that Engineers in county boroughs rarely control a centralized maintenance organization if there is a separate Architect's department. Almost all the authorities where the Engineer was in sole charge of maintenance had no Chief Architect. Where there is a Chief Architect he does not necessarily have sole responsibility for organizing the maintenance services, though very often he is responsible for a part of them. In authorities where there is a separate Works department the Architect usually acts in an advisory capacity.

Non-County Boroughs

The non-county boroughs have fewer Chief Architects and fewer Housing Managers as heads of departments. Since the general scale of operations is usually smaller, there is no responsibility for educational building (apart from the Excepted Districts) and as separate Works departments are exceptional the maintenance organization centres much more in the hands of the Engineer. Out of nineteen non-county boroughs the distribution of responsibilities was as follows:

Officer in Charge of Maintenance	*No. of Authorities*
Engineer	11
Architect	2
Works Manager	1
Responsibility divided between departments	5
Total	19

Among the five authorities with divided responsibilities for repair and maintenance four Housing Managers and one Works Manager had responsibilities for housing maintenance only.

District Councils

Among the district councils there are less than ten authorities

215

with a Chief Architect, six of whom were covered by the inquiry of the Royal Institute of Public Administration. In the 1,000 or so other districts the Engineer is the only technical officer and is generally responsible for all building maintenance. Sometimes the Housing Manager has a separate department with some direct labour. The independent Works department carrying out repairs is very rare.

THE ARGUMENTS FOR AND AGAINST DIFFERENT TYPES OF MAINTENANCE ORGANIZATION

There can be no single answer about the best way to divide or unite the maintenance services. The size of the authority and its responsibilities must exert an influence on the grouping of services under one chief officer or their separation under several. Authorities of like size and kind choose very different solutions to similar problems because they give different weight to the importance of uniting architectural design with maintenance, of treating the human problems of maintenance as a task for the Housing Manager, of giving a Works Manager a more senior status as the head of a separate department or of leaving the organization in the hands of the Engineer. Each authority can argue eloquently in favour of its own solution.

Engineer in Charge of Maintenance

The case in favour of leaving maintenance in the hands of the Engineer in authorities where he is also in charge of the architectural services has been well made by the Surveyor of Carlisle:

> . . . it will be obvious that it is essential that the officer responsible for the design and construction of houses and the officer responsible for their maintenance should collaborate very closely, and there should be a full exchange of information and there should also be a proper understanding of the other's difficulties.

Authorities such as Carlisle, where the Surveyor is responsible not only for the design and construction of new houses, both by contract and direct labour, but also for their maintenance after completion have a decided advantage in this respect. There is a maximum of co-operation not so easily achieved when two or more departments are involved, and there must be kept always in the forefront the im-

216

portant fact that the initial cost must not be pared to the detriment of maintenance costs. Obviously when one is not in a position to wash one's hand of a house after completing it and handing it over one is especially careful not to do anything likely to increase one's work in the future, i.e. maintenance work.[1]

This puts briefly the case for unified control under the Engineer where he is already in charge of the architectural services, and underlines the importance of keeping design and maintenance in close touch, so that mistakes are not repeated.

Organizationally there are well recognized economies in keeping building maintenance in the same department as civil engineering maintenance. By this means transport, storage depots and street services can be shared.

Architect in Charge of Maintenance

The direct connection between design and maintenance and the need for experience on maintenance problems to be passed back systematically to the architects can be used equally well to make the case for placing the maintenance organization under the Chief Architect in authorities where there is a separate Architect's department. The argument is virtually the same as that used for Carlisle. This was stated very clearly by a City Architect during the course of the Royal Institute of Public Administration's inquiry:

I firmly believe that the City or Borough Architect is the appropriate officer to control the Works department, with a Works Manager performing all the usual managerial functions, but responsible to the City Architect. One of the merits of having a works organization in the Architect's department is to bring the architect's experience to bear on maintenance problems and to pass back experience of maintaining buildings to the architects. The architects engaged upon particular committee work learn by their experience of maintenance of the suitability, or otherwise, of the materials and methods employed; their experience is communicated directly between principal assistants or sometimes by the City Architect in an instruction to the principal assistants concerned, as well as through the common link of the Works Manager.

All maintenance work carried out by the Architect's department is under the control of architects. All works orders are perused and

[1] L. J. A. Stow. *Royal Society of Health Journal*, September 1953.

any that require architectural consideration (affecting appearance or requiring some design service) are dealt with appropriately; all colour schemes for decoration and redecoration are designed by architects.

These quotations give the arguments in favour of keeping the services which are concerned with the design of buildings and with their subsequent maintenance in the same department. There can, indeed, be little doubt that considerable benefits can accrue from such close association, and that contact with the practical results of their work when the buildings are in use can give the architects salutary experience. But these arguments do not give the whole picture, particularly for those medium-sized authorities in which the Architect is in charge of the direct labour organization.

In authorities where the Architect's department is responsible for issuing the instructions for maintenance and repairs, while the execution of these instructions is in the hands of contractors, the Architect maintains his traditional role. Where, however, the Architect is himself in charge of the direct labour organization the relationship is not always so straightforward. Maintenance is a different function from architectural design, and there are those who consider that the Architect is a better critic of the direct labour organization, which is, in fact, a contracting organization, than a controller. Execution, they argue, would be better left in the hands of the Engineer or, if the scale of operations is sufficient, transferred to a separate department. It is easier for the Architect to criticize and, if necessary, condemn work which has been done badly by another department than by his own.

This is a difficulty which is not readily admitted, but the Institute's inquiries provided some confirmation of this view. One or two Architects in control of direct labour departments stated that they felt themselves handicapped in this way, and that the dual functions of architect and manager of a direct labour force had its disadvantages.

Housing Manager in Charge of Maintenance

Heads of departments with many buildings in their charge often have a strong preference for controlling their own

218

maintenance organization in order to have complete authority in determining priorities and dealing with the problems peculiar to their departments and its buildings. This is particularly true if there is a direct labour organization, but applies also to contract work.

One of the Housing Manager's most exacting problems is that he is concerned with buildings which are occupied twenty-four hours in the day, 365 days of the year by people who are greatly inconvenienced by the absence of facilities to which they are accustomed and thus intensely sensitive to and critical of any failure in the organization. Failure to complete the painting of a council house scullery or to renew a broken waste pipe can reduce family meals to a shambles and washing the baby to hard labour. With such day-to-day problems to contend with, Housing Managers like to feel that they can control their own maintenance organization, and be certain that urgent repairs are dealt with at once and that the workmen ruffle the tenants' feathers as little as possible.

These problems arise because of the special relationship between landlord and tenant, a relationship which is never easy and whose tensions can be exacerbated by delays or incompetence in carrying out the small day-to-day repairs which are so important to the tenant and uneconomical for the landlord. Many authorities consider that day-to-day repairs are essentially a part of the function of housing management and that the contact between tenant, rent-collector and rent office is the natural link with a maintenance organization run by the same department.

Any decision on this will be influenced by the council's policy on direct labour. Many councils regard direct labour as particularly suitable for day-to-day repairs, and it is widely used for this purpose. Larger maintenance works are more often given to private contractors.

In large authorities which are able and willing to employ an experienced Housing Manager who is technically qualified to manage a maintenance organization, there are considerable advantages in doing so, and the very large authorities can also employ senior staff in charge of maintenance under the Housing Manager. In such cases the Housing Manager is likely to be controlling both a direct labour organization and contract work.

219

In the medium and smaller authorities councils must decide between the advantages in human terms of a separate maintenance organization for housing and the disadvantages of having two maintenance organizations, neither of which can singly afford so well qualified a manager or deploy the same concentration of effort. If the answer is that only a single maintenance organization is reasonable, the authorities must then decide whether to keep maintenance in an existing department, usually under the Engineer, or to set up a new Works department.

In the report *Councils and their Houses* the committee devoted some attention to this matter and recommended that, in cases where the Housing Manager was not responsible for the execution of repairs he

should be responsible for the co-ordinating of requests for day-to-day repairs, for recommending their priority, for indenting for the work to be done, and for following up to see that it is properly done in reasonable time. (Para. 94)

This is a reasonable compromise for authorities where the scale of housing repairs is not large enough to permit the appointment of an officer with sufficient qualifications and experience to run a separate housing maintenance department.

Education Officer in Charge of Maintenance

Educational buildings constitute a large block of buildings with special problems, human and technical, and Directors of Education can marshal strong arguments in favour of a separate maintenance organization. During term education buildings are used with great intensity and holidays are short. Repairs which affect the day-to-day use of the building and may affect several hundred children are therefore doubly urgent. Internal painting and more ambitious repairs must be carried out expeditiously in the holidays. Because of its seasonal nature school maintenance, particularly painting, is not well adapted to a separate direct labour organization. Many authorities carry out most of school maintenance by contract for this reason. Others use contractors mainly for the holiday work of redecoration and have their own staff for day-to-day repairs, so that this work can be specially organized to avoid disrupting school activities.

220

In general it appeared that authorities which expected most of school maintenance and repair to be carried out by contract were more inclined to give the Director of Education full responsibility for maintenance. Where the authority favoured the use of direct labour, the seasonal nature of the work made it better to combine the execution of school maintenance with a central direct labour organization. The labour force could then be deployed in the schools during the holidays and on other buildings during term.

Other Heads of Departments

The role of the Building Manager in charge of a direct labour organization is discussed in the next chapter.

It is exceptional for service departments other than housing and education to have their own maintenance organization. Generally the other chief officers are very willing to leave the supervision or execution of maintenance to the Engineer, Architect or Building Manager.

SOME PROBLEMS OF MAINTENANCE

Since so much maintenance work is carried out by direct labour, the more detailed aspects of its organization will emerge in the next chapter. It is a suitable introduction to that discussion to outline at this point briefly some of the broad problems of maintenance which are not related particularly to their execution by direct labour or by other means. Each of them is of importance, and several of them require more study and research. Some research has already been undertaken by the Building Research Station and by others, but what has been done only serves to emphasize how much more needs to be done.

The following are some of the most interesting issues:

the calibre of the man in control of maintenance;

the programming of structural repairs and periodic maintenance;

reserve funds for maintenance of all types of property;

221

cost control and supervision;

the relationship between capital costs and maintenance costs, and between design and maintenance.

Calibre of Man in Control

This chapter opened with a quotation from a speech by the Director of Maintenance of the Ministry of Works which stressed the variety of qualifications and the calibre of man needed to carry out maintenance operations effectively. He spoke of a 'maintenance officer'. This is not a title commonly used in local government. More usually the responsible officer is the Engineer, Architect, Housing Manager, or a Building Manager. With the first three there is likely to be a Building Manager or Superintendent directly in charge of maintenance in a subordinate position.

The terminology reflects the rather low status of maintenance as a subject for long-term policy decisions, for experiment, or for operational research. Most of the work goes on according to established routines, without much in the way of re-appraisal of methods. Because so much is routine, decisions are taken fairly far down the line of command by subordinate officers, who are not trained to question the general work of the organization. At the top the chief officer is usually running a department with a wide variety of responsibilities of which maintenance is only a modest part. Between the top and the bottom there may be little to spark new ideas or to stir up a new vitality.

If there are critics of the normal arrangements, they usually propose a separate Works department under a more senior and highly paid Works or Building Manager, with a direct labour organization. The merits of a separate Works department with its own head are discussed in the next chapter. Whatever these merits may be, they do not of themselves solve the basic problem of bringing enough thought to bear on the policy issues. The Works department is a contracting organization, and in many authorities it does no more than carry out the instructions of the client committees. It is not its function to question their policy on maintenance or to propose basic changes, though it may have practical suggestions to make. This poses the question of how to stimulate a more intensive examination of the problems of maintenance.

There can be no single answer to this question. Quite apart from the variations in departmental organization from one authority to another, a 'maintenance officer' in the sense visualized by Mr W. T. Jackson is not at present a likely figure in local government. His functions are too much divided between the Treasurer, Engineer, Architect and Works Manager and the client committees. If, however, maintenance efficiency is to be improved in the ways suggested in the rest of this chapter, thought must be given to these questions at a high enough level and intensively enough to produce results. This may mean having a more senior Building Manager, or seconding an architect or engineer for special investigations, or having a joint working party, to include the Treasurer's department, with a more effective voice in policy as well as execution. In every case it means thinking of maintenance in more dynamic terms, and of devoting more attention to the assumptions which underlie its day-to-day organization. Architects, engineers, accountants, works managers and administrators all have a contribution to offer, and methods must be found either under one officer, or collectively, for making this contribution effective. Even if in most authorities there is no 'maintenance officer', charged with responsibility for bringing client, architect and contracting organization into close contact, the same results must be found by other means.

Programming of Repairs and Maintenance

Maintenance involves three main types of operation: day-to-day repairs, painting and structural repairs and periodic maintenance. Of these three the last involves the main policy issues, and on it depends much of the long-term preservation and value of the property. The larger authorities with better financial resources and bigger staff can carry out sufficiently regular inspections to ensure that structural defects are discovered, that the case for repair is well presented and that resources are sufficient to meet both emergency and programmed works.

In the medium and smaller authorities it is not necessarily the case that all properties are inspected regularly for structural defects. Nor do the recommendations of the inspections carried out by a junior officer always carry sufficient weight. It appeared from the Institute's inquiry that long-term maintenance programmes and structural repairs were carried out unevenly as between one authority and another, and that where they were done personally by the Housing Manager, Surveyor or Architect the system worked much better. It is not, however, possible or desirable for senior staff in large departments to carry out such work personally. The problem is to designate staff for this work who are technically competent and able to impress their view of the need for maintenance work, as against other pressures. Without regular inspections it is impossible to preserve property in good repair and to avoid the oversight of what may be important but inconspicuous defects. Without knowledge of what renewals will be necessary over the next three to five years it is impossible to have a programme of work or a budget to pay for it.

With the proper planning of the structural repair of houses, schools and public buildings these can be kept in good condition indefinitely, and can be modernized, if so required, from generation to generation without necessitating major repairs to the basic fabric. It can be argued that school buildings would be better neglected and replaced. But the attractiveness of Tudor cottages and Georgian houses shows how long dwellings can last and how well they can be adapted to modern needs if the fabric has been properly preserved. The same arguments can apply to council housing, even if aesthetically there might not be the same enthusiasm for their preservation. It is in the national as well as the local interest that local authorities should preserve the value of their property.

Reserve Funds

Much of the success of maintenance depends on having the financial resources available to meet demands. Authorities are required to build up a repairs fund for housing. The statutory minimum contribution to the housing repairs account is £8 per dwelling per year but this is usually insufficient to cover expenditure, and in the year 1957–58 contributions ranged from £8 to £27 12s 0d for each house or flat.[1] The Reading committee also revealed that nearly half the authorities covered by

[1] *Councils and their Houses*, page 19.

the inquiry were spending more per dwelling on repairs than they were putting into their housing repairs accounts. Not only does this mean the gradual depletion of any balances in the account but it must discourage authorities from carrying out the repairs that they ought to be doing. A hand to mouth financial policy towards the housing repairs fund must militate against long-term programmes of structural repairs, such as re-tiling, re-painting, re-wiring and re-fencing. Day-to-day repairs, the need for which tenants are well aware, obtain first priority. If the repair fund is getting low, it is the structural repairs which may be put off and this will result in a general deterioration of the property.

There is no statutory provision for repair funds for other types of buildings such as schools. In such cases expenditure is met out of rates and budgeted for at the time of the annual estimates. Since the expenditure may not be required regularly year by year, it may be necessary to meet heavy expenses one year and little the next. In order to even out expenditure and avoid the deferment of necessary work, there is a good deal to be said for having a general repairs fund to even out claims. In any event, all departments should look several years ahead and programme their major schemes of maintenance. To do so has a salutary effect on all concerned and enables the maintenance organization to operate more efficiently. If there is a direct labour organization, this advance planning is particularly valuable, since continuity of employment for the labour force is specially important. Such programming can ensure an even flow of work.

Cost Control and Work Study

Cost control of maintenance operations is difficult to carry out satisfactorily because of the number of small operations, the variety of work and the difficulty of comparing like with like. This also makes comparisons with other authorities unreliable. Authorities have attempted to compare their own maintenance costs with those of other authorities only to find inconsistencies in standards of maintenance and the allocation of overheads between the authorities which invalidate the comparisons. Nevertheless it is extremely important that this matter should be pursued diligently in one way or another.

At present there is no uniform or even commonly used method

H

of cost analysis and control. The Building Research Station has carried out research into maintenance costs but has found it difficult to find comparable records of maintenance costs kept by local authorities. The Institute of Municipal Treasurers and Accountants is now working on the problems of standardized accounting systems and their findings could make the costing of maintenance more efficient.

Quite apart from cost control in the accounting sense there are the more human problems of management. The Girdwood Committee found that 73 per cent of the costs of maintaining houses was attributable to labour and 27 per cent to materials.[1] These figures illustrate the great importance of watching labour costs, and the economies which would result from savings for example in the travelling time of men out on small repair jobs or fetching materials. It is now practicable for authorities to carry out work studies for themselves. These are likely to have more immediate effects than attempts to control costs by cost analysis.

The Royal Institute of Public Administration is sponsoring a project of operational research into the methods of controlling the labour force engaged on repairs and it is hoped that the result will encourage local authorities to carry out similar studies. It is possible that quite small changes in organization and in the methods of briefing and routing individual craftsmen could effect considerable savings in time and therefore costs.

Capital Costs and Maintenance Costs

Maintenance costs are also affected by the type of construction and the quality of materials used at the outset. Good design and specification are fundamental for economic maintenance. Since the war local authorities have been up against serious difficulties in applying sound canons at the design stage and, as a result, maintenance costs of some of the post-war houses and schools are likely to be heavy in the future.

To some extent these repercussions on maintenance were inevitable. The succession of economic crises made it essential to limit capital expenditure and to share out the reduced total among the many claimants. If capital resources are limited, the nation must choose between quantity and quality: between

[1] *The Cost of House Maintenance*, H.M.S.O., 1953.

getting, for example, 300,000 houses a year of medium quality or 250,000 of better quality for the same capital sum. Similarly with schools: the ceiling cost per place could have been raised by lowering the number of places to be provided each year. During the years of most acute housing shortage, or when the school bulge was most serious, few people would have advocated the sacrifice of quantity for the benefits of quality. At the same time many hoped, unrealistically, for the best of both worlds, at least for that section of the economy in which they were most interested.

In the local authority sector the system worked through the control of capital expenditure by government departments. Since the objective of this control was to keep capital expenditure down both local authorities and departments looked primarily at the initial capital cost of each scheme and only secondarily at maintenance costs. In the nature of things the interests of subsequent maintenance suffered. Forced to economize on building costs, methods and materials were sometimes used which were inconsistent with good practice and local authorities are already suffering the consequences. As the result there is some criticism of government departments who are felt to have forced these economies on authorities in their efforts to limit capital costs, and some resentment because it is the authorities who will pay the price for the lowered standards of construction in the long run.

Many of the difficulties were inevitable, but they have been increased by three factors:

lack of sufficient cost planning and research at the design stage to ensure savings where they would be least damaging;

lack of sufficient knowledge and research on the repercussions of capital cuts of different kinds on subsequent maintenance costs;

lack of experience of non-traditional materials.

It has already been explained that the system for controlling the capital cost of most types of local authority building, and particularly housing, lends itself to last minute economies which

227

can adversely affect maintenance costs later on. The only way to reduce capital costs without such damaging results is to cost plan from the outset to a target figure safely within the limits the Ministry may be expected to approve. If this is done, pruning can be carried out at the beginning of the design stage and not at the end, and an authority can decide deliberately on the relative advantages of different types of construction and materials within the cost ceiling. This has been done for school building, and the beneficial results have been recognized. To ensure that maintenance is not jeopardized by last minute changes in specification, authorities must cost plan their designs from the start.

They would do so still more efficiently if more was known about economic design in relation to maintenance. The Building Research Station has done some valuable research on this, but its efforts have been handicapped by the difficulty of obtaining suitable quantitative data.

The effects on maintenance costs of economies in capital costs can be counteracted by a better understanding of what capital savings are least damaging from the maintenance point of view. For example, external painting and repairs to the water services are the two most expensive types of maintenance. Economies in capital expenditure which increase the need for painting work or plumbing repairs will have much more costly repercussions on maintenance costs than savings which might mean the slightly earlier renewal of heating, lighting or cooking equipment which becomes obsolescent in any case.[1] Conversely, the substitution of materials which require less painting or fewer plumbing repairs in place of those used at present will lower maintenance costs much more significantly than other kinds of substitution. An understanding of the relationship between capital and maintenance is particularly important when capital costs have to be pruned. The pruning should be done where it will have the least damaging effects on the lasting usefulness of the building and the need for costly maintenance. Much more investigation along the lines started by the Building Research Station is needed.

The shortages of steel and timber and other normal building

[1] W. J. Reiners. Maintenance and Economic Design, *Chartered Surveyor*, September 1955.

materials at the end of the war compelled the use of non-traditional materials. Rising costs in the 1950s encouraged the continuance of such experiments. At the same time architects attempted to introduce diversity in design by the use of new techniques and materials. There is, inevitably, a long time lag between the use of new materials or designs and the discovery of the maintenance problems associated with them. During a period of rapid change in building techniques there are bound to be difficulties in reconciling design and maintenance. Some mistakes must be accepted as the price of progress and the acquisition of new experience. Without such mistakes progress would be slow indeed.

This brief survey of some of the important issues involved in maintenance reveals how many large problems are outstanding and how much investigation needs to be done. The physical assets in the hands of the councils are so large and much of them of so uniform a character, that investigation into the problems related to the maintenance of, say, housing or schools should be of wide value and yield a rich return.

SUMMARY AND RECOMMENDATIONS

1.   Maintenance is much more important than its usually routine procedures bring out. Local authorities are responsible for very large capital assets in the buildings they own. The efficiency with which they carry out maintenance and repair can prolong the life of these buildings and thus reduce the need for replacement. It is in the national as well as local interest that the maintenance organization should be as effective as possible.

2. Elected members control maintenance at three levels; by decisions on broad matters of policy; by approving annual estimates; and, in some authorities, by Public Works committees which supervise direct labour organizations.

3.   At departmental level the organization of maintenance and the responsibility for it of chief officers is very varied. It depends on the size of the authority, the number of client departments, the existence of a separate Architect's department, and the size of the direct labour organization.

4.   In the urban and rural districts and the non-county boroughs it is most usual for the Engineer to be in charge of main-

tenance. In a number of the larger authorities the Housing Manager may have a separate maintenance organization. Less frequently there is a separate Works department.

5. Among the county boroughs there is a great variety of organization. The main variations are:

to leave building maintenance in the hands of the Engineer;

to hand it over to the Architect;

to set up a separate Works department to execute the requirements of the client departments, wholly or partly by direct labour;

to divide the responsibility between departments.

6. Among the county councils it is almost universal for the County Architect to be responsible for meeting the maintenance requirements of the client departments. One section of his department is usually devoted to the organization of maintenance, usually through private contractors. Very few counties employ direct labour on any scale, and the existence of a separate Works department is rarer still.

7. Each type of organization has its advantages and disadvantages, and there is no single solution which could suit all authorities, even of like kind and size. Variation depends on local circumstances, and the importance given by different authorities to the role of the Architect, Housing Manager and Works Manager.

8. The merits of keeping maintenance in the hands of the Engineer, where he also controls the architectural services, rest on:

the value of keeping architectural services and maintenance services in one department, so that experience on maintenance can easily be passed back to the architects;

the general familiarity of the Engineer's department with a direct labour organization, and the economies of common services, transport and depots.

230

9. The merits of keeping maintenance in the hands of the Architect when there is a separate Architect's department also rest on the advantages of keeping design and maintenance in close contact. These advantages, as with the Engineer, are real. Some authorities do not, however, regard responsibility for a direct labour organization as particularly suited to the Architect and prefer to separate the day-to-day execution of maintenance by direct labour from the architectural services. By this means the Architect can maintain his professional independence from those responsible for the execution of the work, and concentrate more effectively on design.

10. The merits of entrusting maintenance to the Housing Manager depend on the special relationship of landlord and tenant and the close knowledge of tenants' needs. The execution of this service by the Housing Manager is usually associated with the control of direct labour.

11. The maintenance of schools presents special problems also. These are not so easily met by a separate direct labour organization because of the peak work during holidays. Most Education departments who control maintenance make regular use of private contractors.

12. There are disadvantages, however, in dividing responsibility for maintenance between departments. A division means that the officer in each department actually responsible for maintenance is less well qualified than the head of a combined organization. He will have fewer experienced assistants and, if there is a direct labour organization, less specialized plant. Authorities must weigh the relative merits of each method.

13. Authorities which lay special stress on direct labour may set up a separate department. Others usually leave it as an integral part of an existing department. The two methods are described in the next chapter.

14. Because of the routine character of much maintenance work, authorities are inclined to leave effective control in the hands of officers who are not equipped to consider the longer-term issues. Authorities are urged either to employ more highly qualified staff, or to devise machinery for reviewing the more important aspects of maintenance regularly. Some of these are covered by the three recommendations below.

231

15. To ensure the economical and efficient organization of maintenance, authorities need to:

programme structural repairs and periodic maintenance on the basis of regular inspections of all property;

build up reserve funds for the maintenance of all types of building, so as to even out the financial burden and to avoid the postponement of necessary work;

keep a vigilant watch on costs, particularly those of labour, and to carry out work studies or operational research into methods of management.

16. Too little work has been done on the relationship between capital costs and maintenance costs. The Building Research Station has done some investigation, which needs to be extended and made better known. Authorities could also help themselves by cost planning their new buildings in such a way that savings in capital costs were imposed where these were least likely to increase maintenance costs later. As things now are, last minute cuts in capital costs are often made where they are likely to increase maintenance charges later on. This is a matter which would repay study by individual authorities.

CHAPTER 7

DIRECT LABOUR

Scale of direct labour operations for new building and maintenance—types of organization—examples of different types —main issues—Works committees—role and status of Building Manager—purchase of materials—plant—competitive tendering—working conditions—costs—experimental work—future trends.

So much prejudice and emotion surrounds the use of direct labour by local authorities that simple issues can become clouded and facts misunderstood during the course of political argument. This book is not concerned with the political issues. It is concerned with the methods used by local authorities in employing a direct labour force either for new building or for maintenance, and in assessing which of these various methods appear to give good results and at what points difficulties most frequently arise. It is not necessary to be either for or against direct labour to perceive that it is a method which works better in some situations than in others; that it carries with it certain valuable advantages and can also be faced with certain difficulties. This study has brought out a great deal of factual material that is full of interest. It has revealed below the political disputes on the surface a wide area of general agreement on the basic problems and objectives. It has also shown that valuable work is being done by direct labour through very widely different methods of organization. This chapter gives some account of these various methods.

THE SCALE OF OPERATIONS

Some comprehensive information is available from government departments about the scale of operations of direct labour in local authorities. The Ministry of Works has annual manpower statistics. The Ministry of Housing and Local Government has details about the number of dwellings under construction by local authorities. Most of the other material available is now somewhat out of date. The Building Research Station and the Institute of Municipal Engineers carried out surveys in 1952 which produced some information about the maintenance of housing by direct labour. The Amalgamated Union of Building Trade Workers also carried out a national survey at about the same time, which provided many useful facts, particularly about the organization of direct labour.

The inquiry of the Royal Institute of Public Administration covered a wider field than direct labour, and it was not found possible to collect full statistics on this aspect. Simple basic information was obtained from some forty authorities and this was supplemented by an intensive inquiry among sixteen of them, nine of which were visited.

TABLE 11

CONSTRUCTION

Number of operatives employed by local authorities on building work in Great Britain (Thousands)

	New housing	Other new work	Repair and maintenance Housing	Other	Total building work
1948	23	3	34	40	100
1949	23	2	35	41	101
1950	23	2	36	36	97
1951	22	2	34	33	91
1952	24	2	35	30	91
1953	25	2	36	30	93
1954	24	2	39	30	95
1955	22	2	40	30	94
1956	21	2	41	30	94
1957	20	2	44	30	96
1958	19	2	46	30	97

Note: Figures prior to 1955 are on a slightly different basis from subsequent years.
Source: Ministry of Works.

The national picture of the volume of building by direct labour in local authorities can be gathered from Table 11, which covers the years 1948 to 1958. Throughout this period the numbers employed on building in the nation as a whole were just under 1·1 million. The total numbers employed by local authorities on both new building and maintenance averaged 95,000, or nearly one-tenth of the total. This is a proportion of some importance.

Of the men employed directly by local authorities, between a quarter and a fifth have been employed on new building and the rest on repair and maintenance. Maintenance is the major activity. The numbers employed on housing maintenance have risen steadily since 1948, with the increase in houses built by local authorities. In the early years covered by the table some of the other repair work was for war damage which came to an end in about 1951. In recent years this figure has remained steady.

Almost all the new building undertaken by direct labour is housing, most of which has been two-storey houses. The decline in the number of men employed on new building since 1953 is the result of the general decline in house building by local authorities and of the fact that some of the authorities in and round London, who are among the strongest supporters of direct labour, have exhausted the supply of land for new building. House-building by direct labour has declined much less fast than the general decline in house-building by local authorities (compare Table 5 with Table 11). There is no evidence of any fall in interest in new building by direct labour. If anything the contrary seems to be the case. The inquiries of the Royal Institute of Public Administration showed a number of authorities which were expanding their organizations.

These national manpower figures can be filled out by additional information about housing.

The Ministry of Housing and Local Government's figures concern new housing only. They show that in April 1959 there were 137 local authorities building by direct labour. At that date they had nearly 14,000 dwellings under construction covering 465 schemes. Of these 137 authorities, forty-one were building by direct labour alone. The remaining ninety-six authorities had schemes under construction by private contractors in addition to their own direct labour schemes. These authorities varied from those where the majority of house building was by direct labour to others where most of it was built by private contractors. Fifty-four authorities had fifty or less houses under construction by direct labour. Thirty-nine had 100 or more under construction, of whom only fifteen had more than 200.

This building by direct labour must be set against the general picture for England and Wales. In April 1959 there were 117,000 dwellings under construction by local authorities. Thus, about one in eight of all houses under construction by local authorities was being built by direct labour. The great majority of housing was being undertaken by private contractors.

Figures similar to those collected by the Ministry of Housing and Local Government are not available for other types of new building by direct labour. As the manpower figures show, it is much less common for local authorities to erect other kinds of buildings by this method. A few authorities build schools, offices and so on, but quantitatively direct labour for new building other than housing is not significant. Qualitatively it can be of great interest, particularly as a demonstration that direct labour can be used effectively to build schools, offices, flatted factories and other buildings which are both more complicated structurally and not part of a routine programme of a highly traditional kind.

Investigations by the Institution of Municipal Engineers[1] and the Building Research Station[2] had shown that maintenance work by direct labour was widely spread among authorities. The replies to questionnaires revealed that about 90 per cent of the authorities used direct labour for all or part of their maintenance and repair work. These inquiries did not cover the county councils where the use of direct labour on any significant scale is exceptional. It is, however, clear that a high proportion of the borough and district authorities made some use of direct labour at that time. The inquiries of the Royal Institute of Public Administration did not suggest there had been any reduction in the number of authorities who employed labour for maintenance while the volume of work was increasing.

Additional information about the scale of direct labour organizations is available from the survey carried out by the Amalgamated Union of Building Trade Workers in 1953 and also early in 1954.[3] While the information collected by the

[1] Housing Maintenance—Information from Questionnaire to Local Authorities. *Journal of the Institution of Municipal Engineers*, 1953.

[2] W. J. Reiners. Maintenance Costs of Local Authorities. *Journal of the Institution of Municipal Engineers*, 1955.

[3] *Building by Direct Labour*, W. S. Hilton.

AUBTW is now rather out of date, it gives a useful general picture not otherwise available.

Of the 1,287 local authorities and development corporations which replied to the AUBTW questionnaire 661 had direct labour organizations. Of these 523 used direct labour for repairs and maintenance but not for new building, while 138 carried out both new building and maintenance wholly or partly by direct labour. These figures support the general picture of the widespread use of direct labour for maintenance and its much more limited use for new building.

The scale of operations is also important. Discussions about direct labour are inclined to give the impression of large organizations. The reverse is true. Out of 661 authorities, only 166 employed more than fifty men and this included only thirty-seven authorities who employed more than 250 men, and ten who employed more than 500 men. As against these figures, 431 authorities employed thirty men or less. Organizational problems are quite different for a force of twenty to thirty men than for one of 200 to 300. And they are also quite different for a county council with a team of twenty men used as shock troops for emergency repairs, or for a rural district which can carry out all its maintenance work with twenty men. Table 12 summarizes the replies given to the AUBTW inquiry on the size of direct labour organizations.

TABLE 12

SIZE OF DIRECT LABOUR ORGANIZATIONS

(a) Size of department according to operatives employed		(b) Number of departments	(c) Total number of men employed by departments in (b)
1—	10	259	1,411
11—	30	172	3,168
31—	50	64	2,437
51—	100	64	4,613
101—	250	65	10,844
251—	500	27	9,411
501—	800	4	2,191
801—	1,500	4	4,266
5,500—	6,500	2	11,867
Total		661	50,208

237

If the general picture is of a large number of small organizations it is fair to recognize that these employ only a minority of the men. According to Table 12 only a fifth of the manpower was to be found in the 560 authorities who employed 100 men or less. Four-fifths of the men were working for the 100 or so authorities who employed over 100 men.

Taking the direct labour situation as a whole, it is possible to summarize the general situation as follows:

direct labour for maintenance is far more widespread than new building, and employs far more men;

most of the direct labour organizations are small in size but the greater part of the manpower is to be found in authorities employing more than 100 men;

the concentration of effort on new building is on housing and most of this is two-storey houses;

only about forty authorities do all their new house building by direct labour; most of those who build by direct labour carry out only a proportion of their total programmes by this means;

few authorities build more than 200 houses a year by direct labour.

TYPES OF ORGANIZATION

In any discussion about organization authorities divide into two categories:

those that carry out both new building and maintenance by direct labour on a significant enough scale for both to be important;

those that do only maintenance by direct labour.

No authority has been found which uses direct labour only for new building. This is not likely to occur since the new building side generally grows out of the maintenance side and is supported by it. Exceptionally, as in Birmingham, the department carrying out new building is separate from the maintenance organization, but few if any other authorities have this arrangement and even in Birmingham this is about to be changed. Some of the direct labour organizations are of very long standing and date from a time when there was no party political argument concerning their use. West Ham first established its direct labour organization in 1893 and a number were started in the early 1920s. The motive for their introduction was often a dissatisfaction with the price or quality of work carried out by private contractors, particularly painting work, and a desire to attempt to carry out such work better and more economically, without any political overtones. For many years there has been a strong tradition in favour of maintenance by direct labour, and many of the organizations were set up when the Conservative party was in power.

Those authorities with an organization for new building fall into three groups:

the whole-hearted supporters of direct labour who aim to carry out all their schemes by this means;

those who use both methods regularly and fairly equally balanced;

those who use direct labour for only 10 per cent or 20 per cent of their work, either to carry out special kinds of schemes or because they wish to have this experience available in order to feel the pulse of the building industry and to give the direct labour organization the interest and stimulus that a maintenance organization on its own does not provide.

Those authorities with a maintenance organization only, subdivide into four groups:

the enthusiasts who aim to cover almost all maintenance by direct labour, using specialist contractors only for exceptional work;

those who aim to cover mainly day-to-day repairs, and use contractors regularly for much of the painting work and larger structural repairs;

those that give private contractors a fairly constant proportion of their work as a cross-check and stimulant to the direct labour organization and vice versa;

those that use direct labour only for emergency purposes, and otherwise depend on private contractors.

County Councils[1]

Among county councils the use of direct labour for new building is very rare and is the exception even for maintenance. Only a few county councils have built new schools by direct labour since the war, and only some sixteen have any direct labour organization for maintenance, and then usually on a modest scale. The area of a county makes the supervision of direct labour difficult and there is no simple traditional type of building, such as housing, on which a direct labour organization can be based. Even within the compact areas of the county boroughs the use of direct labour for other buildings is much less usual than for housing. It is, therefore, not surprising that only a few of the county councils have built up large direct labour organizations. In most of them both new building and maintenance is carried out by contractors under the supervision of the County Architect. Supervision of large jobs is by a Clerk of Works. Supervision of maintenance work is usually by Building Superintendents, located either centrally or on an area basis.

The inquiry covered two county councils with large direct labour organizations, Glamorgan and Derbyshire. These two authorities show interesting differences in organization, although in many ways they are similar in size and in the scope of the works organization. One has a separate Works department controlled by a Works Manager under the supervision of a Works committee. The other is controlled by the County Architect with no Works committee. The area organization also is different. The decentralization of the supervision of labour,

---

[1] Excluding the London County Council.

which is the main problem in a county area, shows a marked variation between the two authorities.

In *Glamorgan* (Pop. 743,000) the direct labour organization forms a part of the County Architect's department and is supervised by a Building Manager. There is a single direct labour organization of some 600 men employed both on maintenance and new building as the work demands. About one-fifth of the county's new capital building programme is carried out by direct labour totalling some £150,000 per year. The value of maintenance work carried out by direct labour is about £400,000 per annum. New work by direct labour is expanding and contracts are secured in competition with private contractors. This work has been mainly on school extensions, new fire stations and other smaller county buildings such as clinics and ambulance stations.

The organization is divided on an area basis among ten Works Superintendents, each with a force of thirty to eighty building operatives and each responsible for all maintenance within their area. When a new building scheme has been won in competition with private contractors, a general foreman on the direct labour staff undertakes the supervision of the erection of the new buildings, and he controls the operatives who may be transferred from maintenance work or specially recruited. Some 250 of the 600 men employed in the direct labour organization are on the established staff; a proportion are superannuable but temporary, and a proportion are casual.

There is no Works committee.

In *Derbyshire* (Pop. 724,000) the direct labour organization was separated from the Architect's department in 1954 and a new Works department set up. The head is the Works Department Manager, who is a chief officer. The Works department employs some 660 men, who carry out 95 per cent of all maintenance work to a total of some £290,000 a year and 10 per cent of the capital work to a total of about £260,000 a year. Capital work is confined mainly to extensions and adaptations to existing buildings and to police houses. Jobs costing up to £1,000 are undertaken by the Works department automatically. Above this figure work is secured by competitive tender. For convenience local contractors do a part of the minor repairs.

The control of the labour force is divided between three main

241

Diagram 10

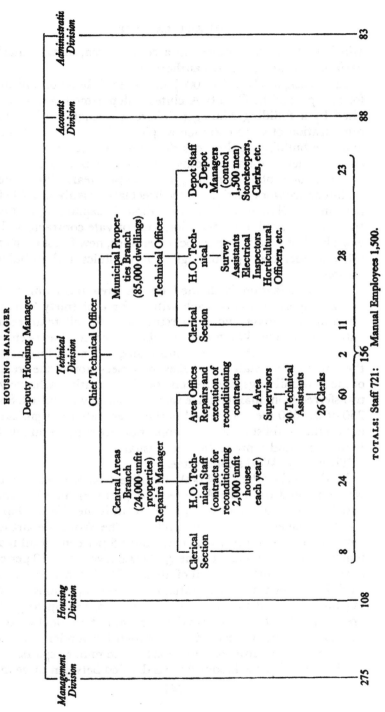

BIRMINGHAM

Housing Management Department

HOUSING MANAGER

Deputy Housing Manager

Management Division	*Housing Division*	*Technical Division*	*Accounts Division*	*Administrative Division*

Chief Technical Officer

Central Areas Branch (24,000 unfit properties) Repairs Manager

Municipal Properties Branch (85,000 dwellings) Technical Officer

Clerical Section — 8

H.O. Technical Staff (contracts for reconditioning 2,000 unfit houses each year) — 24

Area Offices Repairs and execution of reconditioning contracts
4 Area Supervisors
30 Technical Assistants
26 Clerks — 60

Clerical Section — 11

H.O. Technical
Survey Assistants
Electrical Inspectors
Horticultural Officers, etc. — 28

Depot Staff
5 Depot Managers (control 1,500 men) Storekeepers, Clerks, etc. — 23

275   108   2   156   88   83

TOTALS: Staff 721:   Manual Employees 1,500.

Note. New building by direct labour is carried out by a separate department.

depots and two sub-depots. As, however, distances between these depots are large and the whole of the southern half of the county is served from one depot, there is a further sub-division. Groups of men live in different parts of the rural areas so as to reduce travelling time. Supervision is carried out by area foremen sited at strategic points, each with his own van for the transport of materials and of men if necessary. There is thus operational control from the depots and some concentration of labour at these points, but also a considerable dispersal of both supervision and labour in different parts of the county. By agreement the men are paid weekly by cheque, which greatly simplifies the arrangements for wages.

The Works department is controlled by a Works committee, which meets generally every two months.

County Boroughs

The size and concentration of population in county boroughs makes them particularly well adapted for direct labour and it is not surprising to find that the use of direct labour is widespread among them. According to the figures supplied by the Ministry of Housing and Local Government some thirty-five boroughs were building houses by direct labour in 1959. However only two were building all their houses by this means and eight were building more by direct labour than by contract. The rest were building less, and many of these much less.

All the county boroughs covered by the Institute's inquiry carried out some or all of their maintenance by direct labour, and just over half did some of their new building in this way. Others were planning to expand the existing organization and to undertake more new building. One or two had recently reorganized their direct labour work, had created a separate Works department and were hoping to start some new building. Authorities regard the new building side of direct labour as a stimulus and a challenge. It may also enable them to attract a more able Building Manager. Thus while the overall volume of new building by local authorities both by contract and by direct labour had decreased there was evidence that interest in direct labour was increasing.

Among the county boroughs the organization of direct labour

243

is extremely diverse. The following examples give some indication of the variety:

In *Birmingham* the Housing Manager is responsible for all housing maintenance, and has a direct labour force of 1,500 men. Private contractors are used fairly freely in competition on the larger jobs and numbers of small contractors are also employed to assist the large programme for reconditioning older houses which have been acquired in the centre of the city. The direct labour organization for new building is a recent departure and has been set up as a separate department under a Works Manager of chief officer status. It is an expanding organization and is about to take over the maintenance of all buildings other than dwellings. Birmingham has the largest housing maintenance organization in the country with the exception of the London County Council. Diagram 10 shows the details.

In *Liverpool* the City Architect and Director of Housing is responsible for all housing maintenance with a force of 950 men. Apart from 25 per cent of the painting, which is carried out by private contractors because of its seasonal nature, all housing maintenance is carried out by direct labour. There is also a force of some 320 men employed on new housing. These are employed largely on the more difficult sites, particularly where site works make the costing and control of the contractor more complicated. The maintenance organization is controlled by a Maintenance Officer, who is an administrative not a technical officer, working under the Deputy Director of Housing. New building is controlled by the Chief Inspector of Works, who has building experience and works under the Deputy City Architect. The diagram shows clearly the division between the direct labour organization for new building, as an offshoot of design, and the maintenance organization as an offshoot of housing management. Maintenance of buildings other than housing is carried out by the City Engineer and Surveyor, and by certain departments with their own direct labour organization: these include Education and Parks, Water and Transport.

Diagram 11

LIVERPOOL

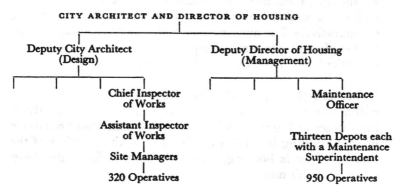

CITY ARCHITECT AND DIRECTOR OF HOUSING

Deputy City Architect (Design) — Deputy Director of Housing (Management)

Chief Inspector of Works — Maintenance Officer

Assistant Inspector of Works

Site Managers — Thirteen Depots each with a Maintenance Superintendent

320 Operatives — 950 Operatives

In *Leeds* the Works department is a separate organization under a Director of Works who is a chartered architect. He has a considerable technical staff, including a Deputy Director, who is also a chartered architect, quantity surveyors, architectural draughtsmen, building surveyors, heating and ventilating engineers, electrical engineers, painting inspectors and a demolition superintendent. The department also controls a large volume of work carried out by contractors as well as by direct labour. It is responsible for the maintenance work, alterations, adaptations and improvements to Corporation properties and has begun to undertake the erection of some municipal dwellings by direct labour. Approximately 40 per cent of the work controlled by the department is done by direct labour and some 630 persons are employed by the department's direct labour organization. The total annual turnover of the department, including the work carried out by direct labour, is approximately £1,500,000. The department has been in existence for twelve years and of late the direct labour force has been increasing.

These three large authorities each have different methods of controlling direct labour. Among the medium sized county boroughs the diversity is just as great.

In *Sunderland* (Pop. 185,000) a new Public Works department was set up in 1957 under a Public Works Manager who controls both civil engineering and building works. So far the direct labour force of 450 for building has been mainly used for maintenance, but the amount of new work is increasing and the organization is being extended. This is one of the comparatively few authorities which combine building and civil engineering in a single separate Works department, and is particularly interesting for this reason.

In *Swansea* (Pop. 163,000) the direct labour organization is within the Borough Architect's department, with a labour force of some 720 men. All maintenance and about one-sixth of new building is carried out by direct labour. Most of the new building is housing, but some schools have also been erected by this means.

In *Middlesbrough* (Pop. 152,000) the direct labour organization is a part of the Borough Engineer's department. Virtually all maintenance, except of schools, is carried out by direct labour with a force of 200 men. About one-fifth of new house building is constructed by direct labour with a force of some 90 men. Maintenance of education buildings is done by contract under the supervision of the Education department.

In *Preston* (Pop. 115,000) the whole of the maintenance organization is under the Borough Engineer with a force of 150 men. About a fifth of new house building is also carried out by direct labour under the control of the Engineer with a force of 80–100 men (Diagram 12).

In *St Helens* (Pop. 110,000) there is a separate Works department under a Building Manager who is a chief officer. Most of the maintenance work is carried out by a force of 150 men. The department is also responsible for a high proportion of the new building, including blocks of flats and the Technical College and has a labour force of 350 men employed on such work. This authority is unusual in having a much larger labour force on new building than on maintenance (Diagram 13).

These five authorities exemplify the wide variety of organization. Direct labour can be run by the Engineer, the Architect or

Diagram 12

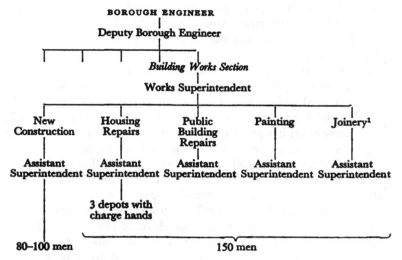

PRESTON

BOROUGH ENGINEER

Deputy Borough Engineer

Building Works Section

Works Superintendent

New Construction	Housing Repairs	Public Building Repairs	Painting	Joinery[1]
Assistant Superintendent	Assistant Superintendent	Assistant Superintendent	Assistant Superintendent	Assistant Superintendent

3 depots with charge hands

80–100 men   150 men

[1] Prepared joinery and wood machine shop

Diagram 13

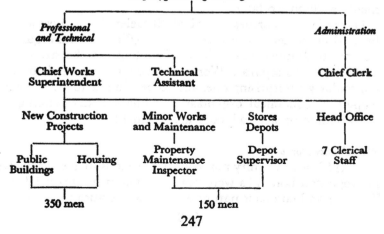

ST HELENS

BUILDING MANAGER

Deputy Building Manager

Professional and Technical   *Administration*

Chief Works Superintendent   Technical Assistant   Chief Clerk

New Construction Projects   Minor Works and Maintenance   Stores Depots   Head Office

Public Buildings   Housing   Property Maintenance Inspector   Depot Supervisor   7 Clerical Staff

350 men   150 men

247

in a separate department. It can cover the greater part of new building as well as maintenance, or it can include no new building at all. Preston is perhaps most typical of the medium, as well as the smaller authorities, who support direct labour but do not wish to have a large organization. Control here is in the hands of the Engineer.

Sunderland, with a combined organization for building and civil engineering in a separate Public Works department, is the most unusual. The experience of Sunderland deserves to be watched with special interest, since it is also one of the Works departments which most closely resembles private contractors and is in the most open competition with them. All works costing over £200 for building work and £1,500 for civil engineering work are publicly advertised and the Public Works department tenders competitively against contractors. As a result the volume of major work fluctuates, and the labour force fluctuates with it. Only about one-third of the labour force is superannuable in order to reduce overhead costs and give flexibility. This procedure is in marked contrast to that of many other authorities who carry out maintenance work with almost no competitive tendering and aim to keep a stable labour force. One of the aims of these arrangements, in Sunderland, is to maintain the normal professional relationship between the architect and the contractor. The Borough Architect advises committees, and, if necessary, will protect their interests and follow up their complaints as he would with a private contractor. The advantages and disadvantages of this kind of arrangement are discussed later.

Of the five authorities described, St Helens is the most wholehearted supporter of direct labour and its direct labour organization has built unusually ambitious buildings for the size of the authority. This separate Works department appeared to be a particularly enterprising one, and to be of a size to give enough scope for economical organization while still maintaining an individual approach to labour management.

Non-County Boroughs

In 1959 just over fifty non-county boroughs including twelve metropolitan boroughs were building houses by direct labour. The size and compact nature of these authorities make it easy to organize a direct labour force, and almost all the authorities which were covered by the Institute's inquiry carried out all or a large part of their day-to-day maintenance by this means.

While it is usual for the direct labour organization to be controlled by the Borough Engineer in the smaller authorities, among the larger authorities there is considerable diversity of practice, responsibility being sometimes divided or, more rarely, given to the Borough Architect or to a separate Works department. Enthusiasm for direct labour is particularly strong in and around London, and as there is a number of large non-county boroughs in this region, there is a particularly wide range of methods used by the metropolitan boroughs and the boroughs just outside the boundaries of the administrative county. The following examples show the diversity.

In *Ilford* (Pop. 179,000) the Borough Engineer controls the direct labour organization and the Building and Maintenance Superintendent is a member of his department. An average force of 100 men is employed on maintenance; none on new work.

In *Woolwich* (Pop. 149,000) virtually all maintenance and all new building is carried out by direct labour under the control of the Borough Engineer. The labour force numbers about 500, being divided equally between new building and maintenance. There is a Building Superintendent.

In *St Pancras* (Pop. 130,000) the Building Surveyor and Manager is a chief officer and runs a separate Works department with some 440 men, of whom 240 are employed on maintenance, 130 on conversions and seventy on new building (Diagram 14). The department has built tall blocks of flats, depots and other such buildings.

In *Edmonton* (Pop. 96,000) the Borough Architect is responsible for the direct labour organization, which carries out a great deal of new building. Some 300 men are employed on new building and 150 on maintenance, each under a Works Superintendent.

249

Diagram 14

ST PANCRAS

Building Department

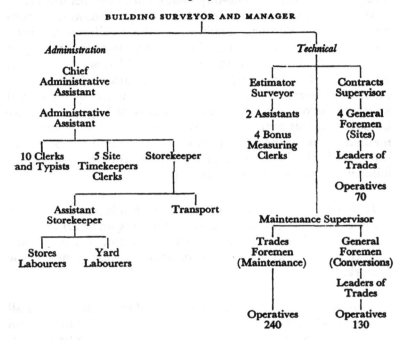

Of these authorities Ilford is typical of the great majority, who do not attempt new building by direct labour. The other three are authorities where there is great interest in direct labour, and a considerable programme of new building by this means. The size of the building programme does not give any clear guide as to whether the authority will choose to have a separate Works department or to combine it with the Architect's or Engineer's department. Support for direct labour has been communicated through different channels.

In St Pancras the Works department carries out virtually all maintenance by direct labour at a cost of some £160,000 a year, but new work, running at about £300,000 a year in 1959, is won by competitive tender and fluctuates considerably. In Woolwich the scale of operations is rather larger with maintenance running at some £180,000 and new building at some

£430,000 a year, but the direct labour organization is in the Engineer's department. There is almost no competitive tendering and all maintenance and new building is undertaken by the authority. The size of the labour force therefore remains very stable and offers the men a valuable security. Thus two similar metropolitan boroughs have very dissimilar organizations. The London area is rich in such variations.

District Councils

In 1959 some thirty urban districts were building houses by direct labour and twenty of these were building by direct labour only. During the same period fifteen rural districts were building houses with direct labour, of which five were using direct labour only. These figures show that only a small minority of district councils use direct labour for new building. It is of some interest that these figures are markedly lower than in 1957. The fall in output is due principally to the general decrease in house building by district authorities since the change in the subsidy arrangements in 1957, and the less pressing demand for council houses.

All or part of maintenance was carried out by direct labour in the districts covered by the inquiry of the Royal Institute of Public Administration, but it is understood that a number of the smaller authorities, particularly the rural districts, use local contractors, since the movement of men over wide areas is likely to be uneconomic for the volume of work undertaken.

In the vast majority of cases the direct labour organization forms a part of the Engineer's department. In a few authorities the Housing Manager is responsible for the execution of housing repairs; in still fewer, where there is a Chief Architect, he may be responsible for new building or maintenance by direct labour. More exceptional still, the authority may have a separate Works department under a Works Manager.

Chesterfield, one of the largest rural districts, has such an organization and the Public Works Manager, who is a chief officer, controls new building, maintenance and some civil engineering works. The authority carries out virtually all maintenance by direct labour, and about a fifth of its new building, most of this being housing. Annual expenditure on new housing built by direct labour is of the order of £150,000 a year. Diagram 15 is of especial interest because it shows how a direct labour force of moderate size can be organized as a separate department.

Diagram 15

CHESTERFIELD RURAL DISTRICT COUNCIL

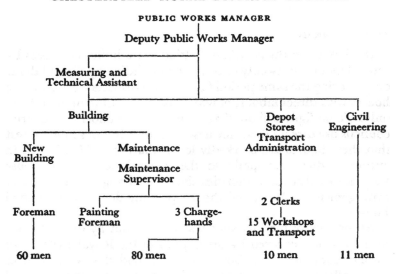

THE MAIN ISSUES

The discussions with local authorities and the information they provided centred on a number of issues of particular interest and importance. Most of the rest of this chapter is devoted to those issues. They cover:

the scope and responsibilities of Works committees;

the status and responsibilities of the Building Manager;

the methods used for the purchase of materials;

the purchase and control of plant;

competitive tendering;

the working conditions of the men;

costs;

experimental work and the general attitudes towards efficiency.

Since the authorities selected to supply detailed information were mainly those with considerable experience of and interest in direct labour the account is biased in their direction, and does not perhaps adequately reflect the views or experience of authorities which carry out maintenance on a more modest scale. Many of the problems are, however, common to them all, and it is hoped that the experience of the authorities which have done most by direct labour will be helpful to the rest.

Works Committees

Some reference has already been made in Chapters 3 and 6 to the place that Works committees occupy among the other committees of a local authority. It was also explained that the existence of an active direct labour organization does not always mean that there is a Works committee. Some large organizations are run by the Engineer or Architect without any regular oversight by a committee charged with special responsibilities to this end. Where, however, there is a separate Works department there is usually a Works committee.

Most of these committees are responsible solely for the direct labour organization and act as the contractors to the client departments. But occasionally their functions are combined with others, such as the control of central purchase of supplies for all the departments of the council. And where the direct labour department controls both civil engineering and building the Public Works committee will also have a dual responsibility. Usually the Works committee is not regarded as one of the senior committees, and it may be deliberately kept apart to maintain its status as a separate contracting organization. A few authorities have given it, or attempted to give it, a more dominant position.

253

This has been done by planning its meetings immediately before those of the Finance committee and after the other committees in the monthly cycle of meetings and by giving it responsibilities for dealing with programmes and building priorities. The attempt has not, however, always been successful since the service committees or the Finance committee may not be prepared to accept the Works committee's authority.

The main business of the Works committee centres on the management of the direct labour organization, and the agenda usually covers routine matters such as a progress report on work going on and numbers employed, the acceptance into the council's superannuation scheme of manual employees who have completed the qualifying period, acceptance of apprentices, individual problems on sick pay or holidays, approval of tenders for supplies and plant, and retrospective sanctions of purchases made by the Works Manager. From time to time more important issues will be raised concerning policy on competitive tendering, types of contract, the methods of calculating and allocating overhead costs or the broad strategy on increasing or decreasing the strength of the department.

Apart from the overall questions of policy it will be seen that the routine work of the committee is not onerous. This can raise problems, since if a committee has not enough appropriate business it may concern itself with the inappropriate and be too ready to interfere with the internal work of the department. It is important that this should not happen, and above all that the head of the Works organization should be free to take on or dismiss staff according to the requirements of the work and to take advantage of favourable market conditions for buying.

Authorities overcome the danger of having too little business in various ways. Responsibilities for central purchase of supplies, or for civil engineering works as well as building may increase the area of the committee's business and overcome the problem of surplus energy in this way. Elsewhere, meetings may be held every two months instead of monthly or be dovetailed with a later committee so that time for discussion is limited. Any authority which has a Works committee or is contemplating one must beware the pitfalls of excessive interference in a department which should be run very much as a business concern in competition with other businesses. Above all it should avoid interference in the day-to-day management of labour. This may mean a careful timing and organization of committee meetings.

One of the problems of a direct labour organization, and particularly of one doing much new building, is to separate it from the normal procedures of local government while yet keeping proper control over its operators. The normal standing orders of committees are geared to very different circumstances, and they can be unduly restrictive when it comes to an organization which is competing directly or indirectly with business under private enterprise. Many authorities allow their senior officers a very limited discretion in spending money or appointing staff. These restrictions become more than ever unsuitable for the conduct of large building contracts.

Advocates of a separate Works committee argue that because it is in closer contact with the problems of the Works organization, it is more likely to insist on standing orders which are liberal or to interpret them more liberally than a committee only remotely connected with the work of the department. This may be so. Unfortunately, the converse is also true. Close contact can beget too close control.

The Building Manager

The decision on whether to have a separate Works department with its own head is an important question of policy. The decision rests partly on the keenness of an authority's interest in direct labour and partly on the size of the organization and the possibilities of combining control of direct labour with the other responsibilities of the Engineer, Architect or Housing Manager. There is no conformity whatever among authorities on this question. Authorities differ according to no criteria of size, volume of work, or balance between new building or maintenance. Each decision appears to be entirely individual. The most that could be said is that authorities with large direct labour programmes including new building are more inclined to have a Building Manager in charge of a separate department.

Building Managers who are heads of departments are however a small minority. The AUBTW inquiry showed that in 1953 only thirty-three Building Managers were 'in complete control of the building section' out of a total of 661 authorities,

255

as against forty-one Architects, 450 Engineers and Surveyors and sixty-five Housing Managers. The remaining authorities had arrangements too diverse to be classifiable. More Architects, Housing Managers and Building Managers have been appointed as heads of departments since that time and the picture must have altered especially in the authorities with large direct labour organizations. It cannot, however, have altered a great deal.

Some of the arguments for and against separating the execution of maintenance from other departments have already been discussed in the preceding chapter. There is no overwhelming balance of advantage in any one system. The only clear lesson to emerge from the Institute's inquiry was the importance of placing the executive control of maintenance by direct labour in competent enough hands. This might call for a more senior appointment, or a separate department.

Because of the variation in responsibilities given to Building Managers there is no nationally negotiated scale and authorities pay very different rates. Exceptionally, as in London, Birmingham and Leeds, the Director of Works or General Manager receives a salary of between £2,000 and £2,500 p.a. Other heads of large departments covered by the inquiry receive from £1,500 to £2,000 p.a. In most of the authorities where the Building Manager works within another department, they are graded at A.P.T. II to A.P.T. V even if they are running quite large organizations.

Some of the salaries seem out of proportion to the responsibilities which the Building Managers ought to be shouldering. The lower salaries are justified by authorities on the ground that the Building Manager is buttressed by specialist staff; by architects, engineers and quantity surveyors, so that there is not the same need to recruit so experienced or well qualified a man. In cases of difficulty, it is argued, the Building Manager can seek the advice of the experts and final responsibility rests with his senior officers. Low salaries are also found where the Building Manager is a promoted craftsman with long service but without professional qualifications. Most authorities consider that they cannot interfere with the relative salary levels of qualified and unqualified staff. Furthermore, professional qualifications are frequently not expected by authorities so that the salary levels may be a rough and ready balance between low expectations and faithful but unambitious service.

While every authority must find its own solution to its particular problems, and no one would suggest that every modest direct labour organization should have its own separate departmental head, there is here a problem basic to the building industry as a whole as well as to local authorities. Local authority organization is merely a particular manifestation of a nation-wide attitude which underestimates the importance of building organization and the possibilities of improvement. As is argued later in this chapter direct labour has not realized some of its potentialities. Part of the difficulty is that a number of local authorities do not appreciate the contribution that a good Building Manager can make to efficiency, and tend to underestimate the costs they incur and the opportunities they waste by failing to attract more able men.

The causes of their failure are easy to understand. The growth of the direct labour organization has often been slow, graduating from small scale to larger scale maintenance, to adaptations and perhaps finally to new building. Sometimes the same man has graduated with the organization and has a wealth of experience but a limited outlook towards new development. The building industry is highly traditional and its productivity has risen very slowly. It is not, therefore, difficult for a local authority's maintenance organization to be as efficient or more efficient than local contractors without itself producing a very brilliant performance.

The situation is similar with new building. Most of the new building by local authorities is of two-storey houses, where the small and medium sized contractor has a firm foothold and much experience. Many authorities only aspire to do marginally better than such contractors. It can be argued that this is all that is needed. But the inquiry revealed possibilities which were being neglected. One reason for this was the relatively low standing of many Building Managers. This would have been improved by attracting a more able man and, where the direct labour organization was large enough, by creating a separate department. There are many Engineers and Architects who are deeply interested in the operations of direct labour and are keenly involved in its problems. But it must be one of many preoccupations. Neither professional training nor their many other responsibilities normally give them the opportunity to become expert in direct labour organization, and for this they must rely on the Building Manager. If he is on a low grade he is not likely to be a strong support.

A willingness on the part of the Architect or Engineer to give the Building Manager wide discretion cannot alter the real responsibility of the chief officer, or give to the Building Manager so great a freedom to engage or dismiss staff or buy materials. Building Managers emphasized the importance of having this freedom to the limit that the Council would permit. Conversely Architects, Engineers and Housing Managers stressed the advantages of combined departments with greater economy of administration and closer links between the professional staff and the Building Manager.

This is not a matter on which anyone can be dogmatic, but in general the inquiry suggested that except in the largest authorities where the Building Manager runs what is tantamount to a department within a department and may be paid accordingly, there was scope for improving the status, salaries and departmental responsibilities of Building Managers and for encouraging thereby a more energetic pursuit of new ideas and new methods.

Purchase of Materials

The buying of materials for maintenance work has to meet demands very different from those for new work. Most of the materials for maintenance are in more or less predictable demand from year to year. Some of them can be ordered in bulk at regular intervals, such as cement, sand, lime, slates, tiles, paint, nails and similar materials. Others, while in equally steady demand, are wanted in great variety and in small quantities, to suit the pattern of door furniture, fireplaces, window frames or sanitary fittings of a particular group of houses or a particular school. Unless the authority has imposed a high degree of standardization the variety of minor items needed for repair and replacement can be very high. Policy decisions on the purchase of materials for maintenance work revolve mainly round the advantages or disadvantages of annual contracts and bulk purchase, and the use to be made of builders' merchants

258

with their facilities for handling stocks as against the storage of a wide variety of small items in the authority's depots.

New building requires a different organization. Many materials are required in larger quantities, within a shorter period, in different proportions, and delivery can be made in bulk to the site without passing through the hands of the authority's or the builders' merchant's depot. The arrangements for ordering bricks by the hundred thousand and standards of timber or washhand basins by the hundred are quite different from ordering supplies for the replacement of small quantities of brickwork, the occasional broken basin or the dry-rotted floor. Tendering procedure, storage and delivery should be adapted to these different demands.

The arrangements for the purchase of materials vary between one authority and another most clearly on the following four main points:

purchase by a central buying department;

bulk purchase and annual tenders;

the use of manufacturers or builders' merchants;

the discretion given to the Building Manager;

Only a few of the authorities included in the inquiry obtained much of their building supplies through a central purchasing department, although two were currently considering the introduction of such an arrangement. Several authorities had central purchasing arrangements for other supplies but excluded the building organization from these arrangements. They considered a central purchasing department was too remote to control the buying of building materials. For these a more detailed knowledge of quality, of the possibilities of substituting one material for another and the need to change buying policy in the light of current market conditions made it important for the Building Manager to exercise his special knowledge and to make quick decisions.

There is scope here for differences of view, but it is fair to say that the purchase of many kinds of building material requires a

259

greater expertize than the buying of some of the other stores required by authorities, such as pencils, school exercise books, towels, soap or stationery. Building departments have a better case for retaining control of the purchase of many building materials than some other departments have in respect of their own particular requirements, since it is unlikely that the central supplies department can be staffed by officers with experience of building materials comparable with that of the Building Manager. In any case, the central purchase of building materials did not appear to be a lively issue in many authorities and its advantages too disputed to make a clear case for centralization.

A number of authorities also considered annual contracts to be too inflexible except for such things as sand, gravel and cement, and preferred to buy when supplies were required or buying conditions were favourable. Emphasis was laid again and again on the importance of taking advantage of the market and for the arrangements for purchase to have all possible flexibility. This applied particularly to supplies for new building, but could also apply when the building department needed to buy piping, timber and other materials for repairs when market conditions looked favourable or a consignment had recently arrived at a local port or a local merchant was anxious for a quick sale. Annual tenders and bulk purchase in advance of demand were regarded as having a theoretical advantage, not justified in practice.

The possibilities and advantages of purchase direct from manufacturers or from builders' merchants in the district depend on local circumstances and the particular material. The size of the orders placed affects the willingness of manufacturers to supply direct at favourable prices, while for some materials the control of prices is much tighter than for others and the manufacturer may not be prepared to give a more favourable price concession than that obtainable from builders' merchants or may even quote a higher price. The builders' merchants may be so eager to obtain the council's custom that they offer very attractive discount rates.

The advantages of obtaining supplies from manufacturer or merchant also depends on questions of storage. The builders' merchant maintains supplies on call by the customer and in certain circumstances it may be more economical for authorities to leave the costs of keeping stocks to the merchant rather than incur storekeeping costs themselves. This applies particularly to small authorities and to supplies used only in small quantities. Authorities are liable to underestimate the costs of storage on their own premises.

Building Managers need as much discretion as possible in buying supplies and accepting quotations so that work need not be delayed or favourable terms lost. Sometimes this discretion appeared to be unduly limited even when formal standing orders are overcome by informal means, such as the practice of getting the chairman's sanction between meetings of committees.

The differences are so wide that there is clearly scope for allowing the more restrictive practices to approach the less restrictive. One city gives the Architect authority to approve expenditure up to £1,000 on non-recurring items and over £1,000 on recurring items, if the transactions are recorded in the requisition book. This is available for inspection at committee meetings. A medium sized borough with similar confidence in its Building Manager allows him a very free hand so that he can operate like a contractor, and place orders for all materials except those bought by competitive tenders which, as legal documents, require committee approval. Orders placed by the Manager are ratified subsequently by the committee, but the Manager feels that he has all the freedom he requires.

Other authorities expect the Building Manager, even when he is a chief officer and in charge of a large organization, to obtain the chairman's approval for every purchase over £50. While this can be a simple matter of a telephone call, it is hardly consistent with paying an officer nearly £2,000 a year, and would be considered ridiculous in private industry. Authorities should have the courage of their convictions and, if they support direct labour and make claims for its superiority over private enterprise, they should permit their own officers sufficient freedom to operate efficiently.

Plant

The need for plant for a direct labour organization which is mainly responsible for maintenance is again quite different from that which carries out much new building. The difference is still more marked if the authority is building numbers of flats. Plant for maintenance of two-storey housing is usually of modest proportions, and provided it is obtained only for average requirements does not present much difficulty. The most expensive item is likely to be transport, mostly of materials but sometimes of men. Sunderland reported great savings in transport costs when vehicles run by the civil engineering and building sections were merged into a single Public Works department. Transport is a particularly heavy item for a direct labour organization in a county or rural district. Even when great efforts are made to locate men at strategic points, much higher transport charges are involved than in a town.

For new building most authorities own the smaller plant: compressors, mixers, dumpers, scaffolding, and usually borrow pumps from the Engineer's department. Heavy plant such as excavators, scrapers, cranes, tubular scaffolding in quantity is usually hired, since demand for these is not continuous. There is, however, no hard and fast dividing line, and each authority makes its own assessment of needs. There are at least two London boroughs building flats which own rail mounted tower cranes.

The merits of hire or purchase depend partly on how easily plant can be hired locally. Chesterfield in an area of open cast mining can hire scrapers and excavators locally at favourable rates. Others may find hire so expensive as to tip the balance in favour of ownership at a different point. The quantity of plant required also depends on the efficiency of its control. For this the authority must weigh in the balance the administrative costs of a system of close accounting as against inadequate incentives for economical use. One authority which had recently introduced a more rigorous costing system, which attributed the cost of plant more accurately to the schemes where it was being used, discovered a striking improvement in turn round. Foremen became eager to return idle plant to the depot to avoid the plant being charged to their scheme. This made possible a more effective use of equipment, which could be re-issued to another job more quickly.

The method of accounting for the use of plant can also affect policy on its purchase. If plant is charged at so much an hour for the duration of its use on a particular job not only will it be used more economically, but there will be a more accurate method of comparing the costs of ownership and of hire. Many authorities appear to be able to charge expensive plant on an hourly basis to particular jobs without it involving excessive clerical work. There seems no reason why all should not be able to do this.

Competitive Tendering

Many authorities do virtually all maintenance work by direct labour, and use contractors only for specialist work. With this arrangement there is no competition.

Even outside the circle of 100 per cent support for direct labour it is unusual for authorities to give much of their day-to-day repairs to contractors, if they have any direct labour organization. Supervision of the contractor on this kind of work is difficult and the possibilities of poor workmanship and materials are greater. Day work rates are common for this class of work and this makes control of the contractors' costs still more difficult. It is widely felt that direct labour is particularly well adapted to day-to-day repairs, especially for houses, and that the kind of repair service which local authorities are looked to to provide makes it more satisfactory to carry it out by men employed directly by the council. A council is expected to carry out emergency repairs, at night, in times of severe frosts or other crisis with a promptness which private owners or tenants would not expect. This, the importance of handling tenants with understanding and tact, and the difficulty of supervising private contractors on small jobs makes the use of direct labour for day-to-day repairs particularly advantageous.

These arrangements normally exclude the possibility of comparisons of costs by competitive tendering. Authorities must depend on the efficient control of labour, work study and other such methods to keep costs down.

Many other authorities use contractors on seasonal work to cover part of their painting programmes or for schemes of reconditioning or structural repairs for which prices can be controlled by competitive tenders. The supervision of this is easier. The authority's own organization may compete for this work. Even if it does not, the use of these contractors gives a yardstick by which to measure the costs of similar work carried out by the authority's own organization and helps to keep the load of work within the department more even.

Some authorities graduate their maintenance work so that there is competition on the large maintenance jobs but none on the smaller. The cost figures which regulate this system vary greatly. One authority gives the Building Manager freedom to proceed with all jobs costing less than £50. Quotations have to be obtained for jobs from £50 to £200 and the department only secures the job if its estimate is lower than the quotation. Over £200 all work is allotted by competitive tender, the Works department competing with contractors. Another authority arranges that all jobs costing less than £250 go straight to the Works department. For jobs costing £250 to £2,000 the Building Manager submits estimates to the client committee, which can ask for the estimate to be tested in competition if it thinks fit. Over £2,000 the Works department has to submit tenders in competition with contractors.

In their practice in using competitive tendering for new building, authorities divide into three groups:

> those which do almost all their new building by direct labour, and hardly use competitive tendering at all;

> those that build a proportion, perhaps a fifth or a sixth, of all new building by direct labour, but do not tender competitively for this proportion;

> those which secure some or all of their schemes by competitive tendering.

The first group of authorities is fairly small in number but it contains some of the authorities whose work is best known and who have been building for many years. Many of these authorities take a great pride in their organization and are anxious to use direct labour to the limit of the possibilities open to them. All schemes are built by this means and cost comparisons are based indirectly on the work of other authorities or on the approval of estimates by the Ministry. It is argued that if the cost of a scheme is approved by the Ministry, it must compare favourably with schemes approved and built by other authori-

264

ties by competitive tender. The onus for judging costs thus rests on the Ministry.

The second group represents the majority of authorities using direct labour for new building. These carry out a proportion of their work by contract and are familiar with the general level of costs through contractors' tenders. They consider that this experience gives them a sound basis of comparison for judging the costs of their own schemes, even though they do not compete against contractors for these. If the final costs of direct labour schemes work out about the same as those built by contractors, this is deemed to be a reasonable yardstick on costs and tendering in competition with contractors to be unnecessary.

The third group contains authorities who reserve to themselves only a proportion of their programme to be built by direct labour without competition. This is done to secure an even flow of work. Beyond this minimum programme of say 200 to 300 houses a year carried out by direct labour without competition, these authorities are prepared to undertake further schemes if the Works department is successful in competition with private contractors.

This group also contains a small but interesting minority. The inquiry covered a few authorities who reckoned to secure a fairly steady proportion of each year's annual programme in open competition with contractors and allowed themselves no schemes protected from competition. The Works departments of these authorities correspond more nearly than those of other authorities to the contractor's organization. The turnover of labour is higher, the number of superannuated employees is smaller and the Building Manager takes on or dismisses staff more freely according to the volume of the work. Such an organization is in conspicuous contrast to that of authorities who attempt to maintain a labour force of constant size, and to regulate the building programme to keep an even flow of work.

The differences in attitude between these groups is important. Most authorities lay great stress on continuity of work and therefore of employment for their workers, security being for the men a counter attraction to the higher wages which may be offered elsewhere. Their greatest objection to competitive tendering is the threat to this continuity on which labour management and control of overheads is based. The loss of a contract of fifty houses to an organization geared to building 200 houses a year can be serious, if, as with a local authority, there is no other outlet for work. It is, therefore, the more interesting that a few authorities appear to be able to survive the cold world of competition.

The question of competitive tendering raises important issues and touches some of the root problems of a direct labour organization. A local authority is limited to its own schemes and the Works department cannot turn to another client for work if its own building programme falls short. Nor does it operate with a profit and loss account so that it can make a loss on one scheme and recoup it on the next. Estimates may be permitted to be out by a small margin, but the Works department cannot underbid when it is short of work and recover profits later when work is more plentiful. It has, therefore, less room for manoeuvre and is much more dependent on an even flow of work from its own authority. It was for this reason that an icy wind blew down the corridors of many Works departments when the Ministry of Housing sent out a letter in January 1958 stating that

The Minister will as a rule need to be satisfied that the estimate submitted . . . is the lowest price received by the Council after the contract has been offered for competitive tender.

Since it was a period when tender prices were falling and contractors were anxious for work, authorities were apprehensive lest the planned flow of new work by the Works department should be disorganized by competition with contractors who would be willing to reduce their profit margins temporarily to secure contracts.

In practice the wind proved less chilling than was expected. Authorities were not obliged by the Ministry to compete on all their contracts, but only to test the market now and then. And they were reassured to find that, with this limited competition, they did not fare too badly, and that their organizations were not disrupted. It can hardly be doubted that the Ministry's action served a useful purpose. While the special circumstances of local authorities make it important for them to carry out a steady proportion of their building work themselves, the need to face open competition from time to time must be a stimulus to a more rigorous scrutiny of costs and a reassurance to critics and supporters alike that there is no feather-bedding. In view of the hypersensitiveness of the supporters of direct labour and the hypercritical attitude of the opponents it is valuable to all concerned to have as much objective evidence of efficiency as possible. This is a subject on which there is far too much unsupported prejudice on both sides. Competitive tendering for at least part of maintenance and new building is much the easiest way to check costs, to compare efficiency and to reassure the anxious.

Working Conditions

Next to competitive tendering the working conditions of a direct labour force raise the most complicated and controversial problems and place local authorities at the greatest disadvantage *vis-à-vis* the private contractor.

Local authorities have set themselves the task of being model employers and have negotiated terms and conditions of service on a national basis for their manual workers which include superannuation, holidays with pay and sickness benefits. These are negotiated for the benefit of the large and miscellaneous body of workers who carry out the manual work of local authorities, and not specifically for building trade workers. The building trade in the past has been well known for its casual employment, insecurity and loose welfare arrangements. Local authorities have attempted to improve these conditions and to offer their building workers security, pension rights and sick pay as they do to their other employees.

These admirable intentions, which set an excellent example to the building industry, come up against considerable difficulties when local authorities are employing people outside the more protected occupations in local government. Few local authority services have to compete with comparable activities outside and the costs of superannuation and other benefits are normally borne by ratepayers without the burden being clearly visible. These benefits applied to building workers in the direct labour department are met directly out of the costs of the building schemes, and are included in the estimates, in the same way as any other overheads are included by a private contractor in

267

his tender price. Fortunately for building workers generally, and Works departments in particular, private contractors now usually offer a minimum guaranteed week and more and more are offering holidays with pay. But sickness benefits and superannuation are still extra charges borne by local authorities which are not generally carried by private contractors.

The working conditions of a local authority building trade worker usually include:

a guaranteed week of forty-four hours;

sick pay—six weeks after six months' service, and thirteen weeks after a year's service;

two weeks' paid holiday after a year's service, and pro rata for shorter service;

superannuation after a qualifying period of a length varying with different authorities.

In addition local authorities pay the standard, nationally agreed, minimum rates of pay applicable to all building trade workers, but not the higher rates often offered by private contractors. They can however usually offer good prospects of permanent employment as a counter attraction. Bonus arrangements vary from authority to authority and are discussed later.

The extra benefits of superannuation and sick pay add considerably to costs. Authorities vary in their estimates of the amount. Some calculate that they increase labour costs by 3–5 per cent. Others estimate that superannuation alone adds as much as 5 per cent and sick pay 6–7 per cent. A number of authorities gave the extra costs of these benefits as between 7 per cent and 13 per cent. Such an addition to labour costs compared with the private contractor is a formidable handicap, and a Works department must be very much on its toes to compete successfully with private contractors, even when it is not attempting to make any profit.

To limit these special overheads authorities have various ways of restricting entry to the superannuation schemes. The qualifying period varies among authorities from six months to three years. Some authorities admit all workers, subject to age and medical fitness, when the qualifying period is over. These usually have the highest labour costs. Others restrict the numbers, who may be on superannuation at any one time, to a fixed number or proportion. These authorities consider that unrestricted entry into the superannuation scheme would make the direct labour organization uneconomic. By restricting entry they reduce their overheads. Nor must it be supposed that all workers welcome superannuation and the deductions in wages it brings. Authorities reported that some workers could be counted on to leave the authority's employment just before they had completed the qualifying period.

Authorities take different lines on the size of the casual or temporary fringe of workers. Some plan to build up a fairly steady force of regular workers and regret the turnover of temporaries. Others aim at a smaller permanent force and reckon to have a high turnover of temporary employees for new work. Continuity of work is more important to the former than the latter, though for both there are other overheads not directly associated with labour which act as a powerful inducement to keep the level of the work steady. For maintenance this is fairly easy since the volume of work is within the authority's control. For new building, changes in Government policy and the uncertainties of competitive tendering offer a less stable foundation.

Incentive bonus schemes are varied and complicated. They were not investigated in detail in the course of the Institute's inquiry but the following findings confirm other information which has been published. Most authorities now appear to use some sort of bonus scheme for new work. Some do so because they wish to provide an incentive and find it a satisfactory method for increasing output and reducing costs. Others regard it as a tiresome complication, necessary only as a means of attracting workers who would otherwise earn more with private employers. A few reject bonuses altogether as a wrong stimulus, liable to produce work of lower quality. Most schemes seemed well established.

Incentive bonus schemes for maintenance workers present far more difficulties. Supervision of individual men working on small jobs is hard, and the jobs themselves are so variable as to

269

make a standard of measurement of doubtful value. Some authorities have declined to introduce such a scheme, and if they do little new building and are in an area where competition for labour is not very keen they may find it unnecessary to do so. Others report dissatisfaction among the men if there is no such arrangement.

The advantages of a bonus scheme for maintenance are greatest when an authority carries out both new building and maintenance by direct labour. To secure continuity of employment it is important to be able to switch men from one to the other as circumstances demand. This is essential if new work is secured only competitively. If there is no incentive bonus for maintenance work and earnings are lower the switch from new building to maintenance, even if only for a short period, is unpopular. Several authorities reported difficulties on this score. Others claimed that the success of a direct labour organization depended on being able to switch men freely from new building to maintenance and back again, and that the incentive bonus scheme must therefore cover both.

Opinions varied so much about the advantages and complications of bonus schemes that it appears that much more investigation and knowledge is required. If one authority can find a simple and easy system which works it is difficult to understand why others should find the problems insuperable. It would be beneficial if there were a greater exchange of information on this subject to overcome anxieties and to encourage the introduction of simpler methods.

Incentive bonus schemes increase the need for good management, and they may not be suited to the older type of worker who prefers the steadier if less remunerative tempo of work on day-to-day repairs. For new work they provide a much needed stimulus to higher output. If the authority depends on an interchange of men between new work and maintenance, it seems difficult to avoid some bonus arrangement for maintenance as a device for softening the drop in earnings which transfer to maintenance work otherwise entails. St Pancras has overcome this difficulty by having an incentive bonus scheme for all new works and for maintenance jobs large enough to require a separate estimate. This gives enough flexibility for transferring men from new work to the larger maintenance jobs without involving the complications of a bonus for day-to-day repairs. The Building Manager put the position plainly:

> Bonus schemes are essential for new work and large maintenance jobs if you want to attract the right kind of labour. The scheme must be simple and easy to understand. Bonus payments should be paid as soon as possible, preferably the week following the period when the work is carried out. Establish good faith with the operatives and do not try to amend targets once they have been agreed.

This authority competes successfully with contractors for many types of new building including blocks of flats, as well on the larger maintenance jobs.

By setting themselves the objective of being model employers the local authorities largely cancel out the competitive advantage of operating without a profit. They have introduced direct labour for a variety of reasons, but one of them is to 'save' the private contractor's profits. In most cases these savings appear to be absorbed by the additional cost of more generous working conditions. Several authorities accepted the position that the extra labour costs were about equivalent to the contractor's profit and that there was little immediate price advantage to be derived from direct labour. They were equally convinced that the quality of work by direct labour was superior, particularly on maintenance, and brought valuable economies in the long run.

Costs

Any discussion of costs comes up against the difficulty that so little firm information is available. Authorities were asked if they could provide any figures which compared the cost of new building or maintenance with work carried out by private contractors. Very few were able to do so, partly because such information as they had was not kept in a form which made systematic comparisons possible, and partly because where there is no competitive tendering or comparative quotations no firm comparisons can be made. This is unfortunate in so controversial a field where firm information would scotch misunderstandings. Such figures as were available confirmed the general impression that direct labour is neither markedly cheaper nor markedly more expensive in first costs, and that the balance of

271

advantage, if any, is to be found elsewhere. It is, however, impossible to be dogmatic. It would take a much more intensive inquiry into this subject to be able to prove or refute the claims and the criticisms of the value of direct labour in terms of costs.

The costs of any work carried out by a direct labour organization are compounded of four elements:

labour costs;

material costs;

costs of depots, storekeepers' wages, plant, transport and so on;

administrative costs, which cover salaries of the Works Manager and his staff, office expenses, and a proportion of the costs of other departments which are involved in accounting, cost control, technical advice or committee work for the direct labour organization.

The extra costs of labour because of the more generous conditions of service have already been described. The cost of materials is straightforward. The last two elements of cost are overheads and are not linked closely to particular building schemes or maintenance jobs. All building organizations, whether they are owned by private contractors or public authorities, have similar overhead expenses. The particular circumstances of local authorities, however, set these costs in a different framework from those of private industry, and it is to this difference that many of the misunderstandings and suspicions about direct labour are due.

Very little is known about how contractors or public authorities apportion their overhead expenses. It is, however, assumed that when a contractor carries out work his overhead expenses for plant, storage and administration must be included in the tender price. While the possibilities of squeezing such costs and profits from time to time may permit the contractor to quote a lower price for a particularly important contract, over time all overheads must be met by the clients, since there is no other source of revenue.

272

Those who are suspicious of direct labour fear lest some part of the overhead costs of the direct labour organization are not charged to building schemes, but are met by other means. These fears apply mainly to administrative costs such as the salaries of officers in other departments who render services to the direct labour organization, or to the cost of buildings, plant or transport shared with other departments. It is suggested that if these costs are not fairly apportioned, and some of those attributable to direct labour are met by other departments, the direct labour organization has a competitive advantage over the private contractor, and that cost comparisons are not true comparisons.

Nothing short of a detailed investigation of each authority's accounts could refute these suggestions. And because the local authority system possesses the flexibility to make possible some give and take in this way the critics are right to be vigilant. But their fears ignore the other pressures within each authority which are pushing the opposite way. Every chief officer and most of all the Treasurer is attempting to ensure that every other department bears its proper share of overhead costs. No one wants to shoulder the overheads of the Works department, and it is the duty of the Treasurer to ensure that these overhead costs are fairly distributed. Far from feeling pampered, most Engineers, Architects and Building Managers in charge of direct labour organizations complain of the rigour with which the Treasurer fastens overhead costs upon them.

Within an authority there must always be a certain divergence of interest between the Treasurer who wishes to see overhead costs charged fully and fairly to each service, including the Works department, and the department which wishes to keep its running costs down. Within the framework of these competing pressures there may be some differences of opinion on the right division of overheads, but such divergencies would appear to have a minimal effect. They would not invalidate the general picture that direct labour organizations do in general carry their own costs and compete on fair terms with private industry. Suspicion on both sides appears greatly to magnify the differences between direct and contract labour and to exaggerate the possibilities of weighting the scales. Local authorities stress unduly the dangers of underbidding by the contractor,

273

while contractors overstate the probabilities that authorities undercharge their costs.

The differences between estimates and final costs can also cause misunderstanding. In comparing direct labour costs with work undertaken by contractors it is necessary to compare like with like. A tender by a contractor is a legally binding document in which he contracts to do a defined job for a defined sum. If it costs more he must bear the costs himself. Subject to any rise and fall clause in the contract to offset changes in the cost of labour and materials the client knows his commitment precisely. The direct labour organization submits an estimate not a firm tender and if this proves insufficient there is no profit and loss account to meet the extra cost. This must be paid by the authority. This means there is not the same certainty about final costs with direct labour as there is with a contractor.

This difference in certainty can bring with it considerable embarrassments, and it accounts in part for the lack of enthusiasm for direct labour among government departments, quite apart from the political views of the Government of the day. When a Ministry approves a contract for a housing scheme or a new school to be built by a private builder it can count on a legal commitment to deliver the building for this price. When it approves an estimate for a scheme to be built by direct labour it has not the same assurance. While most authorities with experience can estimate with a high degree of accuracy, those instances when an authority has submitted final costs to a Ministry which are well above the original estimate have made the Ministries doubly cautious. The Ministry of Education, which has had a few unfortunate experiences in schools built by direct labour, issued a sharp note of warning on this subject:

The Works department will be expected to claim from the Education department the ascertained cost of carrying out the work. The Minister will not be prepared to pay grant automatically on any excesses over the sum approved at final approval stage. He will, in the first place, judge such claims in the same way as claims made by private contractors, i.e. as if a Royal Institute of British Architects' form of contract, or any other form of contract habitually used by the authority, applied, and a full explanation of any excesses will be required for consideration by the Minister. There should be a clear understanding of this point by the Works department when they are

274

formulating a lump sum quotation and by the Education department when they are considering both the quotation and the final ascertained cost.[1]

The importance of maintaining this rigorous attitude is increased when the contract is won by the direct labour organization in competition with private contractors. Private contractors are naturally incensed if they lose a contract in competition with a direct labour department only to hear that the final cost was in excess of their own tender price. Most experienced direct labour departments try to avoid such an invidious situation. And some which do not compete directly but maintain cost comparisons by doing only a part of the work themselves may deliberately over-estimate in order to avoid criticisms on this score. This is not, however, a course open to departments, who are competing directly with contractors, unless they are of exceptional efficiency and are confident of underbidding the private builder with a safety margin of this kind.

It is unfortunate for the reputation of direct labour that so little is made known about its costs, and that the political overtones of most discussions about those costs tend to distort the picture. The critics are ever ready to highlight every occasion when final costs exceed estimates. The supporters, who are on the defensive, consider that the more favourable results when the final costs are below the estimate are not given their due, and are fearful lest minor failure will attract excessive publicity. Neither attitude gives direct labour a fair run.

Experimental Work

A direct labour organization provides a unique opportunity to bring together the experience of the designer, the contractor and the user. It should make possible a co-operative effort which is impossible when the three functions are divided into watertight departments. It could be an 'all-in' service with the added advantages that the client is 'in' as well, and that the teams can work together over a long period of years and pass back the user's experience of different buildings to the direct labour department in a way not possible in the usual relationship between contractor and client. Such an unusually close and

[1] Addendum No. 1, to Administrative Memorandum No. 548, April 1958.

275

continuous relationship should make possible considerable advances in building methods and encourage:

experimental work on the use of new materials;

the use of new building techniques;

recording of maintenance costs so as to compare schemes built by direct labour and by contract;

cost research and pre-planning to enable the Works department to make a contribution to the design of the building and to the organization of the contract on the site.

Authorities were asked if they had experience of any of these methods of advancing knowledge on building, and if they used the direct labour department to further new development.

It is disappointing to record how little progress there appears to be on any of these fronts. A number of authorities keep records to enable them to compare different makes of paints, and watch the performance of different types of fireplaces, windows or staircases. Only a minority use non-traditional materials and even these not usually in the spirit of controlled experiment. Few keep maintenance records from which maintenance costs of different contracts can be readily compared. Almost all the authorities brought in the Works department at some stage during design, and some claimed that the department's suggestions made a valuable contribution to economic design. But only one authority covered by the inquiry stated that the Works section or department had been encouraged to pre-plan with the architects from the outset of the scheme. None appeared to have made proposals to the architects which could effect radical economies in the organization of the contract. The last is perhaps the most disappointing. The Works department is in an unrivalled position for producing suggestions on how simplifications in design and specification can make for a more economical use of plant and manpower during the execution of the contract.

Now that the experience of the Ministry of Education on cost planning and control is becoming better known, the London County Council is attempting development work with direct

276

labour, and the Ministry of Housing is setting up a development group, the situation might change. Selected direct labour departments could now take part in experimental work on pre-planning and site organization, in collaboration with the Ministry of Housing's development group, as well as private contractors. There could be no greater stimulus to Works departments as a whole.

FUTURE TRENDS

The inquiry was not intended to prove or disprove the claims and allegations about direct labour, but to investigate the position dispassionately. Some authorities expect criticism and meet inquiries defensively. It is the more pleasing to record how helpful they proved to be once the object of the investigation was made clear, and how much valuable information they provided. No scandals were unearthed. None were sought. On the contrary the record is one of faithful, often hum-drum, service; of greater zeal and enthusiasm than the contractor-client relationship usually produces, and of much of honest, competent work.

The real failures are failures in ambition, in the quality of leadership, in the ability to see the opportunities direct labour offers. In part this is due to the absence of sufficient competition to keep the organization on its toes; in part to lack of understanding about the special problems of building organization which need different treatment from the ordinary ones of departmental control. Most of all it is due to a failure to rate the importance of building high enough and so to recruit officers who are sufficiently able. This is a failure common to a large part of the building industry and is not peculiar to local authorities.

It is of value to consider the probable long-term trends of direct labour both as this affects local authorities and the building industry as a whole. To do so it is necessary to distinguish clearly between new building by direct labour and maintenance and repair.

The future of new building depends partly on the volume of local authority building permitted or encouraged by the Government of the day, and partly on the political views of local councils. Neither of these factors can be predicted with any

277

assurance. The general trend of house building by local authorities is still falling, but there are large programmes of slum clearance to be carried out and many of these are in areas where at present the use of direct labour is favoured. It may be that the level of new building by direct labour will not fall very much within the next few years. On the other hand the importance of new building by direct labour for the building industry as a whole is small. Less than 2 per cent of the national building labour force is employed in this way, and any increases or decreases in numbers will only be of marginal importance to the general balance between public and private building.

Whatever the future of new building by direct labour, local authorities will continue to build by one method or another. This means that the stock of buildings owned by local authorities will continue to rise year by year. With it will rise the demand for maintenance and repair and, therefore, for larger direct labour forces for maintenance.

Authorities are so emphatic about the advantages of running their own repair services, particularly for housing, that it is unreasonable to suppose that there will be any marked change in their practice in the near future. As their building programmes follow year after year, the number of men they employ for maintenance and repair will rise in parallel. One has only to look at the annual increase in the number of houses owned by local authorities (Table 6) to realize how the use of direct labour for maintenance will grow.

Quantitatively it is this trend which is significant. There are already 75,000 men employed by local authorities on maintenance and repair work. This is a sizeable proportion of the total building manpower engaged on this class of work. It will almost certainly rise gradually to 80,000 or 90,000 or even higher. This growing sphere of operations means that in terms of total manpower and resources local authorities will have an important share of this sector of the building industry.

SUMMARY AND RECOMMENDATIONS

1. Nearly one-tenth of the country's building labour force is employed directly by local authorities, one-fifth of it on new building and four-fifths on maintenance and repair. The num-

278

bers employed on new building have been falling with the decrease in the volume of house-building by local authorities. The numbers employed on maintenance and repair have been rising steadily.

2. It is estimated that about 90 per cent of all housing authorities do some maintenance by direct labour, and many do a large proportion of their work by this means.

3. Works organizations operate with and without Works committees. Neither system appears superior to the other. It is essential that the Building Manager should have sufficient freedom. Restrictive standing orders are not compatible with competitive enterprise.

4. Direct labour for new building is used mainly for two-storey housing where the technical and organizational problems are relatively easy and little specialist manpower is needed. Hitherto only a small number of authorities have attempted to build schools, offices, flats or other more ambitious buildings by direct labour.

5. Direct labour is particularly well adapted to the execution of day-to-day repairs, especially for housing. The costs and standards of jobbing repairs by the private builder are difficult to control. Many authorities regard direct labour as the best method of securing a quick and efficient service and that this is essential if good relations with tenants are to be maintained.

6. On the larger schemes of maintenance and repair and on new building some direct competition with private contractors is desirable. Such competition tests the efficiency of the local authority's own organization and allays anxieties about feather-bedding.

7. Authorities stress the importance of continuity of work, to achieve greater efficiency, keep down overhead costs and to provide reasonable stability of employment for labour and good conditions of service. Continuity is relatively easy to achieve with maintenance work. The limited field in which local authorities operate, with only their own buildings to build, makes it more difficult to secure continuity of work for new building.

8. There is little evidence to suggest that direct labour is markedly cheaper in first costs than work done by contractors.

It is widely felt that the quality of the work is better and therefore long-term maintenance costs lower. Costs of better conditions of service for labour appear to cancel out savings on profits.

9. More Building Managers of a better calibre and with a higher status are needed. A practical way of achieving this is to pay higher salaries. Better men would be attracted as heads of separate departments, but the advantage of such a separation rests on the size of the organization and the burden on other technical officers.

10. For new building an incentive bonus scheme is usually necessary to attract labour. For maintenance and repair work incentive bonus schemes are more difficult, but can give satisfactory results.

11. Direct labour organizations too rarely exploit the opportunities they have for close collaboration with the architects on pre-planning, cost control and more efficient methods of work on the site.

12. The future trends of new building are uncertain. The total numbers employed by local authorities are, however, so small, that they do not affect the building industry significantly.

13. So long as local authorities continue with slum clearance and other housing programmes it can be expected that the volume of maintenance and repair work by direct labour will increase steadily. Quantitatively this is much more important than direct labour for new building, since local authorities employ a sizeable proportion of this sector of the building industry.

CHAPTER 8

CONTRACTS

*Competitive tendering—open competition—selected lists—
time-table for tenders—special contracts—'all-in' contracts
—negotiated contracts—Picton Street—Millpool Flats—
Amersham School—Stevenage—value of special contracts
for developments.*

LOCAL authorities award almost all their contracts to private builders through the machinery of competitive tendering. The authority supplies the information about the work to contractors, the contractors bid for the job, and the authority gives the contract to the builder who has made the lowest bid. This basically simple method of selecting a contractor embodies an important and well established principle of local authority administration. It ensures that the selection of the contractor is fair and free from personal influence, and that the work will be carried out as cheaply as prevailing conditions permit.

A great deal has been written about tendering procedures, and the Institute itself published a report on 'Building Contracts of Local Authorities' in 1958, which goes into this subject in some detail.[1] It is not, therefore, proposed to deal with competitive tendering fully in this book, but only to outline the more usual procedures. The second part of the chapter discusses more fully various kinds of negotiated contracts, which are less well known. Some of them are of special importance because they give an opportunity for the authority and the builder to work together to improve efficiency in a way which is not possible with competitive tendering.

COMPETITIVE TENDERING

Though the general principle of competitive tendering is straightforward, the various procedures which are used to implement it

[1] *Building Contracts of Local Authorities*, R.I.P.A.

vary considerably and can aid or impede the efficiency of the builder in making his tender and lower or raise the price he will be prepared to offer. It is important that local authorities should give the builder every opportunity to be efficient and should not impose conditions or time limits which make his work unnecessarily difficult. Many of the inefficiencies of building operations on the site originate in faults in the methods of instructing the builder and requiring him to start work before all the preliminary arrangements and the organization of the contract are complete. Far more effort and money is saved by reducing the period of building on the site than by skimping the preparatory work or forcing the builder to tender on the basis of insufficient information. Clients pay directly or indirectly for the builder's inefficiency and everything they and their architects do to improve the contract procedures will provide benefits in greater speed and lower costs in the long run.

Competitive tendering falls into two main categories:

open competitive tendering, where a contract is advertised and can be competed for by any contractor;

limited competition from a list of contractors selected by the authority.

Open Competitive Tenders

The most obvious feature of open competition is that it permits any contractor of whatever size and experience to try to win the contract. This means that new firms, or firms new to this class of work or to the district, have an opportunity freely to enter the field, and if they are particularly anxious to secure the work to quote a favourable price. Theoretically at least the authority may secure a particularly advantageous bid. In practice the method can be very wasteful of effort and over a period have unfavourable effects on efficiency. This will depend on local circumstances.

The preparation of a tender is a complicated operation. It involves the contractor and his staff in the detailed examination and pricing of bills of quantities and the study of plans. He must also investigate various local factors, such as the availability of labour, the nature of the site and access. This effort can only be

282

worthwhile if he has a reasonable prospect of winning the contract. If a large number of contractors compete against one another, this likelihood is reduced and the amount of abortive work on preparing tenders is increased. The cost of tendering is an overhead charge and unsuccessful tenderers must seek to recoup this charge on other contracts. Thus one building owner may well have to pay charges for which another owner was responsible. Not only are total costs of all contracts increased, but the burden of meeting these costs will fall unevenly.

There is little doubt that in very many cases open competitive tendering militates against efficiency and that such price advantages as it sometimes throws up are illusory in the wider context of the building industry as a whole. Not only does it add to the contractors' and therefore to the clients' costs in general, it also discourages some of the more efficient contractors from tendering for such schemes, because they are not prepared to be underbid by unrealistic tenders. When this happens the authority can be saddled with an inefficient builder, or with a contract which is so unrealistically low that the contractor is tempted to recover his position by shoddy work or in other undesirable ways. Even the most vigilant architect and clerk of works can never effectively make good the contractor's deficiencies, if these are due to incompetence or financial difficulty.

Authoritative opinion is strongly opposed to open competitive tendering and in favour of more selective methods. The case for more limited competition for tenders has been reported in a succession of government reports and reports from professional bodies.[1] In spite of this agreement among the experts, progress among local authorities, particularly housing authorities, towards this goal has been slow.

Methods of Selecting Contractors

The selection of contractors so that only a limited number compete for each contract is carried out by a variety of methods. The objective should be to give opportunities for new contrac-

[1] *The Placing and Management of Building Contracts*, H.M.S.O., 1944. *Working Party Report on Building*, H.M.S.O., 1950. *Report of the Joint Committee on Tendering Procedure* of the Royal Institute of British Architects, the Royal Institution of Chartered Surveyors and the National Federation of Building Trades Employers, 1954.

tors to compete from time to time, while at the same time limiting the number who tender for any particular contract. Some authorities issue a public advertisement every one, two or three years, inviting contractors to apply for inclusion on the authority's approved lists. Contractors are asked to state the size of contracts they could expect to handle, and to supply such details of their financial resources, capacity and experience as will enable the authority to investigate their credentials and assess whether they can be expected to carry out such contracts with reasonable efficiency. These arrangements allow new contractors to apply for consideration. Separate lists are kept for different sizes of contract and a contractor can graduate from smaller to larger schemes.

Such investigation and verification is a valuable guarantee of the standing of the firm and its ability to do the authority's work satisfactorily. It avoids the possibility of contracts going to contractors who are either inexperienced, have insufficient plant, or are unable to handle the larger contracts. Having made these investigations, the authority then draws on its approved lists and invites contractors in rotation from it to compete for a particular scheme. Usually the standing orders lay down the number of contractors who are invited for small, medium and large contracts. Under such a system each contractor has a fair chance of winning the contract. The expensive work of examining the tender documents, pricing the bills and preparing the estimates is thus limited to the number of contractors sufficient to give a reasonable degree of competition. The wasteful multiplication of this effort among many contractors is avoided.

The number of contractors invited to tender for contracts of different sizes varies from authority to authority. The Ministry of Works, which does not use the system of open competitive tendering, but selects contractors only from approved lists, uses the following graduated scale for inviting tenders:

For contracts below £500	4 firms
For contracts between £500 and £10,000	6 firms
For contracts between £10,000 and £50,000	8 firms
For contracts between £50,000 and £200,000	10 firms
For contracts over £200,000	12 firms

Contractors apply for inclusion on the approved lists. Hertfordshire has a scale which is more finely graduated for the smaller schemes. The arrangements are as follows:

For contracts below £50	1 firm
For contracts between £50 and £150	2 firms
For contracts between £150 and £350	3 firms
For contracts between £350 and £500	4 firms
For contracts between £500 and £20,000	6 firms
For contracts between £20,000 and £100,000	8 firms
For contracts over £100,000	10 firms

According to the Council's Standing Orders no formal contract is required for work under £500.

An alternative method is to advertise each contract as it arises and to invite firms to apply for selection. Competitive tenders are then asked for from a number of the contractors who have applied. Such an arrangement simplifies the preliminary selection. Only those firms who are interested in an immediate contract come forward, and authorities do not have to keep lists of selected firms. On the other hand, it means that the standing of firms new to the authority may have to be investigated at the very moment when the authority is most anxious to press on with the tender procedures and to start the scheme.

In order to encourage the most lively competition among the contractors selected for a particular project, the inclusion of one or two outsiders can be useful. If most of the contractors are small or local, one or two regional or national contractors can give a useful basis of comparison. Conversely, if the majority are large contractors, the inclusion of one or two good local firms can test the market. In either case the confidence of the authority in its selection procedure will be increased.

When local authorities maintain lists of selected firms they usually invite them to tender in rotation. It cannot however always be assumed that all the firms on the list will at all times be ready to compete for work. At any particular moment a firm may be too heavily committed to take on new work or its estimating staff may be too busy to do justice to a new tender. It is, therefore, a common practice to consult the required number of firms next on the authority's list to ascertain whether they wish to compete. If some are unable to do so further firms, up to the necessary number, can then be invited. This procedure avoids sending the elaborate contract documents to firms who will not tender, and also ensures that the field of contractors is wide enough to secure proper competition. It should be made clear to contractors that inability to compete for a particular contract will not prejudice future invitations.

To enable the selected contractors to decide whether the timing and size of the contract for which they are being asked to compete is appropriate, they should be sent full information. This should include details about the approximate size of the contract and what kind of building it is, the site, the kind of contract, and the probable dates for seeking and receiving tenders and for the start and completion of the contract. This information should be given to contractors at least a month before they are invited to compete, in order to give them time to consider the new work in relation to their existing and future commitments. Such advance warning can be invaluable to the contractor in estimating his possible future obligations. Anything which increases his efficiency will assist him to submit more competitive tenders. This month's notice is in addition to the time given for the actual tender.

Advance warning can go even further than a month ahead if an authority is anxious to obtain the maximum co-operation from contractors and the keenest possible tenders. It has been suggested by the Ministry of Education that it is possible to sound out contractors at the very beginning of the design stage, so that they can, if they are interested, hold themselves in readiness. This preliminary approach should be followed up two or three months before contractors will be asked to tender, when fuller details can be given. This allows those who are still interested to come to the Architect's office and to discuss the scheme, visit the site, and make a serious assessment of how they would organize the job and how long it would take them. Having made such an investigation, they are then in a position to tender more efficiently and to submit a price free from the feather-bedding of uncertainty.

Such elaborate attempts to help contractors to tender more efficiently, and to submit lower prices will strike many authorities as revolutionary. Unusual they certainly are. But they are in line with the general policy of the Ministry of Education to improve the efficiency of building operations by giving the contractor every opportunity to understand the nature of the contract. They do nothing to contravene the normal arrangements for competitive tendering, but they bridge a gap in mutual understanding which can be valuable. Perhaps only large authorities can make the attempt. It is a pointer for the future.

The slowness of the acceptance by local authorities of selective tendering is due to several causes. On the one hand there is still a great deal of ignorance about its advantages and the methods of operation. Members are often unaware of the economic costs of abortive tendering and of the ways in which new contractors can be brought in. They may also be apprehensive about arousing uninformed local criticism. In the smaller or more isolated authorities the number of contractors likely to compete may already be small, so that selection would make little difference to the list. In such cases there may well be little to be gained by a change of procedure and something lost in simplicity. In general, however, the advantages of increasing the contractor's efficiency and so of lowering the price far outweigh the objections. Authorities are urged to consider whether they should not make greater use of selected lists.[1]

The Tender

It has been emphasized in chapter after chapter, and in many reports by other bodies, that adequate time is needed at each stage of building operations, if efficiency is to be improved. Haste militates against speed at every point in the building cycle and increases costs. This is as true of the tender stage as of every other. A contractor naturally safeguards himself against uncertainty. Where the instructions are not clear, full information is not available, or the period allowed for preparing the tender is insufficient to permit a full investigation of the scheme, the contractor will hedge against his future liabilities by quoting a price sufficient to protect himself. If an authority wishes contractors to compete keenly, it will reduce uncertainties to the minimum.

---

[1] Those authorities who are not familiar with the detailed procedures for selective tendering should consult *A Code of Procedure for Selective Tendering* published in 1959 by the Joint Consultative Committee of Architects, Quantity Surveyors and Builders. This gives brief, but practical advice.

This means giving the contractor full information about the contract in the tender documents and the time to digest it. The intentions of the architects should be manifest to the builder. This means that each contractor should be given a site plan, $\frac{1}{8}$-inch scale drawings, complete bills of quantities, schedules or specifications if these are necessary, the date for the completion of the contract and any conditions which are attached to it. This information cannot be digested quickly, and if the contractor is expected to rush the job, he will quote a higher figure to cover himself. If for some reason he fails to do so and quotes a price which gives him insufficient cover, he may be tempted to regain his position during the course of the contract in ways which are unsatisfactory for the client. Too high and too low a tender are in the long run equally unsatisfactory, and future difficulties can be avoided by allotting a fair period for the preparation of the tender. The length of time will vary with the size and complexity of the project, but should not be less than four weeks unless the job is a small one.

Most authorities arrange for tenders to be opened by the chairman of the committee concerned and a chief officer. In some authorities and for some contracts two chief officers are authorized to open tenders. In the interests of efficiency as well as courtesy all the contractors who have competed should be notified of the outcome within a day or two of the closing date for the tenders. If they are not so notified, the successful tenderer cannot start preparing his organization to meet the new commitment and the unsuccessful cannot move on freely to new clients.

This notification is not incompatible with the uncertainties or preliminaries which surround the formal acceptance of a tender. Usually the lowest tender is accepted, but with open competitive tendering the lowest tenderer may be found, on investigation, not to be of a size or calibre to undertake the work, and recourse may have to be made to the second lowest tenderer. Or the tender may be too high, so that consultation with the Ministry and negotiation with the contractor may both be necessary before it is finally accepted.

Some method must be found for giving provisional notice of the results of the competition to all the competitors. One device is to inform each contractor of his place on the list; another is to inform the first three contractors of their order and to tell the rest that they have tendered too high and are excluded. Either system conveys to the contractors an immediate picture of their expectations. Only in exceptional circumstances will the second or third lowest tender be considered, but this procedure makes the situation clear to everyone without committing the authority to the lowest tender until investigations have been made.

The Start of Work

Committees are always eager to see the contractor on the site at the earliest possible moment after the tender has been accepted. The arrival of the contractors' huts and heavy plant are for the committee members the first tangible evidence that their long-planned project is to be realized. Their impatience is understandable, but it can be embarrassing for the builder and decrease rather than increase his efficiency. The important date is the finishing date. Before starting operations a contractor should work out the strategy of his work, prepare his site organization and order many of the materials. Nothing is gained and unnecessary costs may be incurred if he is obliged to move on to the site before he is ready. Committees and lay officers must be persuaded to resist the temptation to press for an unreasonably early start. The need for such restraint assumes that the contractor is genuinely getting ready; not that he has taken on more work than he can manage.

Sometimes a token start is made necessary because projects must begin within the programme year for which they have received ministerial approval. Some device to meet this requirement is better than a premature commitment of real resources before the contractor is fully prepared to start. This problem is really the outward symbol of some unrealistic programming or loss of time earlier in the building cycle. Either ministry consent has been received too late to give time for the preparation of the scheme, or the Architect's department has been too optimistic about the amount of design work it could undertake, or there has been some other impediment to normal progress. Whatever the reason, every effort should be made to avoid forcing the builder to add to the difficulties by obliging him to deploy men

K 289

and plant on the site before he has had reasonable time to plan his campaign.

It is difficult for architects, and much more difficult for lay members and officers, to appreciate the ill effects they can have on building efficiency if their contract arrangements are not well devised. Clients, and these are not only local authorities, are all too ignorant of the builders' problems and all too prone to regard complaints and requests as special pleading or a short cut to higher profits. But a builder cannot be efficient without an efficient client, and local authorities can help to increase this efficiency by their contract procedures. What is also needed are more ways for clients, architects and contractors to work more closely together, not on committees, but on actual building projects, in order to understand one anothers' problems at first hand. The rest of this chapter is devoted to descriptions of four ways in which this has been done.

The standing orders of most local authorities lay down very explicitly how building contracts shall be awarded to the lowest tenderer as the result of open or selective competition. Competitive tendering has in the past been a valuable protection against less impartial or even corrupt methods of awarding contracts, and it provides a straightforward means of deciding between one contractor and another. The procedure for advertising or inviting tenders and for the opening of the tenders on the appointed day is usually rigidly controlled, and elaborate precautions are taken to ensure that the arrangements are scrupulously fair. These measures, introduced in an earlier period, have served to build up the integrity of local government and to prevent abuses.

These procedures will continue to be necessary for the great majority of contracts. There is no suggestion that competitive tendering is outmoded. The balance may shift from open competition to the use of selected lists, but competition of one kind or another will remain the general rule. There are, however, a number of new developments which have been made possible only by a change in the standard contract procedures. These new developments have been permitted by the use of negotiated contracts instead of contracts won by competition. These negotiated contracts are described at some length in the rest of this chapter. The fullness of the description is due to their unusualness, interest and importance. It does not mean that such contracts are likely to be employed for any but a minority of schemes.

It will be apparent from other parts of this book that some of the most interesting building developments now taking place have emerged when client, architect and contractor were able to discuss their problems together from the outset of a scheme and co-operate in design and in the organization of the contract. Private enterprise is well aware of this and often works in the closest collaboration with the contractor. It is no accident that the most progressive and enterprising building authorities in local and central government are those which have been prepared to use negotiated contracts for experimental or development work. A much larger circle of local authorities could benefit in the same way if they were prepared from time to time to waive their standing orders on competitive tendering and to permit an experiment in close co-ordination with a selected builder. This applies to the smaller authorities as well as to the larger, to housing as well as to schools. At its simplest, the collaboration is a means of educating each side in each other's problems. At its most ambitious it can result in the development of new building methods and techniques.

Types of Negotiated Contract

Negotiated contracts are of three main kinds, only two of which are of significance to the present inquiry.

The first and commonest might be called a 'continuation' contract. A building firm may be already at work on a school or housing scheme adjacent to a site where further extensions or a new housing scheme is planned. It is often more economical for an authority to permit the same contractor to continue on the site, where he already has his organization in operation, and to carry on to the second part of the scheme, than to start again with a new contractor who must bring in a new organization, site agent, huts, plant, building compound, and so on. This usually involves a new contract negotiated on the basis of the previous one. It is a sensible continuation. It does not constitute in itself any particularly interesting new principle.

291

The second type of negotiated contract covers the wide range of proprietary systems of building, prefabricated and otherwise, and various kinds of 'all-in' contract. These contracts are usually preceded by cost comparisons between the various alternative methods or some kind of preliminary tendering. The final contract is usually negotiated because the use of the proprietary system for a special type of building makes it impossible for the authority to go out to competitive tender on the basis of the usual designs, specifications and quantities. This type of negotiated contract is widely used and has a number of interesting facets.

Thirdly, there are those contracts which are finally settled by negotiation at the end of a long period of collaboration between the client, the architect and the contractor. Such negotiated contracts are exceptional, but they are the foundation of experimental work and can result in important new developments. While they will remain exceptional because they involve an extra investment of effort by both sides, they are proving important for future progress. Single schemes where this method has been used can have widespread effects inside and outside the authority which inspired them.

Contracts for Proprietary Methods

Most of the proprietary types of building use special systems of prefabrication or special methods of erection on the site. They have been developed by large contractors who either design and erect the buildings themselves, or act as the main specialist sub-contractor under a general builder, as in the case of structural work.

In using these methods of non-traditional building, authorities have to make two main decisions. First, they must decide which of the various proprietary systems to use, and secondly, what degree of standardization to accept. Choice of contractor must depend on which type of structure the authority prefers, and which contractor appears likely to give the most favourable price and quickest delivery.

Speed of erection is usually the most important factor. Many authorities use these special systems for schools and houses almost entirely because they seem likely to mean earlier completion than traditional methods of building. The cost advantage over traditional building is considered to be only marginal, if indeed it proves cheaper at all. Savings in erection time and in the demands on the design staff in the authority's own architectural office are the main motives. To authorities with long waiting lists for houses or overcrowded schools these savings have been of the utmost importance. Many families and school children are indebted to these alternative methods of building for their greater comfort and better schooling.

It is obvious that if a proprietary system is to be used price comparisons with other methods can only be on the basis of some kind of preliminary assessment. The final price must be negotiated with the particular contractor on the designs and specifications of his own type of building.

An authority's objective must be to ascertain which is the best designed, cheapest and most quickly built system from the various firms who offer specialist methods of construction. The aim should be to obtain a fair basis of comparison without imposing so rigid a design and specification that the various firms cannot offer their particular products. For a small authority this is not easy, and such authorities may rely on approaching only one or two of the well-known firms who produce such buildings, particularly houses, by these highly specialized methods. These firms are at least as well aware as the authority of the costs which are likely to find acceptance with the Ministry concerned. The contract will then be negotiated with the firm which appears most likely to meet the authority's requirements. For housing and schools most of these firms have already discussed their designs and methods with the appropriate government department and can offer an assurance that their specialist systems and designs have received a general blessing, if not formal approval.

For the larger authorities, who may have bigger schemes to offer to the selected firm, a more rigorous comparison of the alternative systems is possible. For example, some authorities invite several firms with specialist systems of construction to submit formal preliminary offers. These are based on a standard block, say of flats or houses, to the authority's outline design and in accordance with a standard outline specification. The contractors are asked to supply only the minimum information necessary to decide which offer would be most advantageous to the authority. These details include sufficient drawings to

293

indicate each system and its external appearance, a detailed specification, a schedule of rates for external work and foundations and a price for the superstructure. An estimate of the time required to complete the programme for a specified number of houses or flats is also given. Having obtained these preliminary offers, the authority chooses the most suitable and negotiates the final contract with the selected contractor.

This is a contract procedure which works in two stages. To avoid giving the authority and the contractors unnecessary work, the information to be contained in the preliminary offers should be rigorously limited. The purpose of the first stage is to provide the authority with a fair basis of comparison and the contractor with a fair basis of competition. The aim should be to ensure that only one contractor is called upon to complete the full details of the scheme after the preliminary offer has been accepted.

Almost any system of preliminary estimating runs the risk that contractors may have to do a great deal of abortive work. There have recently been cases of authorities who have involved three, four or more contractors in such work including the preparation of outline plans and costs. The overheads of the unsuccessful firms will be carried over to subsequent contracts, and inflate later tenders. Authorities with more experience claim that these preliminary estimates are unnecessary. In their view systems can be compared, in terms of function, by examining the systems themselves and their components. They can be compared in terms of costs by comparing elemental cost analyses for recent and similar types of buildings of each type of construction. Such methods of comparison make it possible to select a particular system without involving a number of firms in the special details of the project to be carried out.

Most specialist firms claim to be able to produce by their own process a building more quickly and more cheaply than by the traditional building methods. But implicit in this claim is the assumption that full advantage will be taken of the standardized designs and components, so that prefabrication and the advantages of mass production will be utilized to the full. Some methods require a higher degree of uniformity of design than others, if the full cost economies are to be achieved. Much of the disappointment over the final costs of such specialized methods

294

of construction is due to a lack of understanding of the price, in terms of time and money, which must be paid if the standard methods and components are changed.

Most authorities have special preferences in the designs of houses and flats and are anxious to incorporate points of design which they have found to be successful locally. Such preferences must be exercised with the utmost caution in the face of non-traditional methods of building. Some systems can be easily adapted. Some of the best known cannot without a serious sacrifice, which may well negate the whole cost advantage of their use.

What may appear to the Housing committee to be minor changes of design may mean the re-tooling of factory machines, the re-making of moulds, the substitution of special for standard components, or manual operations on the site when otherwise factory-made parts could be directly used. If an authority is not fully aware of the technical implications of the changes for which it is asking, it may well receive a rude shock when the tender is finally negotiated. Alterations in the contractor's standard designs should only be made with great caution and when the authority is satisfied they are essential. The task of convincing a committee of the cost and time advantages of the standard designs can be difficult, but it is important.

'All-in' Contracts

Many of these specialized systems of construction are offered to clients at an 'all-in' price to include the professional services of architects, engineers or quantity surveyors and others, to whom the client normally pays separate fees. The 'all-in' service is also used by builders who offer traditional types of houses for sale, but this is outside the field of local authorities. The main advantages of the 'all-in' service are two: its financial simplicity, and the possibilities it provides for closely integrated work between those who are responsible for the design and those who are responsible for the erection of the buildings. Some of the negotiated contracts which have already been discussed come into this category. A local authority having selected the specialized type of building can negotiate a price with the contractor, which is inclusive of all professional services and fees, these professional services being provided by the contractor.

295

This financial arrangement has an attractive simplicity. The client knows at the start what his total financial commitment will be, and he is relieved from the complications of dealing separately with architects and other professional people. It is particularly welcome to small businesses whose contacts with professional firms are limited. And it avoids those sometimes unexpected expenses for fees which arise at the conclusion of the work. For local authorities the attraction is more in the relief to the authority's own staff. In time of pressure it is valuable to pass on the detailed architectural work to the contractor, and to be saved the complications of the quantity surveyor's work and the final accounts. The 'all-in' price should take most of this work off the authority's shoulders.

While the 'all-in' contract may be a convenience to authorities in times of great pressure, they have sufficient professional experience to make the use of such contracts undesirable in normal circumstances. From the client's standpoint the 'all-in' contract has two serious dangers. First, it deprives him of the services of an architect, who is independent of the contractor, to safeguard his interests. Secondly, there is the risk that the client, in handing over responsibility for the more routine functions of design, will also hand over his responsibility for settling the requirements of the building. This is more especially a danger for schools for which the requirements are less standardized than for housing. It would be a serious situation if the contractor usurped the client's functions. This is a real danger with the 'all-in' contract.

In spite of these dangers the 'all-in' contract cannot be dismissed out of hand. While unsuitable for most local authorities it remains a challenge. It is a challenge because of the development of a closer relationship between the designers and the builders within the contractor's own organization.

Builders have long used professional firms or professional staff to help them, but often on a very limited scale. The larger contractors, who are now developing new building techniques, are providing their own special kind of development teams. By bringing architects, engineers, quantity surveyors and the contracting side of the organization under the same roof, they can learn about each other's problems and dovetail their work in a way which is much more difficult when the different elements are quite separate. In terms of architectural design some of these new buildings may leave something to be desired. In terms of the efficiency of the building organization the combined team-work which lies behind the 'all-in' contract is a most interesting development.

The 'all-in' contract is one manifestation of the pressing need to get the different sides of the building industry into closer contact, so as to give one another more help in raising efficiency. The rest of this chapter is devoted to a description of methods by which public authorities have attempted to break down the same barriers by other means. The more these problems can be tackled by different people in different ways, the greater the stimulus to improvement will be.

CONTRACTS FOR DEVELOPMENT WORK

The ordinary procedures for competitive tendering put the architect and the contractor into two watertight compartments. The contractor begins when the architect leaves off. The architect does not know which contractor will be doing the job and cannot consult him about his special techniques and methods of organization, and so adapt his design to fit them. The contractor in turn tenders on the basis of a fully worked out scheme and regards the drawings and specifications as more or less inflexible instructions. The rigidity of this system is an important barrier to progress. What is now required are more opportunities for the occupants of the two compartments to share their knowledge and experience.

Work carried out by the London County Council in a housing scheme in Picton Street, Camberwell, by Birmingham in multi-storey flats at Millpool Hill, by the Ministry of Education's development group on a number of schools and by a few other authorities show how valuable such collaboration between the designers and the builders can be.

In such cases it is necessary to make a dispensation from standing orders so that competitive tendering can be waived for a particular scheme, and a contractor nominated for the job as soon as the architects are starting on the design. It may also be necessary to secure the approval of the appropriate Ministry.

The object of this kind of negotiated contract and the nomination of the contractor are:

to enable the architects to take full advantage of particular techniques and plant which the contractor has available. These may vary from one contractor to another, and to achieve maximum efficiency the scheme should be adapted to a contractor's special facilities and methods;

to enable the contractor to suggest simplifications or alterations of design which make erection easier;

to encourage better site organization by permitting the contractor to prepare more thoroughly than is usually possible.

The examples which follow illustrate how these advantages have been secured from close collaboration between the contractor and the architects. The first two schemes concern housing where high density and tall buildings were important; the third is a school and the fourth is two-storey housing.

Picton Street Housing Scheme, London County Council
Among the main reasons why special systems of construction are not used more often nor made the subject of experiment is the contractual problems which are involved. There may be prima facie reasons for expecting some new method of building to bring valuable savings in cost and time, but an authority is discouraged from trying them because the new techniques cannot be superimposed upon a design of traditional construction. The London County Council had already found that to convert blocks of flats designed for traditional methods of construction to any other system produced only an unsatisfactory compromise. If the full possibilities of new constructional techniques were to be exploited, this meant that their possible influence on design had to be known from the outset. To know this it was necessary to know the contractor and his particular method of construction from the beginning. It was also necessary that he should collaborate with the architect's design team from start to finish.

To achieve this, standing orders were waived, normal competitive tendering was dispensed with and a contractor with a non-traditional method of construction was selected. The nomination of John Laing and Son, Limited was made after a number of firms had been interviewed and their organizations considered in relationship to their suitability for the job.

The scheme provided for the construction of nearly 700 dwellings in Camberwell, 320 in the form of eleven-storey maisonette blocks, nearly 300 in sixteen four-storey maisonette blocks and the rest in three-storey flats and a few two-storey houses. There are also a few shops, a clubroom and playground. A scheme of this size was considered large enough to provide for a good deal of repetition work, which would permit considerable economies in design and the use of plant.

Work started on the site in January 1955 and the contractor's representatives joined the design team about fourteen months before this. The scheme was divided into two phases, and lessons learned in the first could be applied in the second.

Contract Arrangements. The contractual arrangements were devised so that the contractor could withdraw at the end of the design stage, but a target price was fixed from the outset and both sides aimed to improve upon this figure.

An estimate of the cost of the scheme was prepared by the Council's quantity surveyors on the basis of the known costs of comparable accommodation in current contracts which had been let after normal competitive tendering. This estimate was adopted as the target estimate for the work. It became the 'target price', the maximum amount which the Council would be required to pay, subject to adjustments for certain defined variations such as wage rates and materials. The contractor was given and availed himself of the opportunity of checking this estimate at an early stage, so as to satisfy himself that it was reasonable.

On completion of the design stage, bills of quantities were prepared for Phase I and priced independently by the Council and by the contractor. At this point the contractor was given the option of withdrawing if he considered the 'target price' was inadequate. The scheme, moreover, having been divided into two phases, a break clause was included in the contract documents to allow the contractor the opportunity of withdrawing from Phase II if, for instance, he came to the conclusion that the actual cost of Phase I would exceed the 'target price'. Agreement to continue with Phase II was reached later.

Payment was made to the contractor on the basis of actual costs up to an agreed maximum, plus a fixed percentage for overheads and profits. Any excess of actual cost over and above the 'target price' was to be borne entirely by the contractor. Any savings which could be achieved by keeping actual cost below the target figure were to be shared between the contractor and the Council. Both parties therefore had a strong incentive to keep actual costs as low as possible. The procedure for variations, the definitions of 'target price', 'prime cost' and 'overheads' were defined in the formal contract which was an extensive document.

The Design Team. The composition of the design team and the investment of effort in finding the right solutions were exceptional. In addition to the architect, quantity surveyor and contractor members, the team included representatives of the consulting engineers and of the Building Research Station. Every item of the designs of both tall and low buildings was kept continuously under review during the course of the job at regular meetings of the design team. Many suggestions for economy were made by all members of the team and put into effect. As a result of these modifications, the later blocks cost less than the earlier ones.

The early nomination of the contractor resulted in his knowledge and experience of building techniques and materials, of plant and of site organization, and his views on how building time and costs might be reduced, being available to the architects and engineers at the design stage, and exerted due influence upon the design. For example, the decision at an early stage to use a tower crane of known size and capacity for the erection of the eleven-storey blocks enabled the design to proceed on the basis of large prefabricated components, suitable for economic handling by this crane. Again, as a result of joint discussion, an early decision to attain as much speed as possible in erection time by reducing to a minimum such wet trades as plastering, 'in situ' concrete and brickwork fundamentally affected the design of the walls, partitions and floors. There was also another

300

and unexpected outcome of the team's work. It was discovered that the contractor had a large quantity of used steel shuttering. This enabled the structural walls of the four-storey blocks to be made more economically in low grade concrete than in 9-inch brickwork.

Towards the end of the design stage a prototype of a two-storey maisonette unit of the eleven-storey block was built at the contractor's works. This gave useful experience in the handling of the main structural elements and shuttering units by crane, in assembling and fixing other components, such as panel walls and plumbing units, and in certain plastering experiments.

During the design stage cost investigations of alternative designs were made for most components of the buildings. These cost estimates were prepared independently by the quantity surveyor members of the architect's team, by the contractor's staff and by the Building Research Station surveyors and the results subsequently compared. The structural engineers prepared alternative designs for the structure with column and beam frames, with frames combined with walls and with both at varying spacings. A highly original scheme was also prepared by the engineers for precasting the concrete walls in the form of staggered two-storey height units which would interlock with the precast floors. These schemes were discussed with the contractor's plant specialists and production engineers in relation to the use of large cranes and alternatively of light cranes rising with the building.

A number of different designs were also prepared for the floors—in precast concrete, 'in situ' concrete, timber with and without beams and so on. A variety of materials was considered for the design of the lightweight external wall panels, the cost target for which was taken as the traditional brick-cavity clinker panel wall. The plumbing was considered in terms of copper, cast-iron and galvanized steel, and quotations for comparable systems in these materials were obtained.

Assessment. It will be clear that the Picton Street scheme involved all the parties in it in a heavy investment of time and effort. This is not the kind of effort which can be attempted for every scheme, but its value in breaking new ground is very great. The London County Council considers that the work has

301

already been of great value in influencing the form of design of later schemes in the Council's housing programme, and the volume of experience and technical information derived from it has fully justified the Council's hopes of the results of collaboration at design stage between architects and their technical colleagues and the contractor.

Millpool Hill Scheme, Birmingham

The City Council had for some time been concerned about the cost of multi-storey development, because it had not been found possible to reduce costs to what was considered to be a reasonable figure. After much study it was considered that it was the cost of the structural frame which was out of proportion with the total cost of the dwellings and that special efforts should be directed to reducing this element. The House Building committee was, therefore, asked by the City Architect if they would waive normal standing orders on competitive tendering and allow a selected structural firm, a builder and his sub-contractors to be appointed to co-operate right from the start in the design of a group of multi-storey flats. The structural firm, acting as the builder's sub-contractor, was of special importance: it combined the functions of the consulting engineer and the specialist reinforced concrete contractor.

The City Architect first prepared outline plans of the flats and asked the structural firm to prepare a study involving a series of grids, column sizes and other alternatives with a cost analysis of each variation. Having settled the most economical size of grid, meetings were then held between the Council's architects, the builder, the main sub-contractors and the structural firm to obtain the most economical method of building and of servicing the building with plumbing, drainage, hot water and lifts. Adaptations were made to suit the problems of the different members of the team. The actual procedure for preparing the scheme and organizing the building work was also agreed.

A director of the structural firm had visited America and investigated 'plate floor construction'—that is the use of the floor as the actual beam. This type of floor was successfully developed and included in the contract. Many problems were solved by the use of this type of floor with its level soffit which allows considerable freedom of planning. It has since been found that even greater freedom is possible and columns can be moved to a limited degree out of the grid. The use of this floor simplified shuttering problems and speeded up building. Before the floor was accepted for use a typical bay of columns and floor was erected and tested to destruction. The result was completely satisfactory.

Because of the violent changes of ground level, it was not possible for building purposes to use the normal type of tower crane on a rail track. A climbing crane was therefore used and the lift shaft was designed to make this possible. This meant that the shaft had to be slightly modified to take the crane and central enough to permit the boom to reach well beyond the perimeter of the building. The crane was thus an integral part of the building operation and foreknowledge of its potentialities was an essential part of the scheme. The crane was used to lift most of the building materials required. Prefabricated components were used as much as possible, and the weight that could be conveniently handled by the crane was a deciding factor in determining the size of these components.

The final layout of the flats to achieve maximum economy in plan, plumbing and heating suggested that an internal bathroom was desirable and this plan was adopted. This type of bathroom, though common on the Continent, had not been widely used here. Ventilation problems were studied with care and overcome. In some ways the ventilation used is more positive than in ordinary bathrooms relying on ventilation from an air brick.

Throughout the work the quantity surveyors had advised on the many costing problems involved. When the preparatory stages were complete they prepared the bill of quantities of all the materials and labour required to build the flats, and a tender was officially invited from the selected builder. The structural work involved was included in the bills of quantities as a prime cost sum. The structural firm of Truscon, who had taken part in all the discussions, was nominated as the subcontractor for the work.

The tender, when received, was highly satisfactory and showed a saving over previous traditionally built flats schemes of several hundred pounds per flat. It also showed a saving of about £50 a flat compared with other similar non-traditional schemes.

303

As with the Picton Street scheme both the authority and the contractors devoted an exceptional amount of time and effort to the preparations of a single scheme. The investment of effort cannot expect to be recouped from a single scheme, even though in this case the savings in cost were considerable. The benefits were and still are being spread over later schemes as the result of the lessons learned in this one.

Amersham Junior School, Buckinghamshire[1]

This school was designed by the development group of the Architects' and Building Branch of the Ministry of Education in collaboration with Buckinghamshire County Council. Reference to this project is made elsewhere in this book. As the scheme involved co-operation from an early stage with a nominated builder, it is also of special interest in the present context.

The school was a two-form entry school and of traditional brick structure. This size of school and type of construction were specially selected to make it possible to select a firm of medium size rather than one of the national firms of contractors, and to gain experience of traditional building rather than of prefabrication. The contract was for some £50,000 and both in size and complexity varied very much from the two flat schemes just described. The technical problems were simpler than for Picton Street or Millpool Hill, and the experience of working with a local contractor corresponded more closely to that which might be gained by a medium size authority working on a school or housing scheme with a local builder. In doing so, it is not suggested that such an authority should attempt on its own the full scale investigation techniques of a development group. But co-operation with a nominated contractor for a scheme of modest size has been shown by the Ministry of Education to be worth while. It can provide valuable lessons for the contractor as well as for the authority.

The aim was to find a firm which employed most of its own tradesmen and labourers so that as far as possible the organization of the labour force should be under its control. It was also necessary for the firm to make the director and the estimating, buying and site staff available from the outset of the preparatory work so that they could offer their practical experience. With a

[1] Building Bulletin No. 16.

304

firm of medium size and limited staff it is not easy for these men to be spared from the current work to join in discussions about future projects. Detailed practical advice was needed at the design stage and this sometimes proved difficult to get, particularly from the agent and site foreman. It is suggested by the Ministry that in any 'future collaboration of this kind the builder should be prepared to make available the advice of the agent and foreman for a limited period during the design stage'. There was, however, specially helpful advice from the contractor's manager which enabled the architects to avoid specifications which involved the use of scarce tradesmen.

At first it proved difficult, simply through inexperience, to find the right medium whereby both sides could contribute to the design. The customary relationship between architect and builder was not conducive to the kind of collaboration required in a negotiated contract. Rightly or wrongly—and frequently, it must be admitted, wrongly— a builder does not usually question the contents of an architect's drawings, and regards it as his duty to interpret these as best he may, in spite of difficulty, and in spite possibly of preferring an alternative method of construction. Conversely an architect may be able to suggest better ways of carrying out work which the builder, seeing no reason to depart from previous methods, has not thought of. As discussions continued, however, it became clearer how both architect and builder could combine their skills in the best interests of the job. Collaboration became most effective when discussion of general principles gave way to consideration of specific points in rough drawings and in approximate quantities prepared for cost checking purposes, when the combined effort of working to the cost plan stimulated discussion and suggestions from all sides.[1]

The collaboration covered many sides of the builder's work. He was asked, for example, at the outset, what type of bill of quantities, specifications and drawings he would prefer, and during the course of the joint discussions it was found that one kind of bill was more suitable than others. The programme for the buying of supplies was also considered jointly. The job was a small one and tightly programmed and the late delivery of supplies would have thrown it out of balance. In an ordinary contract the builder can only start buying when his tender has

[1] Ibid, p. 122.

305

been accepted. In this case preparations could be made in advance. Some of the components for which delivery was likely to be slow were ordered by the authority ahead of the acceptance of the tender.

Although the builder was nominated at the beginning of the design work, neither the authority nor the contractor was committed until a satisfactory tender had been accepted. Co-operation was, however, so close that by the end of the design period the cost of the work was virtually known. Cost checks had been made throughout the scheme, and the final drawings and quantities could be prepared with near certainty that alterations would not be necessary. The submission of the tender became almost a 'final presentation of what was already known'.

The co-operation of the builder from the beginning made it possible for him to understand all that was involved before work started and to plan for a more rapid execution. These were great advantages, but the experience of this scheme suggests that the builder may not be able, at a first attempt, to take full advantage of the possibilities. In this case the builder was not used to working to a detailed programme and to a tight schedule and he did not adapt his organization sufficiently to the new circumstances. This is the sort of difficulty which other authorities might meet. It does, however, show what potentialities for improvement there are, and how local authorities can co-operate in raising building efficiency. The very fact that the builder found it difficult to adapt his organization to the possibilities shows how much could be achieved if this kind of joint effort was more common.

Housing in Stevenage

The account which follows differs from the previous ones because in the final event the contracts were awarded by competition and not by negotiated tender. The preparatory stages were, however, carried out in co-operation with contractors and their suggestions were an integral part of the investigation. Such co-operation without the assurance of a contract at its conclusion would probably not have been possible if these contractors had not already done a great deal of work for the new town Corporation and were likely to benefit indirectly in the future from the greater efficiency of the Corporation's design organization. Other authorities who wish to carry out a similar investigation with the help of a contractor would proceed by a negotiated contract. It is not reasonable, in normal circumstances, to expect a contractor to do a lot of extra work without the prospect of securing the contract.

The motive lying behind the attempt of the Chief Architect's department at Stevenage was to stabilize or reduce the costs of housing and at the same time to maintain or improve standards. It was felt that under pressure from the Ministry of Housing and Local Government space standards and specifications had reached a level which made further economies impossible without producing sub-standard housing. If costs were to be kept down, some method had to be found for doing so without lowering standards. Part of the problems were solved by methods of cost planning and cost control and the close co-operation of the architects and quantity surveyors from the outset of the scheme. For the purposes of this chapter it is, however, the co-operation of the architects with the contractors which is important.

As the first step in the new experiment, it was decided that a few architects with some years of experience of large-scale housing contracts should investigate with one or two of the national building contractors the methods by which the site organization could be improved and the buying of building materials made more efficient. The object of the investigation was to make the architects more familiar with the builders' problems, so that they could avoid specifying things which were wasteful of the contractor's resources.

During the preliminary investigations it was seen that the potential savings to be derived from a closer integration with the builder would make it unnecessary to consider the reduction of costs by a reduction in space standards. All the schemes planned from then on were on the basis of 950 square feet for a three-bedroom five-person house, with a suitable adjustment for larger or smaller numbers of persons. The reduced area or 'people's house' could be forgotten.

The discussions with the contractors showed the points where the architects could most easily help towards more efficient and therefore more economical building. They covered specifications, manual work on the site and general site organization.

Many architects do not appreciate the bottlenecks and difficulties they may cause in an otherwise standardized design by insisting on certain minor variations which break the rhythm of operations on the site. Variety of design is valuable, but it can be uneconomical if it is incorporated at critical points in the building cycle. How to make or break the building rhythm depends on the architect understanding the builders' problems much more clearly than he usually does. As the result of this particular co-operation, variations in elevational treatment, for example, were confined to changes of design which could be employed without affecting the main structure. More fundamental variations of design were used for different schemes rather than within the same scheme.

Generally speaking, labour in the factory is cheaper than labour on the site and the houses were planned to make maximum use of this advantage. Wherever possible standard sizes of timber and other components were used to avoid trimming and other site work. Window and door openings and lengths of wall were of brick dimensions to reduce brick cutting to a minimum. Great care was taken to specify fittings and components according to the basic sizes in which they were made, and the contractors were able to advise about the components, which usually gave trouble in this respect and would most reward careful specifications to avoid wasteful cutting on the site or other uneconomic use of labour.

Good site organization means that plant can be kept fully utilized and that deliveries can be timed so that the sequence of operations follows smoothly, and men are not held up for lack of special components. The use of mechanical plant must be taken into account at the design stage so that it can be used economically. This is very important for the excavation of foundations and drains. These problems formed the subject of detailed research and a special method of excavating and levelling was worked out to avoid spoil being carted to or from the site. It could be argued that such problems should be within the normal competence of an authority's own engineers and architects. In practice the builder can and did add much from his own experience to show how from the point of view of plant management some schemes are more economical than others. An authority cannot normally expect to be expert on plant management problems, and the contractor can give valuable advice on how to adjust the scheme to make the use of plant more effective and economical.

The other main point of attack on efficiency was to standardize the basic dimensions of the buildings and of components, so that the various parts were interchangeable in all the houses for a single scheme. The object was to simplify labour operations on the site and so to accelerate them, to reduce delays if certain components were delivered late, to eliminate unnecessary work and to simplify bonus payments. For example, all the staircases in one scheme were the same; all the work could be done in the joinery shop without trimming on the site and costs were almost halved. All fittings, such as cupboards, kitchen cabinets, shelving and meter cupboards, were designed to be identical and completely interchangeable in all the houses. All plumbing runs were identical, and thus boilers, cylinders and tanks were constant throughout the job, and baths, basins, and sinks were fixed in a standard position.

The gain in terms of cost of these changes has been considerable. The estimated cost of the first project of 268 houses, based on considerable experience with normal housing contracts in the area, was approximately £470,000. The target of the cost plan was to reduce this by 10 per cent. In fact the lowest tender accepted for the work was £410,000, or a saving of 12·7 per cent on normal costs. The second scheme of 400 houses, of different design and higher standard than the first, showed a saving on the same basis of 13·3 per cent. Other schemes are also being prepared to show similar savings, and contractors are finding very considerable advantages from this rationalized approach to their work.

One general conclusion from this experiment is that co-operation with the contractor from the start of the design of the scheme is of great value but that it is not necessary to have it every time. The lessons from one such exercise can be applied to a number of subsequent schemes. As building techniques, architects and builders change, another such effort would serve to bring ideas up to date with later building developments. Such close practical contact between the designers and the builders is by far the best way of making building more efficient and Stevenage has demonstrated that it pays handsomely.

309

Encouragement of Negotiated Contracts

These examples show how valuable this kind of development work, based on a negotiated contract, can be. The examples are all drawn from authorities with large resources. They are closely akin to, or in the case of the Ministry of Education and the London County Council, are a part of the work of a development group. Such work need not, however, be solely the province of the large authorities. Some of the medium sized authorities could attempt to bring the architects and builders closer together by means of occasional negotiated contracts of a less ambitious kind.

The Ministry of Education raises no objection to the use of negotiated contracts provided the standard cost limits are not exceeded. It has stated:

In order to associate the contractor with a project from the earliest stages of planning an authority may wish to negotiate with a nominated contractor for the building of a project, or even, in suitable circumstances, for a number of projects. The Minister will not object to such arrangements . . . where it seems likely that speedier or more economical building will result . . .[1]

The existence of cost limits makes it easier for the Ministry of Education to agree to negotiated contracts of this kind. But quite apart from this particular advantage, the whole attitude of the Ministry is orientated towards such attempts to bring architects and builders closer together, so that they may both be more efficient. This kind of negotiated contract has been used by some education authorities. It could equally well be used by more housing authorities.

Selection of the Contractor for Development Work

Details were given earlier of methods of choosing contractors for special types of building. That kind of two stage tender is less appropriate for negotiated contracts where development work is planned. Any selection of a contractor for a negotiated contract must require subjective judgments which do not arise when there is competitive tendering. For a development contract the quality and interest of the contractor is all-important.

[1] Administrative Memorandum, No. 548, 1957.

While there may be a ceiling price to control costs it is essential to find a firm whose directors are capable of sharing fully in the enterprise and who are willing to put their staff at the disposal of the authority. The criteria for selection will vary from one scheme and one authority to another, and there may not be a wide choice of contractors willing to participate. But if firms who are being considered for the larger schemes are asked to give the following information an authority will have a clear idea of their comparative potentialities:

size of the company, financial resources, plant;

programme and organization of the contract—time usually being an essential element in the competition;

existing planning staff. Unless a contractor has an experienced planning staff, he cannot undertake work of this kind;

seniority and pay of site manager, to secure first-class supervision;

prices of a recent contract for a similar class of work, to provide a basis for costing.

For smaller schemes and contractors a simpler version would be required. The experience of Amersham School shows that the smaller contractors have no set planning organization, and that they will have difficulty in freeing staff to do the preliminary work with the architects. There are, nevertheless, potentialities here which ought not to be neglected, and many authorities should be able to find medium sized builders locally who would be keen to co-operate.

SUMMARY AND RECOMMENDATIONS

1. This chapter has dealt only briefly with the normal methods of awarding contracts by competitive tenders, because so much has been written elsewhere about these procedures. They were recently covered by another inquiry of the Royal Institute of Public Administration. The chapter has, therefore, dealt much

more fully with special contract procedures, and particularly with negotiated contracts for development work. The balance of the chapter must not be construed as suggesting that the day of competitive tenders is over.

2. Competitive tendering will continue to be the general rule for the vast majority of contracts. The integrity of the methods of awarding contracts depends on the widespread use of such arrangements.

3. Competition can be open to all, or restricted to a selected list of contractors. The use of lists of selected tenderers reduces the number of abortive tenders and saves clients the expense of meeting these additional overhead costs. Efficiency would be increased if more authorities would make use of selected lists of tenderers. Authorities are urged to give more serious consideration to the use of selected lists and to take greater advantage of their possibilities.

4. Even on the standard procedures for competitive tendering there is great scope for improvement. There is a need for greater understanding of the builders' problems, so that authorities can help contractors to be more efficient.

5. The improvements most needed are those which affect:

the information the contractor has at his disposal;

the time he has to consider it and to organize his work.

The more detailed and complete the contract documents and the more the time allowed to consider them, the greater the contractor's certainty. The greater the certainty, the keener the competition.

6. It is well known that contractors make allowances in their tenders for clients and architects who are known to be above or below average in efficiency. The authority or the architect who is known to be business-like, to supply plans on time, to demand few variations and to settle outstanding problems promptly, can expect keener competition and a lower tender. Local authorities have a duty to be such clients and to reap the price benefits such a reputation will secure.

7. Negotiated contracts for specialized methods of building are widely used because the nature of the work prevents ordinary

312

competitive tendering. These types of building are usually used to accelerate the rate of building or to economize in the use of technical staff in the authority's own office. Building costs are seldom as favourable as they could be if authorities would abstain from making alterations to the standard designs. These often vitiate the cost advantages of the system used. Authorities need to be more aware of their implications and to adjust their requirements more realistically to the building system they have chosen.

8.   The 'all-in' contract which includes professional services for an all-in price has an attractive simplicity for the client who is not accustomed to using professional staff. This does not apply to local authorities. They are well equipped with professional officers and accustomed to using private architects, engineers or quantity surveyors. The independent status of these professional men enables them to protect the client's interests. The challenge of the 'all-in' contract is, however, a real one. It permits a closer co-operation between designer and builder than is normally possible. It should be treated by authorities as a stimulus to achieve equal efficiency and integration by other means.

9.   The time has come for the wider use of negotiated contracts, both for development work and on more modest projects. The work done by a few authorities has already had valuable results, and has shown how much can be achieved in reducing costs and developing new methods. The major schemes such as Picton Street and Millpool Hill flats can only be attempted by large authorities. But the medium sized authorities would also benefit by the occasional use of a negotiated contract, and the contact this permits with the builder.

CHAPTER 9

RESEARCH AND DEVELOPMENT

Functions of development groups—pioneer work of Ministry
of Education—extension of this work to other ministries—
use of development group for housing—one-of-a-kind
schemes—Building Research Station—Consortium of local
authorities—development by London County Council—ex-
tension of work—cost planning and control.

UNTIL recently the building industry had made slow progress
in improving its efficiency. Productivity in building has increased since the war more gradually than in many other indus-
tries. The reasons are manifold, but one of the most important
is the large number of small firms which have not the managerial
skill nor the financial and technical resources to develop new
methods nor to use the more expensive plant. Most of them are
engaged on work of a highly traditional kind, particularly two-
storey housing, and their building methods have changed little
in the last forty years. It is with these firms that many local
authorities have their building contracts.

A second reason for the slow increase in productivity is the
high proportion of the industry employed on maintenance and
repair. A large part of this work is concerned with small individual jobs on which the ratio of labour to materials is high.
Many of the most significant improvements in building productivity arise when mechanical processes take the place of manual
ones. This is less easily realized in maintaining and repairing
buildings than in erecting them. Indeed the most important
economies in maintenance and repair are not likely to come in
the future from the more efficient operation of these services,
desirable though this is, but through the use of building materials which will require less maintenance during the life of the
building. Local authorities are responsible for a large volume of
maintenance and repair work, but the close control of the capital
costs has discouraged efforts to reduce maintenance costs by

the substitution of materials and components which, although more expensive initially, require less attention after erection.

The rather depressing picture of the building industry is now beginning to change. After a long period of slow progress the industry at last looks like being on the edge of a revolution. Even the last five or six years have seen a transformation in the use of large plant for excavation, transport and erection. Short-wave wireless transmission and closed-circuit television are increasingly used in their operation. On a more modest level mass produced components are taking the place of manual operations on the site, and such manual operations as remain are assisted by powered tools which reduce the physical effort and can increase the speed of work. Technological progress in producing new materials and improving older ones is also increasing rapidly. The development of plastics and aluminium as building components are examples of the first: light-weight aggregate for concrete or large hollow bricks of the second. New materials and new methods of handling them are appearing every day.

These changes increase the importance of good management and of men with the managerial and technical skills to plan the schemes with care, to control their costs and to deploy the new machines efficiently and economically. As buildings get larger, the foundations deeper and the superstructure taller, costs are a matter of greater and greater importance. Both client and contractor can save large sums if the schemes are well planned and organized, and this can give a much needed incentive to the methods of planning and executing building schemes. Methods used for the larger schemes percolate through in modified form to the smaller ones.

Local authorities are only on the fringe of much of this development. Many of the rural and smaller urban authorities may feel untouched by the operations of the largest national contractors or by the minority of authorities who build tall flats or large schools. But this is not so. Two-storey housing, which is their main preoccupation, can be greatly influenced by the changes which are taking place.

Most of the rest of this chapter is devoted to work which is being done for local authorities or by local authorities to improve their building efficiency. A great deal of it is connected with educational building rather than with house building

315

because this has been the growing point of new ideas and new methods. Much of it concerns the bigger authorities with larger resources. But it would be as wrong for the small housing authority to disregard the changes which have been taking place in school building or in housing programmes of the large authorities as it is wrong for the small builder to ignore techniques used by large contractors. The scope for improvements in design and in the control of costs of two-storey housing is very great and the benefits can be secured by the efforts of the small authority as well as of the large.

The new work which has been going on includes:

development work carried out by the Ministry of Education into the design and costs of schools. This work has now been going on for ten years and has proved so successful that it is being extended to other government departments;

work carried out by the Building Research Station and its Building Operations Research Unit. The technical side of the Station's work is well known. It has also done a considerable amount of work on building costs and on user needs, particularly for housing, which are less well known;

joint action by a group of local education authorities, known as the Consortium of Local Authorities' Special Programme, or CLASP, to pool their resources for the investigation of new methods of school building and for the ordering of materials, for which large combined orders can result in reduced prices;

development work carried out by the London County Council into new building materials and methods;

investigations by the Cost Research Panel of the Royal Institution of Chartered Surveyors into the costs of houses and flats built by local authorities and the methods used by authorities to control these costs.

There have also been the interesting experiments into ways of collaborating with contractors from the design stage of a scheme, so that the contractor can share his practical experience

316

with the architects. These were discussed in the chapter on Contracts.

DEVELOPMENT GROUPS

The development work of the Ministry of Education on school building and the help and co-operation they have received from some of the local education authorities deserve to be more widely known. This pioneer work, starting first in the Hertfordshire County Council and moving thence into the Ministry of Education and then out again to local education authorities in general, has been of great importance.

Organization of Development Groups

The work of the development group of the Ministry of Education has shown how great a contribution can be made to the general body of thought and experience on schools by an exhaustive examination of user needs and costs, coupled with actual experience of erecting a small number of schools on behalf of local education authorities. This pioneer work, which has been recorded in building bulletins, published by the Ministry, has enabled the department to give advice in a form which is more readily acceptable to authorities than that sometimes offered by other government departments, because it has been based on searching examination and practical experience. Coupled as it has been with fixed cost limits, minimum standards and a capital programme fixed well in advance, it has provided a clear administrative framework, and yet left to local authorities a wide and clearly defined field for individual discretion.

The development group was set up to supplement the information already coming in from local education authorities and to ensure, as far as possible, that the advice the Ministry offered and the cost limits it set were reasonable and acceptable. It has been responsible for carrying out special investigations and for building a small number of primary and secondary schools, and has more recently worked on a technical college. The group consists of administrators, architects, engineers, quantity surveyors and H.M. Inspectors, who work in the closest contact with each other and with local authorities. It is divided into teams. Each team is responsible for designing and supervising a particular project, and it acts very much in the role of the private architect to the local authority for whom the building is being erected. Throughout, cost analysis and cost research have played a prominent part in the search for new ideas and value for money, and techniques and new policies have interacted closely upon each other.

The main differences between the work of the development group and that carried out in the ordinary way by the Architect's department of a local authority is in the size, composition and concentration of the team, and in the detail with which costs are investigated and controlled from the outset. These permit a fuller collaboration between the client and the designers, a more thorough integration between the various specialists and a more detailed investigation of designs, materials and costs than is possible in normal circumstances. This heavy investment of effort could only be justified for a single scheme if the lessons to be learned were likely to be of general interest and application and to be widely publicized. This expectation has been fully justified. There is little doubt that as a result of the work of the development group of the Ministry of Education, guidance to local authorities has not only been a stimulus, but stood the test of practicality.

From the point of view of the local authority for whom the development team is designing a building the arrangement can be most advantageous. The authority pays the Ministry only such scale fees as it would normally pay for the employment of private architects, quantity surveyors and other consultants. For this standard fee three or four times as much time and attention is devoted to the authority's project than it could hope to receive in the normal way from its own or from private architects. In addition, its officers are likely to benefit from contact with a team which is able to carry out so exhaustive an examination of new methods.

It is not possible in a single chapter to give an adequate account of what the work of a development group means. For this, reference should be made to the various building bulletins of the Ministry, particularly No. 4 on Cost Control, which is for architects and quantity surveyors and No. 16 which describes in detail the development project of Amersham Junior School. The last part of this should be required reading not only for architects but also for chairmen of committees. It describes how needs were investigated, the work was programmed, costs were controlled and the builder was helped to organize the work more efficiently.

The most outstanding features of the work of a development group can be divided into four.

First, there is the time and thought devoted to the investigation of needs and to discussions with the client. As the result of this intensive examination new ideas and new solutions to old problems are produced, which would not emerge under the usual briefing arrangements and the hurried time-table of the ordinary architect's office. The basic thinking given to some of the problems, the consultations with teachers and H.M. Inspectors and the close working contact between the different technical disciplines and between the administrative and technical staff make possible a unity of purpose, a concentration of effort and a stimulus to ideas quite different from the normal. Among the most impressive parts of the bulletin about the building of Amersham School are the accounts of the investigations which preceded the design of each part of the school, the classrooms and the furniture, the dining and music rooms, hall, library and changing rooms. Schools were visited to watch how children behaved, educational methods were discussed with the teachers and the practicality of new ideas gone over with them.

Secondly, the development group has worked out methods of cost research and cost control which operate from the very start of the scheme. These methods give the quantity surveyors a large measure of responsibility from the very outset of the scheme, and assume that they are able to keep in close touch with the architects' ideas and problems and give them full and expert advice on costs. The Ministry's quantity surveyors are responsible for settling the cost plan, in consultation with the architects, and for conducting the cost checks at various stages during the development of the plans. These arrangements not only make possible a much more thorough examination of costs, but place a much larger share of the responsibility on the quantity surveyor than is usual. The Ministry's methods of cost study are described fully in its bulletin.

Thirdly, the most strenuous efforts are made to complete all

319

the preparatory stages of a scheme before going out to tender. This is done by means of a very strict programme of work and a carefully dovetailed sequence of operations.

Fourthly, there is generally close collaboration during the preparatory stages with a selected contractor in order to make sure that the builder can contribute his practical experience and make known any special facilities of plant or other advantages or deficiencies he may have. This consultation also makes it possible for the builder to plan his part of the operation well in advance.

Experience at the Building Research Station and in many contracting firms has shown that the contract period can be significantly shortened by methodically calculated and applied planning of site operations. The discussions with the builder are directed to making this possible.

The development work of the Ministry of Education has not been confined to schools. Similar work has been done for colleges of further education. The Ministry's group has been building such a college at Preston for the local authority. It has been able to keep its advice on these technical colleges regularly up-to-date by new editions of its building bulletin on these colleges.[1]

It is sometimes argued that there is something peculiar about school buildings which makes them particularly suitable for study by the methods of the development group and that cost control and the fixing of cost limits are much easier for schools than for other buildings. The experience of the Ministry of Education does not support this view. Colleges of further education vary widely in size and in the courses they provide. They have been found equally suitable for study by a development group. Their costs and their standards have proved controllable by similar methods.

The Ministry of Education has been so successful in this work that its methods are now being adopted by other government departments. Development groups are now to be found in the Ministry of Works, the War Office and the University Grants Committee. More recently the Ministries of Health and Housing and Local Government also announced their intention to carry out such development work in these two departments and to set up the organizations for doing so.

[1] *New Colleges of Further Education*. Building Bulletin No. 5.

320

The composition and range of work of the groups already in operation vary from department to department. Although all are concerned with design and standards, not all are working on cost research or on the erection of actual buildings as the practical test of new ideas. Groups which are not responsible for such practical work may perhaps be regarded as in a transitional stage. The basic conception is, however, the same for all: to devote more time and resources than is usually available to a full investigation of requirements and possibilities, and to do this by means of small teams working continuously together in close mental and physical proximity so that the ideas of the technical experts, such as the architect and engineer, interact with those representing the users of the building. By this cross-fertilization of ideas and experience better solutions can be evolved than are possible when each discipline works independently.

Before describing the groups in greater detail some warning is necessary in the face of this burst of new activity. Some years ago the work of the Ministry of Education's development group was little known in other departments. Now it has become the fashionable solution. There is, however, the serious risk that the change will be of title rather than of outlook, of putting a nameplate on the front door, while the work that goes on upstairs is little altered. Even if the new groups bring administrators, architects, engineers and quantity surveyors closer together, the benefits of doing so will only be modest unless each group has a superabundance of vitality and strong backing.

To be successful a development group must contain some people, not necessarily many, intellectually and temperamentally strong enough to question the 'status quo'. They must be able to ask the right questions and tough enough and enthusiastic enough to battle with the inertia which will confront them. Such people are rare. Without them a development group will not produce the ideas or have enough vitality to keep them moving.

A group must also have adequate backing from those who control its terms of reference, organization and staffing and support its recommendations. The effective centre of power is not the same in every department whatever the official hierarchy. But wherever effective power resides, whether this is in the

L   321

hands of administrators, architects, doctors, professors or others it is essential that these people should be enlightened enough to see the need for and potentialities of development work and brave enough to accept, support and, if necessary, enforce the lessons learned. It is quite useless to have a development group under a Chief Architect who is not fundamentally in sympathy with the aims and methods of the group. It is equally useless if those who are responsible for setting the administrative machinery in motion to give effect to the group's ideas are too timorous or too uninterested to do so.

The Ministry of Education has been fortunate in both these respects, and its work has been fruitful in consequence. It cannot be assumed that other groups will be equally fortunate. The rest of this chapter describes the work of the new groups and recommends the extension of this work further afield. In doing so it has not been forgotten that the success of new groups will be dependent on the quality and understanding of a limited number of key people, not on new labels or new machinery.

It will, indeed, be very difficult to find enough of the right kind of people to man the new groups. There is at present an acute shortage of people with the necessary experience. The Ministry of Education has been the breeding ground for architects and quantity surveyors trained in this work, and it is now being called upon to fill key posts in other departments. It cannot do this over too wide a field, and there is considerable danger that the new groups will not have enough experienced members to do their work effectively. It will take several years to train the new teams and to build up sufficient experience to make them fully effective.

It is even more difficult to ensure that the backing will be sufficient.

The Ministry of Works

The Ministry of Works is responsible for almost all the buildings erected and maintained by central government. It acts as the agent of government departments and designs and maintains the buildings they require. To do this it has a large administrative and technical staff.

The Ministry is responsible for a great deal of intensive investigation into user requirements, design, layout and costs which fall outside the scope of this inquiry. It also carries out detailed technical inquiries into building materials and techniques and their findings are made available to the design staff. Apart from this regular work the Ministry has recently turned its attention to the methods and techniques of the development group, and adapted the experience of the Ministry of Education to its own purposes.

There are now two such groups working under the Ministry's wing. The first and more advanced is working in association with the Post Office. The second is less closely associated with client departments.

Joint Post Office and Ministry of Works Group. The development group was set up in 1957, by agreement between the Postmaster-General and Minister of Works, to look into the possibility of reducing the cost of individual buildings and to make the available capital investment go further. The Post Office invests about £10 million a year in new buildings.

The first tasks given to the group were the planning of a 10,000-line automatic telephone exchange building, and a medium-size head post office. The group includes administrative, postal, engineering and finance officers from the Post Office; and architects, surveyors and engineers from the Ministry of Works. They are responsible for all the stages of design, and their work on the planning of the first two buildings was complete or almost complete at the end of 1959. The building of the telephone exchange was due to start late in 1959 and of the head post office early in 1960.

Close examination of the operational and building requirements for these buildings during the planning stages has resulted in quite spectacular financial economies, when comparison is made with similar buildings built in recent years. As a result of the work of the group, the estimated cost of the telephone exchange building is £27,000. This is less than half the cost of any telephone exchange building finished in recent years of the same size. The cost of the post office will be about £63,000 compared with an original rough estimate of well over £100,000. Both buildings are designed with especial regard to function as well as cost, and are expected to be very efficient in use.

This success has been achieved by a closely co-ordinated

323

approach to the problem of building design, by the most careful planning and, in the case of the telephone exchange, by taking fullest advantage of current developments in the field of tele-communications engineering.

Cost investigation has formed an integral part of the group's work on both schemes, and the very large savings in cost are partly due to the methods of integrating cost control with design. The group has, in addition, been investigating the best form of cost control to apply to new post office buildings generally. The requirements and cost of a representative selection of recent buildings have been analysed, and buildings have been visited with a view to relating building costs and economy of planning to quality of treatment and operational efficiency.

These investigations have led to the decision by the two de-partments to put the use of unit costs for the control of new telephone exchange buildings on to a firmer basis than hitherto. The group's investigations have established that there is no con-sistent relationship between any one aspect of the requirements and size of building, so that control will take the form of a maximum cost per square foot gross of building and a minimum ratio of working space to total area. Ancillary buildings will be subject to a lower cost limit and external works will continue to be handled on their merits.

This marks a major advance in the use of unit costs for the control of post office buildings. Previously, diversity of site con-ditions and requirements had been thought to make it impos-sible to use effective overall limits of cost. The investigations of the group have shown that the problem can, in general, be resolved by segregating the costs of the basically similar main buildings from those of the more variable site works and an-cillary buildings.

The group's investigation into the cost control of postal buildings has not been completed. The problem is more com-plicated because individual post office buildings may include different functions. They may, for example, provide space for the public, for sorting or for transport in varying amounts and a single cost limit is unlikely to be practicable. But the aim will be the same: to set in monetary terms a standard of economical and efficient building to meet the operational requirements of the Post Office.

324

This work is extremely interesting in a wider context. The success in reducing costs has not been achieved with unfamiliar buildings. The Post Office has decades of experience of the planning and costs of such buildings. This experience has been embodied in detailed instructions for the designers. Yet in spite of all the work which has previously been done, the special methods and composition of the development group have achieved results which go far beyond those accomplished by conventional methods and standardized codes. This confirms the experience of the Ministry of Education. It suggests that similar cost savings could be found for housing or other familiar kinds of buildings.

The other particularly interesting aspect of this work is the fixing of cost limits before design starts. The Post Office and the Ministry of Works have faced the usual objections to cost limits and have not found them insuperable. Here again their experience provides a valuable lesson for other types of building.

Second Group. The Ministry of Works has also expanded its research and development work by setting up a group to examine buildings for the local offices of various government departments. This group consists of an architect, structural and other engineers, a quantity surveyor, supplies officer, estate surveyor and an administrator. Unlike the joint Post Office/Ministry of Works group it does not include representatives of the user departments. The views and needs of the client departments are expressed through liaison officers nominated by the departments concerned to work with the group at the appropriate stages, and by the inclusion in the group of an estate surveyor who is himself an expert in the requirements of office buildings.

The range of office buildings to which this group is giving special attention includes the local offices of the Ministries of Labour and National Insurance, the National Assistance Board and the Inland Revenue, all of which have an extensive network of offices to serve the local population. A distinctive characteristic of these buildings is that they all conduct a large amount of business with the public and include a public office. By and large they are fairly small, but they present some particularly interesting planning problems in reconciling normal office requirements with services to the public.

The War Office

The War Office has recently started on two types of development work. It is setting up a development group on lines similar to that of the Ministry of Education. The moment is opportune since the War Office is starting on a large programme for the rebuilding of barracks, married quarters, NAAFI clubs and other buildings which affect the personal lives of soldiers. The intention is that the development group should investigate the various alternative methods of meeting these needs and their costs and should be responsible for building examples to test the ideas which are evolved. The field is a large one and closely affects the welfare of serving men and their families.

The War Office is also a member of CLASP, or the Consortium of Local Authorities, already referred to and described in greater detail later in this chapter. This slightly surprising combination of forces is due to the fact that the Director-General of Works at the War Office was until recently the County Architect of Nottinghamshire and a moving spirit in the Consortium.

The Ministry of Health

The Ministry of Health has had a small development section in being for a few years. It has investigated various matters related to hospital buildings, including the design of operating theatres, nurses' homes, out-patient departments and hospital kitchens. A report has been published on the design of operating theatres and another on nurses' homes is pending. The resources of this group did not permit any full investigation of costs, nor has it been able to erect examples of any of these buildings for hospital boards.

A reorganization of the Architect's department was announced early in 1959. Part of the objective of this change was to make possible the setting up of a development group on lines similar to that of the Ministry of Education. This larger group is not yet in full operation but the main lines for immediate development are clear. The intention is that the group shall design and erect a number of schemes in co-operation with regional hospital boards. Sites are now being selected for development schemes for an out-patient department and a hospital kitchen. This practical work will give the Ministry valuable experience both on the design problems and on cost. It is to be hoped that the Ministry will publish its findings in some form which will make the experience widely available. The group may also plan buildings for local health authorities.

The University Grants Committee

The University Grants Committee has also had a small unit in existence since 1957, which has been on the same limited scale as the earlier group in the Ministry of Health. This unit has been responsible for investigating the requirements of various types of university building.

The Committee had been concerned about the fact that buildings of similar functions and purposes, built by individual universities, so often differed widely from each other in requirements, and consequently in cost. While it had no wish to impose rigid standards of accommodation or services on the universities, it had begun to offer guidance based on experience of accommodation which had proved to be satisfactory in use. The development unit is extending the scope of these recommendations and studying their effect on design and cost.

The unit consists of three architects and a quantity surveyor, and has so far examined the requirements of halls of residence, and is studying those of scientific laboratories. These and other types of buildings are being planned or built by many universities to meet the needs of the greater number of students and there are problems of design, standards and costs which are common to them all. The unit has not so far been responsible for the erection of any buildings, but it is hoped that it may be able to act as the architects for halls of residence in one or two universities in the near future. The work it has already done on the design of these buildings coupled with direct experience on actual sites should prove of great value to universities generally.

Extension to Other Buildings

It will be evident from this summary of the development work in progress or starting in government departments that this new kind of intensive examination of design and costs has spread rapidly in the last few years. So far, however, only the development group in the Ministry of Education has been concerned with buildings for which local authorities are responsible.

Early in the course of the Institute's inquiry, and before the changes in the Architect's divisions of the Ministries of Health and Housing were announced, it became clear that there was a need for development work along similar lines for other types of local authority buildings. Discussions with many local authorities of different size and scope revealed a widespread difficulty for individual authorities to devote sufficient time and attention at the early stages of a building project to the investigation both of the user needs of the building and the various technical means by which such needs can be met. While this is particularly true of the less usual types of building, shortages of staff and pressure to complete the buildings rapidly make fresh thought and reappraisal difficult even for large housing programmes.

Local authority buildings fall into two main types: those which are part of continuing programmes such as schools and housing, and those of which only one or two of a kind are built by any one authority over a period of years. A town hall, central library, concert hall, magistrates' court or swimming bath is built only once in a century or a generation. In the case of the less ambitious buildings such as fire stations, health clinics, old people's homes or local libraries, most authorities only build one or two at long intervals and even the largest authorities can hardly be said to have a continuing programme or to have the time and the staff to investigate requirements at great depth. The methods employed by a development group can serve a useful purpose for both these types of building.

Housing

Educational buildings are well catered for. Apart from school building the other and much larger building activity of local authorities is housing. Between 1950 and 1957 expenditure by local housing authorities in Great Britain was nearly £3,000 million as compared with some £640 million spent on educational building.[1] These comparative figures show how, in terms

[1] See Table 4, Chapter 2.

328

of national investment, economy, efficiency and good design are even more important for housing than for education.

While the general body of experience on housing is large, both among local authorities and in the Ministry of Housing and Local Government, it is somewhat surprising that the Ministry had not devoted its resources to the study of housing needs and techniques, particularly in the field of flat construction, with the same vigour and intensity as the Ministry of Education has devoted to schools. The Ministry of Housing has issued a number of housing manuals and other publications which have given valuable advice to local authorities on standards and designs. None of these publications, however, is based on development schemes executed by the Ministry's own architects, and they cannot provide the same direct experience of the problems encountered by local authorities, as that which has enabled the Ministry of Education to achieve that vivid contact with new ideas and practical problems which emanates from some of its building bulletins.

It is likely to be some time before the new development group gets going effectively and several years before new housing schemes will have been erected and the experience published. By that time another half million houses will have been built. There seems to be no convincing reason why such a development group could not have been set up five years ago. By now it would have been in a position to give advice based on first-hand experience and intensive investigations of costs and standards.

The importance of giving fresh thought to the design of housing was stressed by the Nuffield Foundation in 1958, when it announced the giving of a grant to the post-graduate department of Architecture at Edinburgh University to set up a research team to investigate housing needs and costs. The team will also be responsible as architects for two housing schemes. The Nuffield Foundation stated:

For a number of years the Foundation has been interested in the relation between the functions of buildings and their design . . . It is incredible in view of the enormous housing developments in this country before and since the war that so little study of the problem has been carried out in university departments of architecture. Little advance has in fact been made in the last twenty-five years in the

329

technique of planning the individual house or the space around it, or in the grouping of dwellings in relation one to another. And the active housing agencies are so heavily occupied by day-to-day problems of production to a time schedule that they have little opportunity for study and analysis. Thus the exercise of imagination in design is limited and there is a good deal of emphasis on tradition. Yet the need for such study remains, for during the next fifty years there will be large scale replacement of obsolescent houses and the development of new communities.

This initiative is very welcome. The Nuffield Foundation has been a pioneer in the design of hospitals, laboratories, and health centres and it is always helpful when an unofficial agency takes action. Ideas can often develop more freely outside official circles. It is, however, unfortunate that both the official and the unofficial development work on housing should have started so late.

In spite of coming so late into the field, the work of the Ministry of Housing could be of the utmost importance. With the slackening in the building momentum of local authority two-storey housing and the greater emphasis on redevelopment, much of which must inevitably be in flats, the time is ripe to take fresh stock of the situation and to initiate a more intensive investigation of needs, methods and costs. This is the more important, since habits and standards of living have been changing rapidly. With them should also change the traditional ideas about housing design. For example, television, the motor car, and the homework which accompanies more widespread secondary education, all have their impact on space and sound standards inside and outside the home. Equally, changes in building techniques, the possibilities of more efficient cost planning and control and the advantages to be gained from a better understanding of the contractor's problems suggest that a great deal could be learned from the kind of work which a development group for housing might carry out.

To be successful the group must have adequate resources to carry out its investigations, to execute a small number of housing schemes for local authorities and other bodies and to publish the results of its research and practical experience. It will need the support of local authorities and the help of the Building Research Station.

330

The field is so wide and the findings of the group could have so important an influence on design and building costs that every effort should be made to attract first class people. The success of the Ministry of Education's group has been due very considerably to the calibre of the architects who have been attracted to it, many of them from local government service, because they saw the opportunity for breaking new ground. It is essential that an equally able team should be built up for housing; perhaps even more important, since tradition weighs more heavily on ideas about housing than about schools. Bread cannot rise without good yeast and the success of a development group concerned with housing will depend on the quality of the leaven.

It is too early yet to say what kind of schemes the Ministry of Housing's development group will tackle, but a few local housing authorities will be asked to co-operate with the Ministry's design team and to be the clients of the group. Work needs to be done on two-storey housing schemes, on tall flats and on some of the more difficult schemes of redevelopment, where engineering, commercial and housing problems interact. Since the manpower devoted to any one scheme is so high it is clear that only a very small number can be tackled in the first few years. It will, however, be evident from the Ministry of Education's work, and from descriptions, in the chapter on contracts, of work done recently by other authorities, that the results of even a single scheme can be extremely valuable.

'One of a kind' Schemes

Apart from the continuing programmes of housing and schools, there is a great variety of buildings of which individual local authorities erect only one or two within a long period of years. These include:

clinics	municipal offices
public libraries	crematoria
welfare homes	swimming baths
police stations	markets
fire stations	magistrates' courts

Even the larger authorities are rarely able to carry out a sufficiently searching examination of the requirements for such

331

isolated types of building. To achieve a really satisfactory design it is often necessary to carry out a more exhaustive investigation of needs than busy staffs can undertake, and a single building will not provide sufficient data for full cost analysis and control. Inquiries among a number of authorities have shown that without a continuous programme they cannot themselves build up the necessary body of experience and that mistakes in design may be made from lack of knowledge about the essential criteria, or through insufficiently close collaboration between the client department and the architect.

Even when a conscientious authority has spent a great deal of time and effort visiting and obtaining details of existing schemes, it cannot be sure that it has secured the best advice or benefited from the failures of earlier schemes. Nor is it often in a position to know in advance what standards or costs will be acceptable to the Ministry concerned. In the case of the smaller authority, the effort of carrying out these inquiries individually can be out of all proportion to the value of the results achieved.

No standardization of designs or imitation of type plans is inherent in the work of a development group. Every building project should differ in detail according to local needs and conditions. Nevertheless, most buildings which are required to fulfil a similar function have common problems related to layout, room sizes, circulation space, standards of heating and lighting, fixed equipment and so on. Research into the space standards for circulation and reading and the requirements for lighting and heights of shelving would greatly help an authority planning a new library. Similarly, there are problems common to all authorities in building, for example, maternity and child welfare clinics. An investigation into the different kinds of design, layout and equipment which would combine economy and efficiency and yet avoid too institutional an atmosphere would give Health committees and their architects a clearer view of the possibilities. For all such buildings the difficulty of individual authorities is to do an intensive enough investigation of the functions of the building, so as to achieve a solution which is both technically sound and economical as well as humanly satisfactory.

The Institute's inquiry showed that an extension of the system of research and development to these less familiar kinds of building would also be valuable. The development group of the Ministry of Housing and Local Government could be used to examine the design of buildings which fall within its jurisdiction. Valuable experience could, for example, be obtained by the erection of a block of municipal offices for a local authority, or a crematorium. Similarly, the new organization in the Ministry of Health could be used for the design of buildings which are the responsibility of local health authorities. The Ministry of Health is hoping to design health authority premises in co-operation with local authorities.

The Home Office as well has been reviewing its methods of control for police and fire service buildings, but it has not yet produced any comparable proposals for development work. The Home Office has a very small Architect's division compared with the Ministries of Education and Housing, and it would not be easy to graft on the work of a development group. Nevertheless, some departments have quite small units which are doing valuable development work and there appears to be no reason why the Home Office could not follow suit. The need for such work on police stations, fire stations and the like appears to be as great as for labour exchanges, university refectories or health clinics.

This extension of the development group technique raises the question of whether it should all be sponsored by government departments, so that local authorities co-operate only as clients. Can local authorities be associated more actively with this work and should they attempt such work independently? It is clear that not all the various types of local authority building are going to be investigated simultaneously, and there is plenty of scope for investigating some outside the walls of government departments. There may also be scope for some more active kind of collaboration with the work which is now being started in the Ministries of Health and Housing, and which could be started in the Home Office, than the usual architect-client relationship.

BUILDING RESEARCH STATION

Many local authorities are familiar with the technical work of the Building Research Station. Some have co-operated with the

Station on experimental schemes. Others have been advised by it on technical problems. Much of this technical work has been embodied in the Building Research Station's own publications, some is published in articles in the technical press and some is available on request to individual inquirers. A visit to the Building Research Station will reveal the wide range of experimental work going on, as well as the testing of new building equipment and components on behalf of manufacturers and builders.

The Building Research Station has carried out work in the field of cost research, particularly into the building and maintenance costs of houses and flats. This side of its work was expanded in 1950 and it has been a pioneer in this field. It is now associated as well with the work being done by the Royal Institution of Chartered Surveyors and the Royal Institute of British Architects on cost research. This is discussed later in this chapter. It has also carried out research programmes on behalf of the Ministry of Education's development group and the Division for Architectural Studies of the Nuffield Foundation, and has provided them with specialist services for the investigation of technical problems. It will, no doubt, give the new development groups now being formed in other government departments similar assistance.

Less well known than its technical research on materials, structures and physical conditions, the Building Research Station also has active groups working to determine user requirements and building costs. Over twenty research workers are engaged in studying user requirements, and they include architects, engineers, physicists, psychologists and sociologists.

The general aim of this section has been to express design requirements in forms in which they can be used by the architect, engineer and administrator. Evidence is largely based on field surveys of existing buildings, in which occupants are interviewed and their responses are checked by observations and physical measurements. In some instances the surveys are concerned with features introduced experimentally by arrangement with building authorities. In addition, the group has facilities for testing full scale models of buildings or parts of buildings so that modifications of current practice can be tried out under near-laboratory conditions.

This work, which started in 1944 in the Ministry of Works

334

and was transferred to the Building Research Station in 1950, has been mainly concentrated on housing. By now much evidence has been gathered on the relative acceptability of different house and flat layouts, of different engineering services, such as heating, refuse disposal and laundry facilities, and on the particular needs of special groups, such as old people. In addition to research on housing, a substantial and increasing effort is being applied to other fields, particularly to office design. The special problems of drawing offices have recently been studied and attention is now being given to building needs in relation to office punched card installations.

Much of the Station's work in this field is closely concerned with matters which will come under review by the new development group of the Ministry of Housing and Local Government. It is debatable whether the Ministry's group should include experts who can advise on user requirements if this service can be provided by the Station. This is a question of the division of functions between departments. Social investigation is an expensive business if it is properly done, and there is a good deal to be said for drawing the development work done by departments into a closer relationship with the section of the Building Research Station which is equipped to investigate these problems.

Such an arrangement would not prevent the individual development groups from investigating needs, as the Ministry of Education's group has done, but it would avoid providing the Ministry of Housing and the Ministry of Health with experts in social investigation, who are in all too short supply. It would also make it easier to follow up the success of the development projects in later years. If these new projects are to be of the greatest possible value, it is necessary for their failures and successes to be assessed after a period. The team at the Building Research Station might be able to do this more thoroughly than a department which is busy with, and probably more interested in, new projects.

CONSORTIUM OF LOCAL AUTHORITIES

The development groups already described represent one of the most fruitful lines of progress in building design and cost control.

So far these groups are found almost entirely in government departments, or in association with the Nuffield Foundation. Local authorities, except for Hertfordshire, have not been directly involved except as clients. There are, however, other developments taking place in which local authorities are the prime movers. Of these, the Consortium of Local Authorities' Special Programme (CLASP) is one of the most interesting. Both technically and as a method of uniting local authorities in a new way CLASP is of great significance.

The original incentive for this work was prompted by the difficulties of building schools in areas of mining subsidence, where the costs of special foundations are very heavy. The initiative first came in 1956 from Nottinghamshire where the problems of mining subsidence loom large. The Consortium was formed in 1957 and during its short existence its efforts have been concentrated on school building and on the kind of construction suitable to areas of mining subsidence. There is, however, nothing inherent in the type of organization which limits it to schools or to a particular method of construction. The real interest of CLASP is the way in which a group of local authorities have pooled their resources, combined their orders and secured benefits in more intensive technical development, lowered costs and better design.

The description which follows is necessarily confined to school building and to the particular kind of prefabricated construction which CLASP has developed. It should, however, be borne in mind that the same kind of organization could be used to develop other types of construction. The buildings for which CLASP has been responsible are the motive which has produced a type of organization which is of much wider application. In the long run the method of organization is more important than the special kinds of building which have been produced. It has been necessary to emphasize this because criticisms of CLASP sometimes assume that the type of building and the type of organization are necessary to one another. Because an authority does not like the particular type of construction it should not also condemn the type of organization.

Objectives
The objectives of the Consortium have been:

336

to sponsor and control a new system of prefabricated construction for schools. The structure is particularly well adapted to sites where there is mining subsidence, but it is equally useable on ordinary sites and has been used for schools where there is no mining subsidence;

to reduce the costs of building by combining the orders of the authorities who are members of the Consortium. Larger orders have produced lower prices;

to pool the resources of the member authorities in carrying out technical research and development into materials and components. By sharing out such work between authorities it is possible for investigations to be more intensive and to cover a wider range of problems than would be possible for a single authority. This technical work has made it possible to improve the quality and performance of components.

Membership

In 1959 the full members of the Consortium in England were:

Coventry City, Derbyshire County Council, Durham County Council, Gateshead County Borough, Glamorganshire County Council, Leicester City, Nottinghamshire County Council, War Department, West Riding of Yorkshire County Council.

In Scotland arrangements have been made for Lanarkshire County Council to build in the new system and the Scottish Education Department is ready to act as agents for other authorities in Scotland who wish to follow Lanarkshire's lead. The Ministry of Education have agreed to act as agents in England and Wales for authorities who wish to build one or two schools.

Method of Organization

Once a year there is a meeting of elected members representing the authorities in the Consortium to receive the annual report. The technical staff of the authorities work at three levels. Co-ordination of work is carried out at the top by a board of Chief Architects drawn from the authorities who have a major

337

stake in the Consortium. The Clerk of one county council and the Treasurer of another regularly attend these meetings to give legal, financial and administrative advice. The meetings are usually held quarterly, each authority acting as host in turn with that authority's own Clerk, Education Officer and Treasurer present at the meeting, so that other officers can be fully informed.

At the middle level there is a working party which is responsible for the more detailed organization of the scheme. It consists of architects and quantity surveyors from each of the member authorities and meets about once a month. It is responsible for obtaining competitive tenders from suppliers and sub-contractors for the main standardized components which are required in all the schools using the consortium system of construction. The components chosen to be a part of these special arrangements are those which are cheaper if manufactured in quantity and delivered to the main contractors responsible for building the schools in the different areas. The working party also organizes deliveries of components to the different sites to ensure that there are adequate stocks. The other important part of its duties is to direct the programme of technical development, and to ensure that this is divided among the various authorities and that the results are made available to all the members.

More recently it was decided to establish a small and permanent investigation team consisting of four architects and one quantity surveyor to work under the direction of the working party. Each authority is being asked to contribute in staff time or money a quarter per cent of the value of its jobs in the Consortium each year. The exact details of how this team will operate are still being worked out, but it is envisaged that the staff involved will continue to work in their own offices but will come together for whatever time is necessary to co-ordinate the exercises in hand at any one time. It should mean that more technical development work than has so far been possible will be carried out, and that the production programme will be backed by the necessary resources for research investigation to ensure continuous technical progress.

Finally, at the third level, individual authorities are responsible for their part of the technical investigations and for the designing of individual schools in their own programme in each

Architect's department. Both the layout and appearance of the schools built by this method can vary from school to school and authority to authority. The basic elements are a steel frame flexible enough to take the strain of subsidence without disaster and a variety of partitions, upper floors, ceilings and dry cladding systems. Like Meccano it can take many forms and employ the architects' ingenuity in giving architectural variety.

Programmes

It is a fundamental part of the scheme that the programmes should be large enough to give advantages for bulk ordering. Initially, Nottinghamshire committed all the eleven schools in its 1957-58 programme to this method of building to the value of some £900,000. By the time of the 1958-59 programme when other authorities had joined the scheme thirty-one schools were in the programme to a value of £2·8 million, and in 1959-60 it had increased to approximately £3·4 million.

An authority cannot become a full member of the Consortium and a member of the controlling board unless it has three schools within the current programme. For new members this rule has been amended to a minimum of £250,000 p.a. Authorities with only one or two schools may take part, but not as full members.

Not only the total programme, but delivery dates within the programme are important. Authorities must be prepared to accept delivery at the dates they have themselves selected in advance, in order to avoid the accumulation of stocks at the manufacturer's end. Erection itself is rapid and can be carried out by small and medium sized builders without elaborate plant. There is no need to use large contractors with special plant. The selection of the general building contractor is entirely a matter for individual authorities.

Technical Investigations

Nottinghamshire initiated the particular system of construction, and most of the original technical investigations, particularly those concerning the steel frame, were undertaken by it. Since the formation of the Consortium other investigations have been shared out among authorities. One authority is studying the application of the original system to four-storey building;

339

another has examined internal partitions and a third has carried out a general review of drainage systems. Windows have been the subject of an intensive examination to achieve greater standardization, improved quality and lower cost. As a result, there has been a saving in cost value of some 23 per cent, which amounts to £2,000 on a £100,000 contract, and the production of a window of better performance. This development took three architects five months.

The scope for investigations of this kind is very large. Once new solutions have been found the improved designs can be produced by manufacturers in bulk for the whole Consortium. The same methods could be used with equal success for other types of building, particularly for housing, for which the demand for standardized components is potentially very large.

Prices

The prices for most of the components were obtained by inviting competitive tenders for quantities estimated to meet the needs of the whole Consortium. This means large orders and prices are correspondingly favourable. A few items of a highly specialized kind which were part of the original investigation of design and requirements by Nottinghamshire were negotiated in the first place, and larger orders have been placed at lowered prices with these same firms.

A comparison between the prices accepted by Nottinghamshire for its 1957-58 programme when only its own eleven schools and two other projects were involved and the prices quoted for the thirty-one schools in the 1958-59 programmes shows the following reductions:

Component	Percentage reduction on the 1957-58 price
Steel frame	5
Concrete cladding and plinth units	15
Metal roof lights	27·5
Internal flush doors	No reduction but higher quality
Rubber floor finishes	5
Heating and hot water installations	4·6
Sanitary fittings	11·6

These constitute very considerable reductions, and further reductions below these figures were being achieved in many cases in 1959 when sub-contracts were on a fixed price basis. The savings on the steel frame and the heating installations are particularly important in terms of overall cost, since they may constitute 20 per cent of the total price of a school building. Savings on these items are therefore specially valuable and could be still further increased if the bulk orders were larger.

In addition, those authorities in areas of mining subsidence who would otherwise have had to build costly special foundations have been spared this cost by the use of the Consortium structure which has no foundations of the conventional kind. The normal precautions against subsidence add on average about 7·5 per cent to the cost of a school, and the Ministry of Education is prepared to permit authorities to aggregate or accumulate those savings to build an extra school.

Criticisms

Three main criticisms have been made of this scheme. Architects have criticized the schools as mass-produced boxes with little architectural merit. There are those who consider the negotiations with manufacturers of the components, particularly where the product is highly specialized, as dangerously near to creating a producer's monopoly. And there are others again who feel the Consortium is usurping the independence of individual authorities.

On the first point it may well be that the prefabrication limits the architect's freedom of design. But considerable variety is still possible if the architect is skilful, and experience will suggest new methods of combining the advantages of quicker and cheaper erection with greater originality in design. Experience is still very limited, and improvement should be easy. Very soon some of the new buildings will be of four storeys and the extra height will give greater opportunities for variety in design. Some of the defects are teething difficulties. Some must be weighed against lower costs and quicker erection.

As far as the contract arrangements are concerned, most contracts are secured by competitive tender of which there can be no criticism. The component most open to possible objection is the steel frame. This has all been obtained from a single firm,

341

which has been responsible for its development. It must, however, be recognized that where customers require the manufacture of unusual units, which need special development work, a great deal of collaboration between client and manufacturer may be required. This collaboration cannot be obtained through the ordinary machinery of competitive tendering. In the case of the Consortium, the costs of the selected firm were closely examined and the authorities were satisfied that the original price was fair and that the subsequent price reductions for larger orders were favourable. There is also no reason why other manufacturers should not compete in the future if this safeguard was felt to be desirable.

The third criticism concerns the independence of the member authorities in the Consortium. Any such anxiety arises from a misunderstanding of the commitments and relationships within the Consortium. Each authority enters it with full knowledge of the type of building and the general level of costs. Its commitment is only for one programme year. The number of schools with which it enters the Consortium, the starting dates and the individual designs are all within its own decision. And it can withdraw the following year if it so wishes. Each authority is kept fully informed of progress through the working party. And selected representatives have had opportunities for visiting completed schools and for hearing about the operation of the scheme. None of these arrangements usurp the independence of authorities in any significant way.

Advantages

In return for joining the scheme authorities enjoy two advantages of great value. They obtain price concessions from large orders, which they could not obtain singly. And they are able, by dividing and then pooling the technical work of investigation, to improve and develop new techniques in a way which would be impossible for them to do on their own. Both these are significant advantages.

The advantages peculiar to the type of building are of a different kind. To the extent that they solve special problems in areas of mining subsidence their importance is limited to authorities with this particular difficulty. It is, however, claimed that a structure designed for a particular purpose has been

342

found to have a much wider use. As far as authorities in general are concerned the lessons of this method of prefabrication and the means taken to find the most satisfactory solutions deserve investigation. They differ fundamentally from the use of certain proprietary kinds of prefabricated schools and houses which are produced by a single manufacturer or contractor. In these cases, if the authority calls for variations in the basic design many of the economies of prefabrication are dissipated and the cost advantages lost. Furthermore, many of them demand the highly developed organization of a large contractor and exclude the use of local firms. The buildings of CLASP do not.

Whatever these advantages, the efforts of the Consortium are of greater interest as a method of organization and joint action, and the importance of this is not confined to education authorities. A similar grouping of authorities could be equally beneficial for housing, particularly for those with flat programmes. There are plenty of technical problems which require investigation which cannot be undertaken by authorities singly. There could be large economies in the bulk order of components. There is no reason why other groups of authorities should not form their own consortia and secure similar benefits.

The experience of CLASP suggests that a working party which covers nine or ten authorities is about as large a group as can be handled around a single table. The working party would be less effective if it were larger. There would be advantages in price reductions if the programmes were larger, but not from a larger number of authorities. The aim should not be to make the membership of any one Consortium bigger and bigger, but to create new groups of authorities who have problems in common, just as the problem of subsidence has united many of the members of CLASP.

THE LONDON COUNTY COUNCIL

A development group was established in the Housing division of the Architect's department of the London County Council in 1950 with the specific intention of investigating all the structural elements, services and components in housing work and so to provide better value for money in terms of quality and speed of erection. This development group is kept deliberately small

343

in size with a staff averaging seven in number. By its contact with special negotiated contracts and by introducing practical experiments into running contracts the group is, however, able to carry out an extensive programme of work far greater in extent than its size would suggest.

The scope of the work of the group has so far extended in three main directions:

the design, in collaboration with the manufacturers, of factory made components for standard use;

investigation into the various building elements and the experimental use of new techniques to test their value before general application;

publication of information and supervision of the testing of materials by other departments.

The work on the design of factory components is intended not only to produce components specifically suitable for housing but to reduce costs or give a higher standard of design and finish for the same cost. The door and window furniture produced as part of this programme is now in use by many other consumers and the London County Council's range of pivot hung wood windows has been adopted by the English Joinery Manufacturers Association as a national standard. Examples of other components are drying cabinets, easy-clean hinges, solid fuel open fires, surrounds, an openable stove, and an aluminium refuse hopper. Drawings showing dimensions and fixing details for these standard components are produced by the group and issued to the working sections.

In its investigations into building elements and the experimental use of new techniques, the development group has kept in close contact with the Building Research Station. Perhaps the most successful examples of this collaboration have been the extension of the single stack system of plumbing into multi-storey work, the mechanical ventilation of internal bathrooms and w.c.'s and the practical experiments with branched smoke flues. The group is also fortunate in being able to call upon the services of a wide range of technologists from within the London

344

County Council. These include structural engineers, heating and ventilating engineers, electrical engineers, mèchanical engineers, chemists and physicists.

Thirdly, and acting as a separate group, the Materials and Information section is responsible for the cataloguing of new materials and information on manufacturers' products. It also arranges for the testing of materials, which is carried out in the laboratories of the scientific branch of the Public Health department or the Chief Engineer's testing station, and for the direct or bulk purchasing of certain components where substantial cost savings can be made.

There is also in the department a Development and Materials committee under the chairmanship of the Deputy Architect on which all divisions are represented. Whilst the development group forms part of the Housing division, its functions have a bearing on constructional work generally and, of course, special research problems are also dealt with in the other divisions. The departmental Development and Materials committee is the means, therefore, of ensuring the general dissemination of information on development and research throughout the department, and periodical bulletins are issued to all divisions setting out the results of research undertaken as well as information on the latest materials and constructional methods.

The work of the development group has so far mainly concentrated on the investigation of technical problems and on providing a service to the teams of architects who are at work on actual schemes. The group has not been responsible for the actual design of any scheme. This is now to be modified. It is to be closely associated with more negotiated contracts for development work and will take some direct part in design.

The London County Council has obtained valuable experience about the merits of negotiated contracts with its scheme at Picton Street. This experiment is being followed by further special negotiated contracts which will be carried out in the same way as Picton Street; that is, by various working sections in the Housing division, but they will be under the direct control of the Development Architect. These schemes include multistorey blocks of flats and maisonettes constructed almost entirely of pre-cast factory made components, and a thirteen-storey

345

block of flats in unreinforced light-weight concrete utilizing a continental system of shuttering.

As the majority of the authority's flat blocks up to and including six storeys in height still employ traditional forms of construction, work is proceeding on a 'traditional experiment' scheme. The object of this scheme is to rationalize the technique of traditional construction working with the direct labour building organization of the London County Council. In this contract the development group will be responsible for carrying out the entire work of design, working drawings and architectural supervision within the group. There is always the danger that any development group which is divorced from practical building may lose interest and enthusiasm, besides becoming unrealistic in its approach. This scheme is therefore designed to give the development group the direct responsibility it has hitherto lacked.

This extension of the work of the London County Council development group is trebly interesting. It is the first example of such work by a local authority which extends beyond technical investigations into the field of design. In this it differs from the development team of the Consortium, which is not responsible for the design of any schools. It is also likely to be the first development group to design housing, since the Ministry of Housing's new group will not be in operation quite so soon. Thirdly, it will be carrying out experimental work in conjunction with the direct labour organization. In the earlier chapter on direct labour it was pointed out how little work was being done along these lines by local authorities generally. The existence of a direct labour organization engaged on new building gives the architects an excellent opportunity to bring the design organization and the building organization into closer contact and so to improve efficiency. This opportunity has been rarely taken. It is the more welcome that the London County Council is to do this through its development group.

EXTENSION OF DEVELOPMENT GROUPS OR CONSORTIA TO OTHER AUTHORITIES

So far development groups of the kind outlined in this chapter are limited to government departments and to the London

County Council and are not to be found among other local authorities. The development team of the Consortium is small and concerned with technical problems, not with the design of buildings as the development group of the Ministry of Education has been. So far the type of organization embodied in the Consortium is limited to one group of authorities and experience suggests that the number of authorities belonging to this group is about as large as can conveniently combine together in a joint effort. These two limitations prompt three related questions. Can other local authorities form development groups of their own, singly or in combination? Can they participate in the work now starting in government departments, particularly in the Ministry of Housing and Local Government? Would it be useful if the organization of the Consortium was transplanted to other groups of local authorities?

Present experience suggests that the kind of co-operation necessary for a Consortium is easier to organize than that demanded by a joint development group. Organizationally the one is almost the converse of the other. The Consortium demands comparatively little effort at the centre and spreads the benefits and burdens equitably among the members. It also provides immediate tangible benefits in terms of price reductions, which more than compensate for any extra administrative burdens, and offers a technical service at very economical cost.

The development group works the other way round. The work is concentrated and intensive. It involves a heavy initial investment of effort with no immediate return. And if a group is to build actual schemes, which is an essential part of its experience, it can only build for one, or at most, two clients at a time. It is not easy to see groups of local authorities combining on this basis, although in the long run they might all gain much valuable experience.

If this is so, are government departments to 'go it alone' on development groups, or is there some means by which local authorities could participate in, or contribute to the general advance of ideas on this front? The Royal Institute of Public Administration consulted the four main local authority associations on this matter in 1958, but the associations were not then in a position, either individually or collectively, to suggest means of participation. It is, indeed, not easy to suggest ways by which local authorities, through their associations, could participate in the work of the development groups in government departments.

By its very nature a development team is a close-knit unit which is working intensively in a technical and specialized field. It is the territory of experts and participation is necessarily of an expert and individual kind. Local authorities have, nevertheless, their own experts who could make a valuable contribution to this work. Government departments often have only limited experience of the running of the services for which the new buildings are being planned and it is, therefore, important that the experience of local authorities should be drawn upon.

It is suggested that the best way to make this experience available to a development group would be to arrange for the secondment of individual local authority officers to join in the work. This has already been done by education authorities, who have seconded architects to work with the Ministry of Education's development group. Such an arrangement could be extended to other development groups.

Technical officers would have to be associated with a particular project continuously during the period of design. Officers representing the users of the building, such as a Housing Manager, Police, Fire, or Administrative Officer, might find it sufficient to give only part-time service to the group after an initial period of continuous participation. Whatever system was evolved it would be essential for local authorities to select really able officers with ideas and experience. They would be men and women who were rising up, but had not yet reached the top of the ladder.

The initiative of the London County Council shows that it is possible for the very large authority to build some schemes by a development group. It is, however, doubtful how far other large authorities will follow suit, at least until they are more familiar with the effects of such work on housing design. Another possible line of advance would be for central government departments to give some support to small development teams in individual authorities. It is clear that the new development groups in the Ministries of Housing and Health will not be able to cover their respective fields. And there is no sign that the Home Office is contemplating any development work along these lines. Local authorities individually would find the cost of even a small development group heavy in relation to the benefits directly receivable by that authority. What is needed is some means by which central government could share the burdens and benefits of such work.

With some financial encouragement authorities with large architectural staffs might be prepared to devote the extra time and staff to the preparation of a scheme by an 'ad hoc' development team. The team would be a modified and simplified version of the full development group. But it might be an excellent stimulant for the authority's own staff and it would serve to bring home to authorities the need to study the user requirements and costs much more thoroughly than is now usually done.

The extent of the backing by the government department would depend on how relevant the results of the work of the individual authority would be to a wider circle of authorities. The department would have to make sure that the design, standards and costs of the scheme were likely, in general terms, to be applicable to other authorities. On this assumption a Ministry might make a contribution towards the extra cost of the salaries of those working in such a team, and towards the costs of publication of the results. Publication is an essential part of the process, as the building bulletins of the Ministry of Education give proof. Such backing would go far to spread the ideas of development work and to encourage local authorities to rethink their existing methods of drawing up the brief, evolving the design and controlling the costs.

It would be misleading to pretend that much of this work would be more than tentative first steps. Stress was laid earlier on the difficulty of finding enough of the really able people who can vitalize such work, or of obtaining sufficient backing to make their work effective. While it would be valuable if local authorities could take the initiative themselves, it is important to recognize the difficulties. Already there is a tendency to label as a development group activities which are far from being any approach to the intensive and systematic work carried out by the Ministry of Education.

There is every reason for pressing for the extension of the Consortium to other groups of authorities. This is a revolutionary idea in local government, and for the benefits it gives, is of an engaging simplicity and economy. There would appear to be strong arguments for other authorities to follow suit. The cash benefits are powerfully in its favour. As an example of joint action it is no less valuable. The Ministry of Education strongly supports the Consortium and would, no doubt, support other similar arrangements. It is to be hoped that the Ministry of Housing and Local Government would give equal encouragement to some such initiative by local housing authorities.

COST PLANNING AND COST CONTROL

The need to keep down the costs of housing, schools and other public building has been an insistent theme since the war, reiterated down the corridors of Ministries and council offices and round the drawing board. Its counterpoint criss-crosses the relations between local authorities and government departments. Its development has often seemed but the variations on an insolvable enigma.

For all this preoccupation with building costs and the efforts to control them, systematic methods of doing so have been developed only recently. Exhortation there has been in plenty. Equally plentiful is the number of schemes which have been rejected or modified because the original costs were too high. But the disciplined exercise of the functions of design within a predetermined framework of costs has been too rare. It requires a ceiling or target cost for the building within which the architects must evolve their design. It needs a vigilant watch on the various elements of the building to ensure that undue expenditure on one does not necessitate the skimping of another. It involves close and early collaboration between the various professional members of the building team, so that matters, which will affect costs, have the benefit of their experience and advice before major decisions on structure and design have been taken.

Cost Limits

Those who may doubt the absence of cost targets and the systematic control of costs should refer to the work done by the Building Research Station on cost research and to the investigations sponsored by the Cost Research Panel of the Royal In-

350

stitution of Chartered Surveyors.[1] These investigations revealed such wide differences in the costs of both flats and houses that it was clear that authorities did not subject their schemes to proper cost control. Flats which provided similar accommodation varied in price from 45s 3d to 89s 2d per foot super (1), or as much as £1,000 a flat (2). The variations for housing were not so wide (3), but considering the high degree of standardization of two-storey housing, and the years of experience which authorities have had, they also revealed the inadequacy of current methods of controlling costs.

Similar information for other types of building is not available, but fire stations or libraries or health buildings would almost certainly show as wide variations in cost for buildings of similar size. The cost of schools would be quite different, since there are strict cost limits.

There are many reasons for this lack of cost control, but one of the most significant is the absence of cost targets or limits. The replies to a questionnaire on building costs sent out by the Royal Institution of Chartered Surveyors in 1957 showed that 80 per cent of the local authorities covered did not give their architects a cost limit within which to design a scheme. The exceptions, where cost limits were fixed in advance, were usually among the larger authorities. Elsewhere, authorities operated to less defined targets and stated for example that 'no limit is imposed as homes are designed within assumed Ministry limits', or 'no limit is set as it is always assumed that sound construction and finish are required at minimum cost'.

In their report to the Minister (1) the Royal Institution of Chartered Surveyors were emphatic about the need for local authorities to give their architects 'a clear and unambiguous cost limit . . . within which to design the scheme'. The Royal Institute of Public Administration's own inquiries confirm the widespread absence of firm cost limits for all types of buildings except schools, and the importance of imposing these wherever practicable. Failure to do so inevitably reduces the incentive to

---

[1] The work of both the Building Research Station and of the Cost Researce Panel has been published in a number of articles, of which the most important arh listed at the end of this chapter. Those papers which are referred to in the text are shown by numbers (e.g. (1), (2), (3)). The others are given for more general reference.

plan and control the costs of the buildings. It may also encourage a false optimism about costs, which can be most damaging to the scheme, if cuts are necessary in the final stages. Authorities are urged to do all they can to fix the cost limits of schemes before design work starts, so as to encourage a more disciplined approach to costs and more economical building.

Desirable though it is for local authorities to fix their own target costs, they can have no assurance that these limits will secure Ministry approval unless the Ministry's own limits are known in advance. Various procedures for early consultation between the architects of authorities and Ministries exist, but these are far from successful in controlling costs. Experience shows that it is an immense advantage if a government department can itself publish cost limits. It has already been explained that at the present time only the Ministry of Education has any system for fixing cost limits published in advance and applicable to the country as a whole. There are no published cost limits for houses, flats or any other type of building for which local authorities have to seek the approval of government departments. It was recommended in Chapter 2 that the use of cost limits should be adopted by other government departments.

Cost Planning and Control

If the cost limit gives the goal it is the designers and their colleagues who are responsible for achieving it. The terms 'cost planning', 'cost control' and 'cost research' are recent comers to the building world. Costs have been implicit or explicit in all building since the Pyramids, but a systematic approach to cost control in the design and execution of building is a recent development.

It is the Ministry of Education which has been the pioneer on cost planning and control. And it is the Building Research Station which has done most of the cost research for housing. The example of the Ministry of Education is now being followed by a number of education authorities and its general approach to cost control has stimulated architects and quantity surveyors outside the field of education to examine their own methods. These efforts are, however, of recent origin.

In 1957 the Royal Institute of British Architects invited architects in private and public offices interested in cost research and cost control to give information or evidence on their experience. The result was disappointing. The R.I.B.A. reported:

It would seem to be a reflection on the absence of any widespread use of systematic cost control in architectural practice that only one contribution was received in response to the Journal invitation. This and the fifteen other contributions, both written and oral, received as the result of a direct request for evidence is thought to cover the major part of the profession's experience.[1]

Since that time there has been a growing interest in the subject, and the Royal Institute of British Architects has set up its own Cost Research committee. It has been active in stimulating discussion. General acceptance of the need for such work and the exploration of the various methods of doing so is, however, gradual and much of the work is still tentative.

Almost at the same time the Royal Institution of Chartered Surveyors set up its Cost Research Panel. Since 1957 this Panel has been active in carrying out inquiries into building costs and in stimulating interest among members of the quantity surveying profession in cost research. A liaison committee has been formed between the R.I.C.S. and the R.I.B.A., research is being carried out into the costs of commercial buildings, and various studies are being made into quantity surveying techniques, including cost research during the earlier stages of design. The series of articles already listed at the end of the chapter gives the fruits of some of this work.

The words 'cost planning' and 'cost control' have no single definitive meaning. There is indeed some dispute between the different professions as to the correct terminology to express the underlying intentions. Within the context of this book it is enough to emphasize the need for a more methodical approach to design and costs. The aims should be:

to give the client, in this case the client committee, greater confidence in the way costs are estimated and to ensure that the cost targets are achieved;

to design buildings so that they give good value for the money spent.

[1] R.I.B.A. Journal, February 1958.

To achieve these results the interaction of design and costs must be watched with relentless concentration from the earliest stages of the scheme. The pattern of the roads and services, the most economical use of the land, the height of the buildings, the type of structure, the alternative use of materials all affect over-all design and costs as well as the more detailed parts of the design. Cost planning can be carried out by a number of different methods. All the methods involve a close collaboration from the beginning of the design between architects, engineers, quantity surveyors and others.

Such work has been done in the greatest detail within the framework of full-scale development groups. It is being attempted for schools by about thirty local education authorities and by a small but unknown number of local housing authorities. But cost planning and control can also be attempted on a more modest scale within the smaller local authority office or between private architects and private quantity surveyors. There are indeed private quantity surveyors who can offer a highly developed service along these lines. The difference between the more usual methods of design and the more recent techniques of cost planning is in the more systematic approach to costs, and the closer understanding between the different professions. The future of well designed and economical building depends on both.

SUMMARY AND RECOMMENDATIONS

1.   Development groups have now been accepted by the Government as a method of improving the design of building and of getting better value for money. The Ministry of Education's efforts have shown how valuable this work can be. Not only has it had a profound influence on school building, but it has led to the setting up of similar groups in other government departments.

2.   Of the new development groups now being created the most significant for local authorities is that concerned with housing in the Ministry of Housing and Local Government. National expenditure on housing is so large and housing conditions so important a part of human welfare that the effects of such development work could be far reaching. This group should be given the strongest support.

354

3.   Apart from the large-scale needs of housing and schools, local authorities build many other types of building. Many of these are schemes of which each authority will build only one or two. It is suggested that such buildings should be investigated by development groups, which should be responsible for the erection of one or two actual buildings. The new development groups in the Ministries of Housing and Local Government and Health could be used for such a purpose.

4.   There is no sign that the Home Office intends to set up a development group to cover the buildings in its control. It is recommended that the Home Office should undertake, sponsor or support work of this kind inside or outside its own Architects' division.

5.   In spite of the value of development groups it will not be easy to repeat the successes of the Ministry of Education. Success depends on the qualities of a few key people and on sufficient backing in departments. Neither are easy to secure. Without them such groups will be ineffective.

6.   So far there is a clear line of division between the development groups inside government departments and the local authorities. Generally speaking departments have only limited experience of the running of the services for which these buildings are intended. It is, therefore, important that ways should be found to make the experience of local authorities available to the development groups.

7.   As far as action by local authorities is concerned the Consortium (CLASP) is the outstanding example of joint collaboration. In its own field the Consortium is as great a step forward as the Ministry of Education's development group has been.

8.   There appear to be excellent reasons for other groups of local authorities to adapt the model of the Consortium for their own purposes. This applies to education and housing authorities alike. An extension of this form of joint action would bring financial and technical benefits which are out of the reach of local authorities singly.

9.   To design buildings efficiently the planning and control of costs from the outset of a scheme are essential. This involves the fixing of a ceiling or target cost when the architects are first instructed, and the systematic control of costs throughout the

period of design. The Ministry of Education has been a pioneer in this field.

10. It was recommended in Chapter 2 that government departments should make greater use of cost limits to guide local authorities about costs before design work started. In the absence of such limits authorities are urged, wherever possible, to give their architects cost targets. This is likely to encourage a more disciplined approach to design and more economical building.

11. Cost planning and cost control during design are so far practised only in a small minority of public and private offices. Such work involves close collaboration between architects, engineers, surveyors and other experts. It is recommended that local authorities should do all they can to encourage it.

REFERENCES

(Numbers in brackets refer to text of Chapter 9)

Building Research Station

C. N. Craig, 'Factors Affecting Economy in Multi-Storey Flat Design'—*Journal of the Royal Institute of British Architects.* April 1956.

J. C. Weston, 'Architectural Economics'—*Journal of the Royal Institute of British Architects.* July 1956.

[2] W. J. Reiners, 'Cost Research'—*The Chartered Surveyor.* September 1957.

C. N. Craig, 'Value for Money in Flats'—*Proceedings of the Royal Society of Health Congress.* April 1957.

Offprints of these articles can be obtained from the Building Research Station.

Cost Research Panel of the Royal Institution of Chartered Surveyors

All the articles below have appeared in *The Chartered Surveyor* as the result of the work sponsored by the Panel, and from information provided by government departments, local authorities and architects and quantity surveyors in private practice.

Questionnaire on Building Costs	February 1958
Factors Affecting Relative Costs of Multi-storey flats	March 1958

Indices of Building Costs by Trades		April 1958
Planning the Cost		May 1958
(^{1})	Report on the Cost of Flats and Houses in England and Wales. Submitted to the Ministry of Housing and Local Government June 1958	July 1958
	Studies in the Cost of Housing and The Tender Prices of Local Authority Flats, by W. J. Reiners	August 1958
(^{8})	The Cost and Design of Two-storey Housing. A case study	April 1959
	Cost Analysis. Its Application to Cost Planning and Cost Control Techniques	June 1959

Offprints of these articles can be obtained from the Royal Institution of Chartered Surveyors.

CHAPTER 10

CONCLUSIONS

Outstanding findings of inquiry—importance of local authority building—control by central government—control by committees—division of functions between Architect and Engineer—contribution of private architects—role of quantity surveyors—cost control—maintenance—direct labour—contracts—development groups and CLASP—competition and collaboration.

THIS chapter summarizes the most significant conclusions and recommendations of the report as a whole. It makes no attempt to be exhaustive, but highlights those findings which are of special interest or of particular value in helping local authorities to improve their building organization.

THE IMPORTANCE OF LOCAL AUTHORITY BUILDING

Local authorities will continue to be large users of the building industry in the foreseeable future. The most acute period of housing shortage has passed, but local authorities have large housing programmes before them, particularly for slum clearance. School building is still running at a high level; the replacement of the older schools has hardly begun and is much needed. For twenty years a wide variety of other types of local authority building have been starved of capital. Services such as the health, fire and police services would greatly benefit from more and more up-to-date buildings. There are also many ways in which local authorities could meet the social and cultural needs of their areas if they could provide buildings for them. These demands, collectively, will add up to large and varied building programmes for local authorities.

The change in emphasis from two-storey housing on virgin land to large programmes of slum clearance, and the higher proportion of more specialized types of building will change the

358

balance of local authority building activity. Two-storey housing is highly traditional and, therefore, familiar to authorities and builders. In future the designers will have to take into account less familiar demands from the client, and more complicated building structures. This will also affect the demands on the builders. This change may require some realignment of ideas and methods and will give local authorities new opportunities.

The stock of buildings owned by local authorities has been rising rapidly since the war and will continue to rise. Local authorities are now property owners on a large scale. This means they also have growing responsibilities for maintenance. They use directly or indirectly a considerable proportion of the nation's building resources for this work and the efficiency of their maintenance organizations is a matter of public importance.

The balance of local authority building activity has changed considerably in the last ten years, with the rapid expansion of school building since 1950 and the recent fall in house building. The whole period has been one of both sudden and long-term changes. Changes will continue quite apart from short-term financial emergencies. The birth-rate is rising again. Standards of living are rising also and with them the demand for better services and more living space. The population continues to shift from north to south. These fundamental changes will affect local authorities and will demand new responses. Buildings are one of the most visible evidences of this kind of challenge and response. (Chapter 1.)

CONTROL OF BUILDING BY CENTRAL GOVERNMENT

It became clear during the course of the inquiry that the methods used by different government departments to control the capital expenditure of local authorities greatly affected the efficiency of the local authorities themselves. These methods vary widely from department to department and from one type of building to another. While some variety of treatment is inevitable, due to differences in the buildings themselves, in the methods of financing them and in the powers and duties of central and local government for each service, the variations are much wider than can be justified by these differences and suggest scope for improvement.

The aim of any system of control of building by central government should be to give the greatest degree of certainty as far in advance as possible, and to allow local authorities the maximum freedom within clearly defined limits of cost and standard. Changes in capital programmes and uncertainty about building requirements and cost limits prevent efficient planning and increase the risks of abortive work, delay and friction.

Only the methods of control over local authority building used by the Ministry of Education satisfy the requirements of certainty and clarity, and leave a wide measure of discretion to local authorities. The Ministry of Education fixes building programmes two and a half to three years in advance. There are minimum standards for different kinds of building and clearly defined cost limits which are known before design starts. Within the framework of advance programmes, minimum standards and maximum costs authorities can plan with certainty and with a large amount of freedom. It is no accident that school building has been outstandingly successful and that public expenditure gives remarkably good value. The right stimulus to economize and to show initiative in design have been built in to the structure of control.

The adoption of similar methods by other government departments would enable local authorities to organize their work more efficiently and therefore economically, and would reduce the points of friction between departments and local authorities. Local authority building cannot expect to be insulated from the general economic situation of the country and must suffer its share of cuts when times are difficult. But more advance programming for other kinds of buildings as well as schools should be possible and would enormously help local authorities to improve their own building services. Similarly, better guidance on cost limits and standards could be given. Nothing is more wasteful than last minute changes in design to secure superficial economies in cost. Nothing encourages self-discipline better than a clear definition of objectives at the start. It is encouraging that other government departments are now following the Ministry of Education's lead. (Chapter 2.)

CONTROL OF PROGRAMMES BY COMMITTEES

Local authority committee organization is very diverse. The inquiry did not show that one kind of organization for the control of building was better than another, even for authorities of similar size and with similar responsibilities.

It did, however, reveal that arrangements for settling co-ordinated long-term capital programmes and priorities are exceptional. Few authorities do this for more than the year immediately ahead. Failure to co-ordinate capital programmes is due partly to the strongly centrifugal character of committees, who resent any encroachment of power by a central co-ordinating committee. It is also due to the many changes and uncertainties in capital programmes controlled by central government. After suffering a series of set-backs and changes of programme some local authorities have abandoned the attempt to plan ahead on any co-ordinated basis.

This result is unfortunate. Authorities need to look at their programmes as a whole, to gauge future commitments and to compare the demands of the different services. The absence of such a procedure gives insufficient protection to the services which may need few buildings but need them at least as urgently as housing and education. Authorities are urged to review their arrangements for making co-ordinated long-term capital programmes.

They are also urged to ensure that the chief officer who is in charge of the architectural services, whether he is the Engineer or Architect, is responsible clearly to one particular committee for these services, and can turn to the chairman for advice and support. Where such an arrangement does not exist, the chief officer may be subject to pressures from committees on priorities and other matters, which can be difficult to meet equitably. (Chapter 3.)

DIVISION OF RESPONSIBILITIES BETWEEN ENGINEER AND ARCHITECT

All local authorities must face from time to time the problem of when to keep several functions under one chief officer and when to sub-divide departments. This problem is constantly changing as the functions and responsibilities of authorities grow and alter and chief officers retire and are replaced.

In the context of an inquiry on building organization the most important manifestation of this problem was in the division of functions between the Engineer and the Architect. This proved to be a growing point in the pattern of building organization and one to which local authorities are giving a good deal of thought. Since the war the number of Chief Architects with separate Architect's departments has increased sharply among the large and medium-sized authorities and many counties, county boroughs and some of the larger non-county boroughs have effected this change. The inquiry also revealed a number of authorities who were currently considering such a change or who altered their departmental organization in this way during the period of the investigation. Among the smaller authorities the overwhelming majority have and will continue to have the architectural services under the control of the Engineer.

This is a matter on which opinion among authorities of similar size and functions is sharply divided. There are those with combined departments who emphasize the advantages of co-ordination under a single head and the economies of administration within one department. Others, with separate Architect's departments, emphasize the importance of encouraging architectural quality by having a Chief Architect. There can be no doubt that the existence of a separate Architect's department enables an authority to attract an abler Chief Architect and better junior staff. The inquiry underlines the merits of dividing the architectural services from the engineering services and of appointing a Chief Architect, if the size of the authority and its building organization justifies the separation. (Chapter 4.)

THE CONTRIBUTION OF THE PRIVATE ARCHITECT

Local authorities make frequent use of private architects, but mainly to tide over shortages in their own staff and to meet sudden rushes of work. In this role private architects have proved indispensable. Most authorities deprecate the regular use of private architects and many of them are critical of their experiences of using private architects. Private architects are also sometimes critical of local authorities as clients and particularly of the hurried time-tables and rushed work, which they so often demand of private architects.

These difficulties may arise from a variety of failures on both sides. But there are two particular causes of difficulty. Too few authorities appear to plan the allocation of their architectural work far enough in advance. Private architects tend to be called in too late to give the architect time to plan the scheme properly. Hurried work is almost certain to give rise to mistakes and mutual criticism. Except in emergencies, authorities should be able to apportion their work between private and official architects according to a prepared plan of operations, and thus to commission the private architect in good time. Only in this way can the private architect give of his best and satisfy his client.

Secondly, few authorities recognize the value of the private architect in helping to stimulate fresh thought and new ideas on familiar problems. Under the pressure of regular programmes and standardized requirements it is very easy for local authority building, and particularly housing, to become monotonous and stereotyped. The official architect often needs the private architect to help him to break new ground, to overcome local prejudices and to challenge accepted ideas. The separateness of the private architect from the official routines makes it easier for him to have a fresh approach. It is recommended that large authorities should regularly give a proportion of their work to private architects for this purpose and that the smaller authorities should commission them from time to time. To do so is no confession of failure. It is the more progressive and vigorous authorities who most welcome this contribution from the private architect. (Chapter 5.)

THE ROLE OF THE QUANTITY SURVEYOR

Local authorities make regular use of both official and private quantity surveyors for the more routine or traditional side of their work. The inquiry revealed no opposition to the use of private quantity surveyors, such as was shown to the use of private architects.

Usually private quantity surveyors are appointed after sketch plans and preliminary estimates have been approved by a committee. Sometimes they are not called in till after working drawings have been prepared. This is much too late to enable quantity surveyors to make any contribution to cost planning and to the most important problems of design and cost. The most vital decisions which affect costs are usually made at the sketch plan stage.

Many architects do not welcome the participation of the quantity surveyor in these early stages, nor are quantity surveyors always anxious to share in such work. The pioneer work of the Ministry of Education and of some local education authorities and private firms has revealed the value of teamwork from the earliest stages of design. In this way the architect can benefit from the specialized knowledge on costs of experienced quantity surveyors and can design his building more economically and with a more accurate knowledge of final costs.

These benefits are at present usually derived from teamwork between architects and quantity surveyors on authorities' own staff, where the architects and quantity surveyors have easy access to one another. Similar benefits can only come from the use of private quantity surveyors if they are appointed early enough to give their advice during the preliminary stages of design. It is recommended that authorities should encourage early collaboration between architects and quantity surveyors to ensure a more accurate planning and control of costs.

It is not enough to encourage architects and quantity surveyors to collaborate together. They must be given time to do so and to complete all the preparatory stages of the design before the schemes go out to tender. A very large proportion of a quantity surveyor's time is now occupied in tying up the loose ends of contracts, which should have been settled earlier before sending the schemes out to tender. He would be occupied to much better purpose if he spent more time with the architects in the early stages of design and contributed to the control of costs. Authorities are urged to see that the time-table for designing their building schemes is sufficient to permit this joint work and to complete working drawings and bills of quantities before going to tender. In the final event time, building costs and fees will be saved. (Chapter 5.)

MAINTENANCE

Maintenance is of much greater importance than its rather

hum-drum routines suggest. Except in the very large authorities or where there is a separate Public Works department, the officer in day-to-day control of maintenance tends to be insufficiently qualified and too junior to press the larger issues of maintenance. This means that the more important policy questions may be neglected or examined too infrequently. The scale of ownership by local authorities warrants a more positive approach to maintenance problems by officers able to support the claims of maintenance with knowledge and vigour.

Authorities vary greatly in their maintenance organizations. Some are centralized; some divide the organization departmentally; many have housing maintenance controlled by the Housing Manager. One of the merits of a single organization is that it can afford to place a more senior officer in charge and thus to provide a more expert service. On the other hand, many authorities regard housing maintenance as a social service as well as a building service and justify a separate housing maintenance organization because of the special relationship between landlord and tenant.

Whatever type of organization authorities select, they are urged to:

carry out regular inspections of property and to programme structural repairs and periodic maintenance;

build up reserve funds for all types of building and not only for housing;

keep a vigilant eye on costs and to use cost comparisons or operational research methods from time to time;

examine the relationship between capital costs and maintenance costs and to plan the design of new building with maintenance costs in mind. (Chapter 6.)

DIRECT LABOUR

The volume of maintenance carried out by direct labour is large and is growing steadily with the increase in the number of buildings owned by local authorities. There is no reason to expect a reversal of this trend. Indeed direct labour is particularly well adapted to the execution of day-to-day repairs, especially for housing, and carries many advantages for this class of work.

The volume of new building by direct labour is quantitatively small compared with that carried out for local authorities by contractors. It is limited mainly to housing. The volume of such building is falling with the general decrease in house building by local authorities, but a number of individual authorities are increasing their direct labour organizations. It appeared that much solid, conscientious work was being done by direct labour and that it provided authorities with valuable experience of building methods. There was no evidence that work carried out by direct labour was markedly cheaper in first costs, but nearly all authorities claimed that the standards of workmanship were better and that subsequent maintenance costs were, in consequence, lower.

Authorities can allay much criticism of direct labour if they tender competitively against private contractors for at least some of the new work and for the larger schemes of maintenance. This provides an added stimulus to their own organizations and is a proof of efficiency. The need to ensure reasonable continuity of work for an authority's own organization, within the restricted field of its own buildings, makes it difficult for authorities to tender competitively for all work. But some competition from time to time or for a proportion of the work is highly desirable from every point of view.

In spite of the special opportunities which a direct labour organization offers for collaboration with the architects, and for carrying out experiments in building methods, very few direct labour organizations exploit these opportunities to any significant extent. The inquiry showed that one cause of failure was the status and salary of the Public Works or Building Manager. This is generally too low to produce the best results. The findings suggest that authorities would be well advised to secure Building Managers of better calibre and to give them a higher status. (Chapter 7.)

CONTRACTS

The efficiency of builders and therefore the prices at which they tender can be greatly affected by the contract procedures of local authorities. The completeness of the information given to the builder before tendering and the time allowed for the preparation of the tender by the contractor will affect the price. If the contractor has incomplete plans, or the expectation of changes in design or specification or insufficient opportunity to understand the full implications of the contract, his price will reflect his uncertainties. Local authorities have a duty to ensure that they receive keen tenders because the contractors have been able fully to appreciate their commitments.

The use of selected lists of tenderers as opposed to open competition also encourages efficiency. It reduces the amount of abortive tendering by contractors, for which clients must ultimately pay. It increases the client's certainty that the contract will be carried out by a reliable and experienced firm. Authorities are urged to make much greater use of selected lists of contractors than they do now.

While negotiated contracts for development work will remain exceptional, their use is one road to the better understanding of the problems of building. At present the gulf between the designers on the one side and the builders on the other is too wide, and the bridges between them too few. The experience of a few authorities and of the Ministry of Education has shown the value of arrangements whereby the builder can give his advice during the period of design and gain experience of the architect's approach. These methods have produced better designs and more efficiency on the site. These results can be achieved through negotiated contracts and it is suggested that authorities should use such contracts from time to time to secure these benefits. (Chapter 8.)

DEVELOPMENT GROUPS AND CLASP

Great importance is attached to the work of the development group in the Ministry of Education and to the extension of this work to other government departments. This is one of the most valuable and stimulating centres of activity in the whole field of public building. The pioneer work of the Ministry of Education's group has profoundly affected school building. Its existence has made it easier for the Ministry to modify its building standards and to fix cost limits, and thus to simplify the

367

machinery of control over local authorities. The first-hand experience of the development group in building schools for local authorities has given the Ministry's building bulletins and technical advice an unrivalled authority and expertise.

These methods are now being adopted by other departments, both those concerned with local authority building and others. The setting up of development groups in the Ministry of Health and the Ministry of Housing and Local Government is to be welcomed even if this start comes very late. No such action has yet been taken by the Home Office.

The work of a development group for housing could be of outstanding value. So far insufficient thought of a fundamental kind has been given to the design, costs and planning of houses and flats and such work is long overdue. It could have a very important influence on the standards and costs of housing in the future, and could simplify the control of local authority housing by central government. Other types of building, such as fire and police stations, swimming baths, clinics or libraries are built in smaller numbers. But intensive investigation into the basic requirements, by the techniques of the development group, would enable government departments to give authorities better guidance on current developments and a clearer picture of the standards and costs which would be approved.

Such work would require co-operation with the local authorities. Generally speaking government departments have only a limited experience of the running of the services with which the new development groups will be concerned. It is suggested that local government officers with special experience of these services and therefore of the buildings needed for them should be seconded to join in the work of the development groups for limited periods.

CLASP or the Consortium of Local Authorities' Special Programme is an outstanding example of collaboration between local authorities. Its benefits have been striking. Not only has it achieved great savings in the cost of schools. Organizationally it is an important new development among local authorities and sets a valuable new precedent. It is hoped that other groups of authorities will set up similar organizations, and for housing as well as schools.

The Ministry of Education has also done much work on the

cost planning and cost control of schemes planned by its development group. These methods are now being adopted and adapted by some local authorities and private concerns. Local authorities are urged to encourage more of this kind of work for their own building schemes. (Chapter 9.)

COMPETITION AND COLLABORATION

Two general points deserve special mention as pointers towards development in the future.

The inquiry brought out very clearly the virtue of relying on a variety of methods and the competition between them. What local authorities need is a touchstone by which to judge their efforts, and this is seldom available if they select only one method of operation. The use of private architects, for example, stimulates the official architects and reduces the risks of complacency and monotony. Competition between direct labour and private builders evokes greater efforts from both sides. It is all too easy for any organization to become fixed in its habits and to form a defensive shield which unconsciously resists innovations. The authorities who aim to do all their work by direct labour or by their own staff, remove a valuable stimulus. Authorities have to make deliberate efforts to keep themselves fully abreast of changes in the building world, and competition is a surer means of doing so than any other available.

The other issue which emerged again and again throughout the course of the inquiry was the importance of collaboration between the different members of the building team; between clients, architects, engineers, quantity surveyors and builders. This applies just as much to other public authorities and to private enterprise, but it behoves local authorities to make their contribution to the new ideas and new methods.

In local authorities the divisions are at their most rigid between the designers and the builders. Contract arrangements reduce the opportunities for architects and contractors to understand each other's problems. At present there are serious barriers to technical progress because the two sides work in watertight compartments. The Ministry of Education encourages local authorities to work with contractors on negotiated contracts. Some of the most interesting developments by CLASP

369

and by the London County Council have been evolved by this means. More authorities must make the attempt to bridge the gap and to make building more of a co-operative effort.

If more collaboration is needed between designers and builders, more is also needed between the various professional members of the design team. The outstanding success of the new development group in the Ministry of Education has been due largely to the intimate working partnership between architects, engineers, surveyors and other members of the building team. In this joint effort professional divisions have been submerged.

Modern building is complex and expensive and it needs a wide variety of expert skills. Buildings will never be as well designed or as economical as they might be unless the various professions pool their ideas and are prepared to work much closer together than in the past. Local authorities are potentially well adapted to encourage this teamwork. Many of the professional officers already have a single employer and have similar interests in the success of the buildings. This gives them an excellent opportunity to work closely together. (Chapters 7, 8 and 9.)

THE END

9780367684242